To Life

Books and pamphlets by Elmer Gertz

Frank Harris: A Study in Black and White (with A. I. Tobin)

The People vs. *The Chicago Tribune*

A Handful of Clients

Moment of Madness: The People vs. Jack Ruby

For the First Hours of Tomorrow: The New Illinois Bill of Rights

American Ghettos

Books and Their Right to Live

Joe Medill's War

That Saturday at Chikaming Goat Farm: A Profile of Carl Sandburg

Play

Mrs. Bixby Gets a Letter

In anthologies

"Henry Miller and the Law" in Henry Miller and the Critics

"A Lawyer 'Uses' the Press" in Mass Media and the Law

To Life

Elmer Gertz

McGRAW-HILL BOOK COMPANY
New York   St. Louis   San Francisco
Düsseldorf   London   Mexico   Sydney   Toronto

Book design by Marcy J. Katz

Copyright © 1974 by Elmer Gertz.
All rights reserved.
Printed in the United States of America.
No part of this publication may be reproduced, stored in a retrieval
system, or transmitted in any form or by any means, electronic, mechanical,
photocopying, recording, or otherwise, without the prior written permission
of the publisher.

123456789BABA7987654

Library of Congress Cataloging in Publication Data

Gertz, Elmer, date
  To life; the story of a Chicago lawyer.

    1. Gertz, Elmer, 1906–   I. Title.
KF373.G47A37   340′.092′4 [B]   73-16018
ISBN 0-07-023160-5

For
the two glorious women in my life,
Ceretta and Mamie,
and
our children and grandchildren

contents

	Specimen Hours—A Prefatory Note	ix
One	Pictures Out of My Past	1
Two	A Very Serious Young Man	19
Three	The Law	33
Four	Beginnings	45
Five	My First Books	55
Six	Growing into the Middle Years	73
Seven	Carl Sandburg	83
Eight	Race, Religion, and the Law	93
Nine	"Mr. Housing"	109
Ten	President Truman	119
Eleven	Out of the Depths—A Personal Tragedy and Its Happy Aftermath	131
Twelve	A Literary Boom	139
Thirteen	Litigating for and against the Police	161
Fourteen	Writing a New Constitution for Illinois	167
Fifteen	Nathan Leopold—After Stateville	187
Sixteen	Fighting the Death Penalty	199
Seventeen	The Many Lives of Libel	217
Eighteen	A Sabbatical Leave-taking	247

SPECIMEN HOURS—A Prefatory Note

No book about any man can be complete. In a sense, a man writes only of specimen hours, typical moments, when he does his memoirs. The real man is viewed, if at all, by indirection, through the interstices, so to speak, of the narrative.

Perhaps no one, not in my position, will care about the omissions, but they trouble me greatly. I am tempted to list those friends, cases, writings, organizations, incidents that I have left out. Some of them were once in this book. Their spirits still hover over these pages.

I think of George Herman, Eli Fink and Leo Rosten, whom I have known for more than fifty years—each a distinct personality with different life experiences. They traveled with me from the grades to gray hairs. We have savored and endured much together, but scarcely a hint of this survives in my book.

A whole untouched era in my life is represented by the name of that dynamic and lovely woman, Lois Weisberg—the Shaw Centennial, the Shaw Society, *The Paper*. And through her I recall actors, authors, characters of every hue and shade. All these subjects and persons were interconnected with the Adult Education Council and its gifted executive directors, Esther Fain and Robert Ahrens. It is a feat to write of my life and not deal with them, like excluding myself from my autobiography.

I think of the Kurgans family who have been parts of my life for a generation; Peter Pollack for a longer period; John Ligtenberg; Jack Cowen; Alexander Isaacs; Ralph G. Newman; Carey McWilliams and Louis Adamic; Wayne Andrews; so many others. I think of the members of my family—brothers, sister, children, aunts and uncles, cousins. Some men and women have been close to me for a moment and then have vanished with scarcely a trace. Some are as unreal as if they had never existed.

There is a special role for the group of friends known collectively as the book club and discussion group.

One is always tempted to go on a sentimental journey if one has my temperament. Let it suffice for me to say that they and others are invisible threads of this story. So, too, the unmentioned colleagues and antagonists in countless unmentioned cases and controversies; the persons who have worked with me, especially Gladys Fuller and Wayne B. Giampietro, life-savers in times of stress.

The facts of my career, the chronology and vital statistics, are found in *Who's Who in the World* and other reference works—the organizations I have headed, the awards I have received, many miscellaneous items. Here I put flesh and spirit on some bare facts.

I say to the reader and to myself: Here is more than a glimpse of a person of many vicissitudes and passions. He would tell more, but that cannot be, for reasons too involved to relate. I plan for other occasions and in other incarnations.

———ELMER GERTZ

one

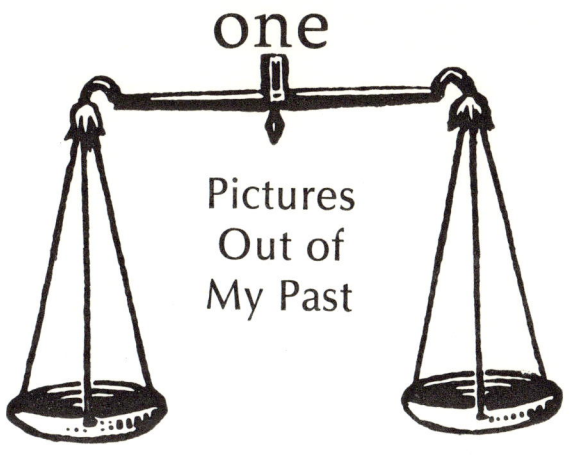

Pictures Out of My Past

In our family we all firmly believed that our paternal grandfather, Aaron Gertz, lived for 115 years. At the funeral service, the old and respected Rabbi Ephraim Epstein said that, many years before, when the rabbi himself was a mature man in the Old Country, our grandfather was already well advanced in years and both affluent and pious, than which there was no better combination unless learning, too, was added. No one ever accused Grandfather of book knowledge, other than Holy Writ. But all admitted that he was shrewd and sometimes wise. One of his family was the chief rabbi of Lithuania, a man whose reputation looms large in the folk histories.

Grandfather was a man's man, which means that he was, also, a lady's man, tremendous in size, sturdy, clear-eyed. This big man was matched for marriage by his parents, before he had a chance to see her, to a woman who was so small and unpretty that Grandfather was tempted to flee when he first met her on the bridal day. Like a good Jewish son, he went through the ceremony and was a faithful and provident husband as long as Grandmother lived. By then he could stray only with his eyes and his thoughts. Until his last day, his first comment about any woman pertained to her looks, rather than other qualities. He seemed to assume that, if she was pretty, there was no point in further inquiry. I am happy to say that this good sense has been passed down to his descendants.

Despite his age, Grandfather looked forward, rather than to the past. His interest was in the very young, and not in his contemporaries. He was a veteran of the first Crimean War, which was over before our Civil War had begun, but he never referred to it, save in answer to questions. He was intrigued only by what was going on, rather than what was over and done. He had more curiosity about his grandchildren and great-grandchildren than about his sons and daughters. He used to say, "My children are not too bright, but my grandchildren are very smart." He was brusque with his offspring, when they were in their seventies and beyond, but he treated their children and grandchildren with great respect and affection. He was proudest of the doctor, my brother George, and the lawyer, myself; the titles suggested an earned position, which meant even more than the wealth for which he also had a worldly man's respect.

We never knew our grandmother. She could not come here because of some ailment, so Grandfather remained in Lithuania during her life. Then World War I made it impossible for him to travel. It was not until he was an old man that we saw him for the first time. The only one of his children who had remained with him was my father's younger brother, Walter, and he, one of the Czar's hapless soldiers, was killed early in the war. Uncle Walter's wife died during that wretched time, virtually of starvation, and Grandfather was left to care for her three young children. We were told that much of the time while armies devastated the country Grandfather's family lived on grass. Finally, in 1920, he took the boys with him and journeyed to America. He was able to carry on, despite his very great age, his complete ignorance of the English language, and the responsibility of watching over three youngsters. We first saw him in Aunt Sarah's Chicago apartment, back of a Roosevelt Road delicatessen, not far from where I had been born. With his snow-white beard and dignified manners, he seemed like a patriarch transplanted from the Biblical past to an improbable new world. We took to him at once, and he to us. Although at his age it was hardly to be expected that he would learn our difficult language, and some of us were equally ignorant of the tongues that he spoke, there was no insurmountable problem in communicating with him. Somehow, we always made ourselves understood. Language, it seems, is only one overt form, scarcely more effective in translating meanings than gestures and love.

In one sphere, no one could persuade him. The doctors thought that he was too old and heavy to stuff himself with potatoes, his favorite food. In the manner of physicians, they wanted to make sure that he would not die young or happy. His youngest daughter, with whom he lived, was determined to follow their orders and would not prepare potatoes for him in any form. So he would get up in the middle of the night and surreptitiously boil a pot of spuds for himself; this he would wash down with good whiskey, even in prohibition days.

Nor was it wise for him to partake of sweets, although he had never visited a dentist and still had the remnants of his original teeth in his mouth. He solved this impediment to his happiness by hanging around the corner drugstore and acting as a sort of sergeant-at-arms over the children who congregated there. They delighted in this ancient drugstore cowboy. As a reward, the pharmacist would fill him with milk shakes and malteds, concoctions that he had never known abroad, but which he easily learned to love. It was difficult to determine which he preferred—whiskey, or the sweetened milk products beloved of children.

Grandfather toured the homes of his progeny between extended stays with his youngest daughter. He was the pride of young and old, a neighborhood exhibit wherever he went. The universal question inevitably was, "Is he really past 100?" He had so much of the very old in him and yet was so very well preserved that one just could not be sure about him. All delighted in photographing the celebrated head of the family. The cameras snapped him alone and in company with his children, grandchildren and great-grandchildren, and strangers. Grandfather was invariably serious about such things. I know of no smiling picture of him, particularly in association with the generations. A cousin of mine once bedecked him in formal attire, tails and all, and stood him next to the famous St. Gaudens Lincoln in the northside park. The photograph showed that Grandfather was at least as solemn as the martyred President, and bore a striking resemblance to Robert Todd Lincoln in his last days.

In Grandfather's honor, we created a cousins' club and met regularly. Never before or since had opposites found so much to hold them together. He was our darling despot and we hovered over him. But there came a time when it was best for him to live in a nursing home; then the cousins' club died.

Grandfather made friendships easily in the nursing home, but he cultivated one feud—with the doctor in charge, no less. Perhaps it was because he believed that there was no doctor in the world equal to my brother George, whose name became something like "Judge" to him. George, or "Judge," would minister to the growing needs of our grandfather, but each day the old man picked new quarrels with the nursing home physician. One morning Grandfather attempted to hit him with his heavy cane. The cane was taken from him, and he thereafter discussed with me the possibility of suing the doctor! I concluded that it was best to humor Grandfather, to give some excitement to his last days. So we would plot together the details of the suit that was to be filed and the division of damages. Grandfather seemed in no hurry to have the suit on file. It was enough to talk about it, and in this he showed considerable mental agility. While we were still discussing the litigation, Grandfather lapsed into his last earthly sleep, the result of old age, not illness. He seemed to be aware of the presence of his beloved "Judge" at the end.

His children now were on the way themselves to extreme old age. Sturdy as oaks they were, and it took great natural forces to fell them. They owed this, and more, to Grandfather. Myself, I owe great memories to him and links with a past in a land otherwise unknown to me.

My father was very much his father's son. Years before Grandfather arrived in America, I was intrigued by my sturdy and warmhearted parent.

In those distant days, when one had to depend wholly upon an inadequate public-transportation system, we lived in Roseland, which, though nominally a part of Chicago, was like a faraway country. Father traveled back and forth to work in the downtown area six days a week. He left our home before daybreak and returned after dark. We younger boys were generally asleep when he left and when he returned. On those rare occasions during the week when we were able to see him, we hovered close to him. He would place me upon one of his knees, and my brother Bob on the other knee. We looked lovingly at the big and handsome man, who carried himself with such grace in well-tailored garments.

Even when we were grown-up men, the eldest in his fifties, we all kissed him whenever we met or left him, never with matter-of-fact carelessness, always with a love that was reciprocated. For he was tender in his ways when he was not losing his temper. He could be like a hurricane in his angry forays, and anybody could be the victim. When the storm subsided, he was abashed. Sometimes, he broke a dish or mirror; then he would mend it, if he could.

One day, in a tough southside neighborhood to which we had moved from Roseland, Mother and I got on a streetcar ahead of Father. For no reason at all, the conductor insulted Mother. Father heard his nasty remarks as he got on the car. He proceeded to pummel the conductor, buffeting him from one end of the car to the other. When the motorman sought to interfere, my father cautioned against such foolish conduct. "You don't want to receive the same sort of licking that I'm giving this bum," Father said, soothingly. The motorman remained neutral.

Mother was never too well, and Father insisted upon her dropping all household chores on Sunday, his one day away from the Hart, Schaffner & Marx shop. He tidied up our home and cooked the dinner. He took pride in his roasts and soups and pies.

When our parents had first met, they were engaged to others. Father then spoke little English, and Mother less Yiddish. These barriers were insignificant. Mother taught him the English language, and he taught her Yiddish; both learned to read and write the other's tongue with considerable fluency. The marriage was by no means placid, but they loved each other with the sort of intensity that suggested that their years together were not going to be numerous. She was only thirty-eight when she died. He survived her by thirty-five years and was thereafter a much married man, but he never ceased to recall her with great tenderness.

Father always made each of his relatives feel that he, or she, was his particular favorite. "I have come to town, just to see you," he would say, and he would mean it at the moment. Not having time to see all of them, he would to choose that day's favorite. They all loved to be with him, and each cherished his own favorite story of Uncle Morris and his quips and fancies. He seemed to be on his way out almost as soon as he arrived. He was one of the few persons I knew who was more impatient than I, more punctual, and so energetic that when he lived in South Bend, hours away from us, he might be waiting for me in front of our apartment before seven in the morning, which meant that he had started from home at three or four.

He had the wonderful gift of taking his six children at their own valuation. If I considered myself the intellectual, the literary, the creative, the Puritan, Father accepted my assessment happily. He read everything that I wrote, no matter how difficult it was for an unschooled person, and he carried around newspaper clippings about me, which he insisted upon reading to his friends, with or without invitation.

Yet, he could view me, at times, with a surprising degree of objectivity. No one imagined that I could sing, but Father phrased it more exactly. "Elmer, you have a good foot for music," he once said to me.

When he had a clothing store, he used to bemoan the fact that I could not be more useful. "High-school graduate," he would say, sadly. "You can't trim windows!" He himself would show much grace, despite his size, in arranging the displays. And he was an amazing salesman. I often wondered why he failed to amass a fortune with his great gift of persuasion. It was probably because his general optimism was marred by a persistent pessimistic streak. When I came to the store after school, I often found him listing the assets and liabilities of the business. He easily persuaded himself that he was going bankrupt.

One day, while he was pressing a coat in the rear of the store, he noticed that a man was hiding some trousers in his jacket. Father hurried to the front of the store and handed a garment to the thief. "Mister," he said, "you have forgotten the coat." He then proceeded to mess up the man in the fashion of Everett True, a comic-strip character of that day who assaulted boors and others he disliked with an umbrella.

At that time, he had an employee named Ed Kelly, who sometimes managed to be sober. At such times, he was a good salesman. But he had the quaint view that, if he were known as Father's senior partner, he would be able to sell more. Father permitted him to print cards with the legend: "Kelly and Gertz, Clothiers." Father did not let vanity stand in the way of results.

So, for many years, we took great joy in him, and he in us. He had great strength and, like his father, might have passed the century mark had he not been overtaken by cancer. My brother, George, the physician, tried to arrest the disease by surgery. Just before going into the operating room, Father turned to my brother Bob and me and gave us the names and addresses of two men to whom he was indebted. "Be sure to give them every penny," he said. "They have nothing to show for what I owe them—no note, nothing." Thinking of them made him forget his pain and fears. Then he turned to me and said, "Give Bernice the watch that my synagogue gave me last year." This was his choicest possession.

Father survived the operation by more than two years. He was often in very great pain, but the love that he received from everyone compensated for this. He once said to me, "Elmer, I am the happiest man—in pain." Shortly after his operation, when he was optimistic about things, he turned to my sister and said, "I guess I am going to live, Bernice." Then, with a laugh, he added, "You had better return my watch to me."

No matter how much agony he suffered and even when bedridden in his very last days, he insisted on being shaved and clothed immaculately, and wore a handkerchief jauntily in his pajama pocket. He sat, uncomplainingly, near a window and read his favorite detective stories, now and then putting down the book to observe the beautiful flowers in his garden, brightened by the sunshine.

On his last day of life, he passed into a coma; but when I put my hand in his, he squeezed mine as if in tender recognition, although he could not say a word. He died in his eighty-second year, a man of unfailing humor and infinite love.

Recalling my grandfather and father and, later, as we shall see, my father-in-law, I could note, regretfully, that they belonged to a departed race—the immigrants who helped to create the nation we now cherish. They were men and women with originality and strength and poetry in them. With their departure, we have lost much that is irreplaceable.

If I am my father's son, I am no less my mother's, although her physical presence in my life was of much shorter duration.

When one has lost a parent during the first years of one's life, one is forever after in the painful process of seeking to recall and to recover and even to recreate one's unknown forebear. Those whose parents have survived into their maturity do not experience, nor can they truly understand, what this means.

I was in my tenth year when my young mother died. Normally, I would have been old enough to have formed some definite impressions of her. But my mother had been ill and in hospitals for several years prior to her death, so that it was as if she had passed out of my life when I was only seven or so. I can recall a number of incidents about her, and can even sketch her character and personality in broad lines, with enough deftness to persuade others that I really knew my mother. The sober truth is that I did not.

In a vague sort of way, I recall her rather tall and thin figure, her ample auburn hair, her smallish glasses, her fondness for reading. Sometimes I can imagine her voice or, at least, snatches of her speech. I know, in a general way, her love for certain foods. I remember bits out of my babyhood when she nursed me through a siege of pneumonia. I recall when she cautioned me not to touch a cup of cocoa that she had placed before me, and I ignored her advice and scalded myself badly. There is a vague sort of impression of her taking me to the hospital on two or three occasions; once leaving me there, on the promise that she was presently going to return with some ice cream. On my sixth birthday she took me to an ice-cream parlor and bought me a soda, sitting alongside of me while I gobbled it. One day I am going to write of half a hundred similar half-realized recollections, and I will do so only because of this irresistible yearning to find the lost one. All of my life I have sought to give materiality to the maternal spirit that has only vaguely hovered over me.

I was probably eight years old when I was told one day that my mother was going to return from the hospital. I was so stirred with happiness that I could scarcely remain seated in the house. I ran outside to be at hand the moment that Mother arrived. Suddenly, a woman appeared. I did not recognize her, so ravaged was she by illness. She took me in her arms and cried, "My Elmer does not even recognize me!" It is, perhaps, the sharpest and most painful recollection of my youth. It has run through my mind during the decades since then.

For many years I dreamed of writing a novel about my mother. I was going to call it, "Grace Was Her Name." I thought of her as having a gracious personality to match her name. All of my older cousins, my older brothers, my father, my aunts and uncles assured me that she was the dearest person that ever lived. This I believed. Gradually, the idea of the novel vanished, just as the image of my mother receded. On May 4, 1974, it will be fifty-seven years since she died. I am sad in a vague sort of way, because of the tragedy of not really remembering. That is a void that cannot be filled by wishful thinking, by an active and satisfying life, by words, by anything that I know. Now, this seeking for the unattainable, this effort to materialize one's shadow parent may give a spiritual quality to one's life that might otherwise be lacking. At the same time, it is maiming. It is as if one had come into this world incomplete and rootless.

I was born on September 14, 1906, on Blue Island Avenue, near what was then 12th Street, on the East Side of Chicago, in an area where immigrant Jews and their children often lived in those days. I was the fourth child, the third son, born to my parents, Morris and Grace Gertz. Two other sons were later added to the family, making an even half-dozen children. Although two-thirds of the way down in the family roster, I was in the middle according to age, seven years younger than the oldest, Edward Milton (then usually referred to as Edmil), and seven years older than the youngest, George (whose full name was resounding indeed—George Joseph David—but whom we called Yookie). We were a close knit family, even in our differences. As the years went on, we became more, rather than less, devoted to each other.

I can illustrate the close relationship of my only sister Bernice and myself by an episode from my high-school years. It tells much, too, of my brother Robert Sidney, twenty-two months my junior, and born in the midst of Fourth of July fireworks. He and I, companions as well as brothers, had gone together to the Pageant of Progress at Navy Pier when "Big Bill" Thompson was mayor of the city. We stopped eagerly at every booth, picking up pounds of literature and samples, gobbling down free food, and enrolling in various prize competitions. It was great fun, but forgotten until months later when I received a letter and a $500 check from the Gulbranson Piano Company—I was one of the prize-winners! I rushed to the office where Bernice and Bob were both employed, so that I might share the excitement with my sister. Then all three of us hurried to the bank where I had a small savings account. I would deposit this mammoth amount in my account. All three of us babbled happily. Just as we were about to enter the bank, Bob confessed that he had gotten hold of Gulbranson stationery and checks at the Pageant of Progress and faked the $500 award. "What if I had deposited the money without seeing you and Bernice?" I demanded sternly. "I know you, Elmer." he responded. "You were certain to rush first to Bernice with the news. You always tell her everything."

We moved from one neighborhood to another from time to time. I remember neighborhoods better than I do the flats we lived in, which all seemed to be comfortable, never luxurious, gas-lit, coal heated, generally without telephone, and the younger children, including myself, were bathed in a washtub, the water heated on the stove. Of course, we had no automobile. The only times that we rode in a car were when warmhearted Uncle Dave Belson, the affluent member of our family, occasionally visited us, gave us each a dime, and took us out for a ride.

From Roseland we moved to Halsted near 51st Street in the "Back of the Yards" area, the one Jewish family surrounded by the Irish, Germans, and Swedes. We were scarcely aware of the odors of the slaughterhouses that thrived before World War I. To the youngsters the Yards were a place to steal resin, for uses that I cannot recall and probably never knew. O'Leary's Public Market and Luna Park, across from our hardware and crockery store, attracted crowds with the circus atmosphere. The nearby carbarns had been the scene of the exploits of the once-famous bandits led by Webb. Dietrich's bank, at a nearby corner, had not yet become a symbol of the depredations of the private bankers. Immigrants used to invest their meager savings with the banker of their ethnic group, confident that he would cherish their precious dollars. Often enough banks and money would disappear.

The cabbage patch around the corner was the spot chosen by the competing Irish and Germans for a weekly shindig. Outsiders like ourselves were eager observers of the brick battles, unaffected by the loss, one Friday, of a contestant's eye. I had worked at the cabbage patch, which we thought of as a farm, for a nickel a day, but I was promptly fired when I placed a bushel basket over a fleeing baby pig and forgot to remove the covering until it was discovered that it had suffocated.

The clubhouse of Ragen's Colts on our block was an increasing attraction to us. We loved to watch, through the store-front window, the pool tables, the punching bags, the bowling alleys, the other signs of robust activity, never dreaming that this group of athletes would spearhead, only a few years later, the worst race riots in the city's history, along with other assorted crimes and misdeeds. I felt inconspicuous in this circle of the Irish and was shocked, a generation later, when the leader of the Colts, Frank Ragen, himself, greeted me warmly by first name when he saw me in the office where I began the practice of law, under John L. McInerney, whose father had been the alderman of the ward and an undertaker. Shortly after this brief reunion, Ragen was killed while recuperating from wounds in a well- (but not too well-) guarded hospital. I understood then what I did not know as a child—that I was living in a violent world and that it would not take much of a push to send one downhill to prison, a hangman's noose, sudden death, a drunkard's grave. My brother, Ed, big and powerful, was welcomed by Ragen's Colts, despite our being Jewish. My brother, Sol (Circus Solly, as he was called because of his wild ways) shot craps with the janitor at the Dewey School around another corner, and heaved rocks at Diamond Tooth, the big cop who had hurt his dog.

I would invariably explore any new neighborhood to which we moved and invariably I would get lost. I would romp around, preoccupied with great dreams, and lose my bearings.

My peregrinations were famous in our family circle. Early one morning I wandered off to a spot where I had heard there was going to be a circus. Daydreaming of the event, I was hit simultaneously by two motorcycles traveling in opposite directions. Someone deposited me in our hallway and the screams aroused my mother. I was confined for days. When I had recovered, I wandered again. This time, at Sherman Park, blocks away, I discovered a library. I had never known that there was such an institution. Spellbound, I remained there all day, feverishly going through the shelves of books. When I returned home, I was surprised at the worry my long absence had caused. But thereafter, books were the great essentials of my life, as necessary as bread and air.

I learned at the ripe age of six that there was a delicious experience known as sex. My teacher was an eight-year-old Irish girl, Alice. Years later when I read the first pages of Frank Harris' *My Life and Lovers,* I did not scoff in disbelief, like so many others; my little Irish girl had taught me what Harris himself had learned in Ireland.

More than fifty years later, Henry Miller, who was visiting with us, expressed the desire to see the Stock Yards in order to learn how they looked in their decline. My son Ted and I drove him there. He saw the almost-empty Yards and the ghost buildings as perfect subjects for the photography of his friend Brassaï, illustrator of *Quiet Days in Clichy.* He was delighted as always, expressing himself as he did in his books. I saw only the wisps and shadows of my distant youth. We drove on the very street where I had once lived, and I tried to recall the scenes and personalities of long ago. My memories were clouded and incomplete. "I want to see my old school," I said. I had not seen it in more than half a century. We drove past. It was like a toy school, so much smaller than I remembered it, so much smaller than they now build schools. Were all of the giants of my past in fact pygmies?

As I think of the greatest influence of my youth, I recall words by Bernard Shaw that I read years later.

"I now confess to an episode in my boyhood formerly so repugnant to me that for 80 years I never mentioned it to any mortal creature, not even to my wife." With these words, Shaw began a chapter of his book, *Sixteen Self Sketches,* published just a year before the end of his long life. What was that dread and unmentionable secret? That he was a student, briefly, at The Central Boys' School in Dublin, a sort of classless institution populated by Roman Catholics that distressed Shaw's snobbish Protestant soul.

With the example of Shaw before me, I must confess that, for the first two or three decades of my life, I sometimes found it difficult to mention that I had lived for several years in two orphanages, one in Cleveland and the other in Chicago. When I mentioned the situation, I was quick to add, as if to take off the sting of charity, that my father paid for our residence there, and it was as if we were in boarding schools. Once I began an article in a Boston literary journal with a quotation from the Gilbert and Sullivan operetta, "The Pirates of Penzance." "It is a useful thing to be an orphan boy," they said; and, indeed, it is, as I can testify.

"Experts" say that orphanages are passé, that foster homes are psychologically and socially sounder. So these youthful reminiscences of mine are in the nature of a period piece, a relic of a discarded institution.

In every family there is an arbiter of right and wrong, whose judgments are accepted, not necessarily because they are sound, but because they are voiced in an authoritarian tone. My mother's younger sister Marie Belson filled that role for us. She decreed that my eight-year-old brother, Bob, and I would be better off in an orphanage than in a motherless home and that the B'nai B'rith institution in Cleveland, dating from the post-Civil War days, was the very one for us, although it meant geographical separation from our family. So in the first days of July, 1917, Bob and I took our first train trip, with our aunt and uncle. A group of relatives, undoubtedly commiserating our orphaned circumstances, saw us off at the railroad station, and showered us tenderly with gifts. But it was a gala occasion for us and, with complete disregard of the presumed tragedy, we rejoiced in it. All night long, as we lay in our upper berth, we talked, with mounting excitement, of the adventures that lay before us in a new world, and we chewed deliriously on hard plums, almond chocolates and other confections. Our first night in Cleveland was spent in a hotel, the first one at which we had ever stopped, and we toured the town by trolley car. Then, on July 4, Independence Day, Bob's birthday, we went to 5000 Woodland Avenue, entered the gate (usually kept firmly locked), walked expectantly down the long sidewalk to the office in one of the ancient buildings, and we were part of the Jewish Orphan Asylum of Cleveland. Imagine a name like that! When later the word "Home" was substituted for the fifty-year-old "Asylum," it was as if a revolution had been wrought, just as later when the J.O.H. was renamed Bellefaire, there was, indeed, a new day in a new world.

We were not permitted to go beyond the gates of the home. We ate together in one big dining hall, in which the meals were highly institutionalized and not very tasty, unless an occasional treat was served to mark a special occasion, like the birthday of some very important person. We had schedules for everything —school, worship, play. We had rules of all sorts, with merits and demerits to match. When Bob misbehaved on an occasion or two, he was spanked by the superintendent, who assumed the role of parent. Mail was delivered to us on one night each week. We all sat, expectantly, in a big room and, as our names were called, we received messages from home. When too many packages arrived for us, our families were told to cut down.

One could write an account of the orphanage that would read like a tale out of Dickens—something like *Nicholas Nickleby* or *Oliver Twist*. The J.O.H. could be made to seem like a prison. Later I could understand how Nathan Leopold felt in Stateville. There were some who reacted that way to the orphanage. Edward Dahlberg, a literary figure of some reputation, who left the home as we arrived there, has written in agonizing terms of orphan life; he saw nothing good in it, although he conceived great pages in his books out of the experiences. Neither my brother nor I felt like the dour Dahlberg. In fact, the home was a very stimulating place to us, as it was to Louis Gilbert, the actor, who was our contemporary, and General Samuel Lawton, who preceded us by many years.

The old engineer and handyman at the home, an Indian, purported to be a survivor of Custer's Last Stand at Little Big Horn. He said that, finally, he had learned to like the white man; and he used to tell us countless tales, which we firmly believed, even when he contradicted himself. The art of storytelling was cultivated by many of us in the dormitories and playgrounds. I acquired a reputation for telling highly imaginative tales.

The home had a very large postage-stamp collection, which privileged children were permitted to see occasionally. There, one could journey forth everywhere without leaving the home. I, particularly, wanted to see the lands of triangular and other oddshaped stamps. With such philatelic richness, I was sure that they had much to offer eager-eyed boys.

In our truly excellent school, we learned, besides the usual academic subjects, Hebrew and, until the wartime hysteria put an end to it, German. Military training, in Teutonic style, took its place. I used to hide and read books like *Les Misérables,* while loud voices boomed my name.

We were taken on trips now and then to the Euclid Beach amusement park (where I, fearful of such things, learned that the Velvet Coaster was really as breath-taking and rugged as any ride of more tumultuous name). At the Indians' Baseball park, we saw the great Tris Speaker, Stanley Coveleski and Ray

Chapman (later killed by a ball pitched by Carl Mays) in their heydeys. And on one never-to-be-forgotten day, I saw Babe Ruth, then a famous Red-Sox hurler, pitch a one-hit game and win it on his own triple.

Above and beyond all else, there was the influence of one of the greatest men that I have known—Dr. Simon Peiser, the superintendent of the home. He and I walked through the J.O.H. grounds, he with his arm around my shoulder. We talked of literature and life. He listened to all of my ideas and never belittled them. If he disagreed, he did so gently, as when he suggested to me, a boy not yet in his early teens, that I ought to refrain from reading George Eliot's *Romola,* until I was somewhat older. Many years later, I read an account of Dr. Peiser that captured his character perfectly. "He was at once stern moralist and tender in his spirits," the anonymous writer said, "culturally an aristocrat and a democrat among the children . . ." He became a part of each life, my own particularly.

A few years after I last saw him, he died, overworked on an American mission to war-desolated Eastern Europe. I have met many men in my life—Presidents of the United States, Nobel Prize winners, poets, men of genius and distinction; but no one has meant more to me than Simon Peiser. I count my life blessed because he was my mentor for those few years in the Jewish Orphan Home of Cleveland. When he gave me a copy of Dickens' *Our Mutual Friend* as a prize, I was inspired to read all Dickens' works. Because of him I was familiar not only with Dickens, but with Victor Hugo and other great writers. Inspired, I wrote feverishly. I edited the children's papers at the home when I was twelve or so. I was a thoughtful person, mature, ready for life in many respects. Then in January, 1920, I left the Cleveland home to enter one in Chicago, called the Marks Nathan Jewish Orphan Home.

For years, I lost track of the Cleveland home, and it of me. Then, following my first wife's tragic death, a sort of nostalgia for the past came upon me and I renewed my contact both with the Cleveland home and with my contemporaries of the Chicago home. I began to realize that the absence of one or more parents is not necessarily a tragedy, but the absence of love and happiness, the failure to achieve the satisfactions that make life worth living, are.

My whole method of life and thought stems from the background that has been denied to most children. It is, indeed, a useful thing to be an orphan boy, as the Pirate Chief and I knew.

two

A Very Serious Young Man

Eli Fink, my great friend from those days, a scholar of scholars, likes to recall my experiences in the seventh-grade class of Miss Hampden, an antiquated spinster with the most conventional of viewpoints. She used to regard me as not very bright, an unusual experience for me with any teacher. She wrote a letter to the Superintendent of the Marks Nathan Home that suggested that perhaps the trouble was I needed new eye glasses. My glasses were good enough; in truth, Miss Hampden was outraged that I had disagreed audibly with her when she praised Longfellow's "Evangeline" as great poetry. "Miss Hampden," I said in class, "I don't agree with you about that awful poem. It is much like a jingle. It does not have great thoughts and it does not have great language."

Later, Miss Hampden took a second look at me when it was announced in one of the Chicago newspapers that I was a winner of the Lincoln essay contest. My prize-winning composition was printed in full with my name and address and the school I was attending. No longer did my eyes need correction; **no** longer was I stupid; I had a silver medal from a daily newspaper to prove that I had talents.

Although I could recognize the shoddiness of some of Longfellow's efforts, I was once deservedly rebuked by the judges of a contest for selecting equally shoddy literary merchandise. The home had an oratorical contest that aroused great interest among the boys and girls. I entered the contest, and won, despite my lamentable choice of poems. I was one of those insufferable creatures—a boy orator—until my voice changed and lost its silvery qualities for some years. I tried to pick that poetic piece that would most show off the range of my voice, regardless of the intrinsic quality of the words. I selected—I blush to recall it—Tennyson's "The Charge of the Light Brigade."

Although I had no aptitude for technical subjects, except, somehow, mechanical and architectural drawing, I went to Crane Technical High School, then a school of outstanding reputation in scholarship, athletics, student government, and activities generally. My contemporaries at Crane included Meyer Levin, who was certainly our best writer (subsequently he was my opponent in a famous law suit in which I represented Nathan Leopold), Leo Rosten (with Eli Fink and George Herman, my oldest and dearest friends), Louis Zara, the author and editor, Leo Lerner, who later edited a chain of many neighborhood newspapers, Aaron Bohrod, the celebrated artist, and many others. There were even some who became architects and engineers!

What distinguished Crane Tech in my day was its amazing student spirit. It was an all-boys school, and this may have sublimated the libidos into other, safer channels. We took great pride in governing ourselves. Discipline was left largely in our hands. At one time I was judge of the student court, and a severe judge, too. I did not hesitate to suspend students for offenses against the mores of our community. It was fortunate that Leo

Rosten, the Big Brother of the court, could intercede now and then to soften the punishments I meted out.

I am embarrassed when I recall all of the organizations to which I have belonged at Crane Tech and later in my life. I ask myself at times if this means that, despite any pretensions to the contrary, I am a Babbitt, an inveterate joiner of petty organizations. There may be something in my psyche that requires such often-counterfeit tokens of success. I could resist scholarly honors, but not organizational ones. Why not? Bernard Shaw could have asked himself the same question in connection with his endless committee work.

One of the sensations of our day at Crane Tech was when a teacher was picked up in a police raid at a nearby brothel, often frequented by the more robust students. The daily newspapers covered the story with big headlines. I did not refer to the event in any of my feature articles in "The Crane Tech." Another was an English teacher, a woman amply endowed sexually, who was known to be susceptible to well-developed boys like my brother Edward. She flourished for at least a decade, without getting either pregnant or reprimanded by the principal.

It may be that coeducational schools are better generally than single-sex institutions, but we at Crane Tech seemed to miss nothing. I have often thought that my three and a half years there were more meaningful than my six years at the University of Chicago, great though that school was and is. Schools, like other institutions, develop an ambiance that later may be lost. Crane Tech today does not have the spirit that it had in my day.

I have often thought of the almost mad variety of occupations I have had since my high-school years. There was never a time when I was just a student or, for that matter later, just a lawyer. I ought to tell now of some of these extra-curricular activities before narrating the story of my college days and my subsequent legal career.

I taught English at the Jewish People's Institute during my college days, and the sole dividend was my being present at the inception of the Hyman Kaplan stories; I got the job through Leo Rosten, the creator of the immortal night-school student.

It was at this time that a friend suggested that I had a talent for writing advertising copy. "It is scandalous that you earn so little," he said. "Why don't you apply for a job with one of the big agencies?" He gave me a few of the better names, and I composed my best letter in praise of my own talents, and sent it off to a good firm. By special delivery, sight unseen, I was hired. When I reported at the office, I was unhired. Somehow I got the impression that it was due to my nose, which suggests my Jewish origin.

I associated myself instead with a Philadelphia promoter, who was more trusting than any Philadelphia lawyer. He took my qualifications on faith. My first assignment was to ghostwrite an autobiography of the notorious gangster Al Capone. Capone, whom I never met, was willing, provided I turned the book into a preachment against prohibition. I was willing, too, since my brothers, other than the physician, had long been in the medicinal spirits business. Then Capone changed his mind; I think it was at the time that he found refuge in a Philadelphia prison, shortly before his income-tax indictment.

As a fitting sequel to the assignment, I was given the task of turning old Judge Marcus Kavanaugh's book, *You Be the Judge*, into a series of moving pictures. We took over, rent-free, a courtroom in the Criminal Court Building. We cast Kavanaugh, himself, in the role of judge, and, whenever he was awake, he was fine. We tried to make Pete into a movie bailiff, but despite his forty years of service as the judge's bailiff, he was a flop—utterly unrealistic in the part. Mayor Thompson's city prosecutor, William Saltiel, his hair then jet black, was our prosecuting attorney, and he was so good that we had visions of the gallows when he bellowed forth; Wayland Brooks was to be the defense attorney; he was sweet and mushy, and ineffective, and later found what some regarded as his natural place in the United States Senate. I wrote the script and blurbs and looked important; but the venture flopped. My Philadelphian tried to rescue the situation by promoting what he called a Traffic Tangle. It was so tangled that I cannot explain it to this day.

So, as we shall see, I became a lawyer; but the old yearning for variety in my work would not die. While practicing law with the Arvey firm, I became the director of public relations for the Illinois Police Association, in connection with its promotion of an historical pageant at the Century of Progress Exposition in 1933–1934. I wrote the pageant, secured sponsors for it, including Carl Sandburg, and ran an historical essay contest among the school children of the State.

My ego received a jolt when a client remarked to one of my law associates, "Elmer is a remarkable man—a lawyer and a writer"; and the associate replied, "Half-ass lawyer, half-ass writer." In any event, the police project failed, too.

The financial angel of the police pageant was a man who had always engaged in dubious enterprises. Some might have called him a confidence man. He gave large sums to the police organization for the pageant, however, and interfered not at all; he was content to be repaid in the end with a share of the profits. This was solemnly agreed to; then, suddenly, without warning, the organization canceled the pageant and its debt to the angel. He was never repaid. He said to me: "All my life I have dealt with hoodlums and racketeers and have never been cheated. Then I placed my faith in the police . . ."

My school days, like my later career as a lawyer, were always punctuated with episodes like this.

During much of the time I was attending high school and then college, I lived on that West Side of the city in a vibrant neighborhood populated largely by Jews a notch or two above the poorer people who still lived in the Maxwell Street immigrant area.

Douglas Boulevard was the thoroughfare on which Leo Rosten, my great companion of those days, and I walked and talked for hours on end, back and forth, discussing all of the intimate, literary, and worldly problems that concerned us (and we were concerned and articulate about everything). Occasionally, we would relax in Leo's apartment, where his sharp-eyed tiny mother would make ever-so-lightly textured scrambled eggs for us, while she listened unobtrusively to our conversation, saying nothing, but taking great pride in her very bright son and his dearest friend. "Mrs. Rosenberg" (that was the family name before Leo Americanized it), I would say, with much conviction, "you make the best scrambled eggs in the world!" Later, when I was not there, Mrs. Rosenberg would ask her son, "What in the world can you and Elmer talk about so much?" For Leo and I saw each other, not only every day, but sometimes all day. Our friendship has lasted, but it has not always had the intensity of those early years.

Even then, Leo was an exceptional public speaker. He and his younger sister Helen used to give recitals; she sang folk songs in various languages and he expatiated on them or other subjects. His parents and cousins and I would sit with the audience, beaming approval and wonder. Leo gave lectures at the Jewish People's Institute, where we both worked, on the various writers that we respected, Frank Harris not least. Despite any factual inaccuracies, he would give superbly perceptive and eloquent expositions.

I used to travel each day, by the elevated, from my little room off Douglas Boulevard to the University, miles away. Often, it was the only time I had to study, because of the jobs I held. I had to utilize every moment of my time. I learned how to concentrate in the midst of uproar. There is a classic story of a piano being stolen under my nose while I was supposedly in charge of a recreation room. Preoccupied with reading, I did not observe the mischievous boys removing the piano.

In as great an academic institution as the University of Chicago, there were relatively few faculty members who made a lasting impression on me. I recall some very brilliant lectures by the renowned historian, Andrew McLaughlin, who spoke intimately of the fathers of our constitution. To my amazement, he professed to know little of Thomas Paine, who had so stirred the revolutionary soldiers and contributed to the birth of our nation, but he knew everything about the minor figures. Harold Lasswell was at the beginning of his career as a political scientist. He illustrated what he had to say by distributing to us newspapers from everywhere. He was on the road to acquiring his particular idiom that made simple matters complex. From Harry A. Millis I took numerous courses in labor economics in the midst of the national capitalistic euphoria. Millis was never exciting, but always informative in the field in which he was the most renowned student. Raleigh Stone, an apologist for the established order, carried on a dialogue with me on trade unionism in an extremely useful seminar in which the other students simply sat by while Stone and I argued our diversity of viewpoint. There was one memorable laboratory course in botany given by Professor John Coulter, a world-celebrated botanist, and his son Merle and another assistant. With no special aptitude for the sciences, I was deeply absorbed in this course, perhaps because the senior Coulter had great dramatic ability, making plant life sing and dance in rapture.

One of my most satisfying classes was in public speaking, taught by Professor Bertram Nelson, who was an exciting and exacting teacher. I used to have great fun talking in favor of women's rights, but against intellectual women; for greater economic equality, and against the dead level of conformity. It was easy to learn why some people found me upsetting; they thought I was radical when I said in class that a woman had as much right to smoke as a man. One day Professor Nelson unexpectedly asked, "Is not Elmer Gertz brilliant?" All nodded in agreement, and I beamed happily, until the professor went on to say, ominously: "Yet Mr. Gertz will fail unless he gets rid of his lisp before the end of the quarter." I got rid of it, though now and then, these days, it returns.

No man in my undergraduate days inspired me more than James Weber Linn, generally known to thousands of grateful students as Teddy Linn, because, as some said, he was a bear with the ladies. He taught English literature and composition and made them seem important and exciting even to those who came to the University simply for football. (The U. of C., in my day, actually won the Big Ten championship.) Linn, a nephew of Jane Addams of Hull House, was a football fancier, a golfer, a journalist, a would-be novelist and biographer, a politician; but, above all, he was a great teacher, who communicated his enthusiasms to the dullest. Although his classes were large, they were intimate.

The thrill was unforgettable when Linn wrote on the first composition that I submitted to him, before I really knew him: "I'll be doggoned. Let me take a look at you." Thereafter we took many looks at each other and developed a profound mutual respect. Nobody would call Linn a great writer, but he had an infallible instinct for discovering talent in others. There was not a potential writer who went to Chicago who was not immediately picked out by Linn, and these included Vincent Sheehan, John Gunther, Elizabeth Maddox Roberts, James Farrell, Glenway Westcott, Sterling North, Janet Flanner, Meyer Levin, George Dillon, Leo Rosten, Harry Barnard, and others.

Linn was the sort of man who would have risen from the dead, if he could, to help a friend.

The proudest memento of my college career is a letter he wrote to me in response to my request for a job recommendation. I prized the letter so much that I put it away for security and did not find it again for forty years.

The letter read in part:

> Reached Chicago yesterday and sent in your recommendation today. I said you were one of the most industrious and brilliant students I had ever had, and that if you did not become distinguished I should be surprised; which, so far as I know, I never said before of any student.

Linn was, by all odds, the best man I met at the University of Chicago and one of the most inspiring in my entire career.

In my first year in college I went to an eye doctor for what I thought was a routine examination. I had had such examinations from time to time since I first began to wear glasses when I was ten or eleven. There would be adjustments in the prescriptions, but nothing of a basic nature. Now, out of the blue, the doctor announced that I had to stop reading completely, give up school, adopt an occupation that would remove all strain on my eyes—otherwise, I would become blind! This was like a sentence of death for one of my interests, habits, and temperament. In a state of shock I went to an ophthalmologist of great reputation—Dr. Harry S. Gradle. With trepidation, I told him of the dire warnings given me by the other doctor. He listened quizzically, examined and reexamined me with great care, prescribed new glasses, and told me not to worry—that I could go on as before. I continued at school; I read as much, or more, than ever; I wrote; I was the same sort of student that I always had been. Almost fifty years later, I suspect that Dr. Gradle was right.

In those days we were all closely shaved each day and our hair was well cropped. We wore neat, pressed suits, shirts and ties, despite the poverty of our wardrobe and purses; and the most unconventional of us was not much interested in politics. We were not activists. We shared H. L. Mencken's contempt for our rulers, especially the Presidents of our day, whom we called Dr. Harding and Dr. Coolidge in mocking token of their honorary degrees and vapid minds.

At the University there were men and women of various races and ethnic groups—Negroes from the United States and Africa (they were not called blacks then), Indians, Chinese, Japanese; Jews, Greeks, Irish; all of the world's hues. There were artists, poets, dancers, philosophers, journalists. While there was no political ferment at the school, there were creative fires and yearnings for brotherhood, rather than merely civil rights in the political sense. I became close to all of them. We early enlisted Haridas T. Mazumdar, a Hindu who had written the first book in the English language on his master, Gandhi. Haridas, a very good-looking man, somewhat older than we, brought in his friend Przada, equally good looking, and more energetic. He knew Hindu magic and lore and would perform for us. I did not hear the name of Haridas after I left college, until I was discussing *Tropic of Cancer* with Henry Miller, in 1962, in Minneapolis, and learned the amazing fact that Haridas was the model for the Hindu in some fantastic passages in that highly original work.

It was not possible to dine with men and women of other races in any "white" restaurants or clubs in Chicago at that time. This was true until the end of World War II. We met, therefore, in the home of Barefield Gordon or at the nearby Appomattox Club. Sometimes Professor Linn or other members of the faculty would join us in our discussions of the arts. Poems would be read and criticized, unceremoniously. I remember reading a poem of mine about Wagner before it appeared in "The Chicago Defender," a leading Negro newspaper to which I often contributed. I intoned solemnly:

> As the strains of "Die Walküre" eat into my flesh,
> I think that Wagner drew from Zeus a heaven of thunder
> And from the Himalayan heights something
>   of their unattainable summit.
>
> There clangs in my ears the crassness of brass
> And in my heart the audacity of strange-voiced strings;
> A medley of disharmonic harmonies
> And then a roll and a tide of sweetness,
> And my inmost vessels sail giddily through the body's sea.
> Restless,
>   Startled,
>   Restless!
>
> A crescendo succeeds a seeming crescendo;
> The wrath of Sinai's Jehovah silences the defiance of
>   Lucifer,
> And a chorus of archangels anathematize.
> I twist and turn, lean forward, and back—
> The music ceases,
> I am silent;
> Visions of the Valhalla of artist heroes beautify my
>   sight.

> There struts Wagner,
> Conducting the heroic orchestration of the future;
> There dream I on a solid cloud of rhythmic splendor;
> There you recline at my side!

Immediately everyone tore into it, especially a rather hefty woman of much assurance, who proclaimed the faults of my poem with little effort at softening the blows. Then Fenton Johnson, deep of voice, despairing of manner, would read one of his free verses, which would soon find its way into the anthologies.

To me books were always as important as people. My life was highlighted by my experiences with the printed word.

When I was in high school, I began to see, here and there, very small cardboard bound books, generally in blue, sixty-four pages in length, on a vast variety of subjects. They cost only a nickel, a price within my means, and I bought and read as many as I could find. By the time I entered college, the Little Blue Books came out in torrents and there were stores downtown with whole departments devoted to them. One store sold only Little Blue Books. I spent hours there, as well as at other shops handling used volumes. I craved books like any drug addict. There was hardly a moment that I was without one. I devoured books; breathed books; I dreamed them. Every inch of space in my bedroom was crowded with them. I never had enough. It was a delirious experience, thanks largely to the nickel products that were published in Girard, Kansas, by E. Haldeman-Julius, married to a niece of Jane Addams and thus a cousin of my beloved Teddy Linn.

There were countless books on sex, popular and scientific ones. Through them I first heard of Sigmund Freud and learned about psychoanalysis. It gave new understanding to me in an area that had troubled me from early childhood when my little seductress Alice had introduced me to that wonderful kinetic world.

There were books by and about the major and minor poets and dramatists, American, English, Latin, Greek, French.

Will Durant's "Story of Philosophy" first appeared in this form, and I read it from beginning to end, and the writings of the philosophers to whom he referred—Plato, Aristotle, Nietzsche, Schopenhauer, and others. I found myself particularly influenced in my daily life by the counsels of Schopenhauer.

There were hundreds of titles that I read in this magical form. I discovered Frank Harris and read all that E. Haldeman-Julius published of him—"The Man Shakespeare," "Contemporary Portraits," "Montes the Matador," "A Daughter of Eve," other stories. The name was totally new, the effect phenomenal, as I shall narrate presently.

E. Haldeman-Julius was a great educator, despite his flamboyance. He was the father of the paperback-book industry. He made millions of Americans, myself not least, read without apology and regardless of time or place. He was a comet in my universe and I will not forget him. It grieves me to recall that he took his own life rather than face the disasters that came his way later because of his tax difficulties.

He had been a socialist at one time, but became more interested in other ideas, chiefly the fight against religious dogmatism. Under his influence I wrote a poem which expressed my anti-religious ideology in college days. I no longer have the dogmatism of these words, nor the blasphemous spirit:

I
Take not the name of God in vain;
In Jesus' name, what can you gain?

II
Here's to the sacraments divine;
Oh, while I'm here I'll get mine
And when I'm gone the Lord can do
No more, I swear, than I or you.

III
There's heaven for the rich and one for the poor;
The rich man's heaven has a closed door.

IV
They sing of charity and have none;
They praised the good giver and gave none.

V
Here's to the Church of God who loves;
A few more babes to hell he shoves.

VI
Hark! the herald angels sing:
It does not mean a blessed thing.
The Father, Son and Holy Ghost;
Oh, all they do is loaf and boast.
Thou art Peter and on this rock
I shall erect a cuckoo clock!

In a somewhat more philosophical, less blatant, spirit, I wrote these words during the same Haldeman-Julius period:

> Awakened from the aching past
> And sent pell mell to death at last,
> The shrouded corpses earning then
> The tawdry tears of vulgar men;
>
> One rogue combats another one,
> The foolish gibber never done,
> While idle crowds pollute the air;
> No soulful calm, no rest is there;
>
> No rest until the endless sleep
> Within the wormy, ravished deep;
> There is no meaning—can be none—
> A foolish scene to blur the sun!

three

The Law

One day in 1924 when my father was ill, I was in charge of his clothing store on the South Side of Chicago. Two burly men entered the store. They looked to me like hoodlums. I feared they were going to rob me. One of them said, peremptorily, "Come with us, kid!" "Why?" I asked. They declined to answer. "May I call my father?" I inquired. They curtly refused, and took me in their automobile to the Northwest Side of the city to a police station, miles from my father's store. I was left, unattended, in a locked room. Later, one whom I took to be a plain-clothes detective entered the room. He seemed friendlier than the two who had picked me up. He began to talk with me on the subject everyone was discussing, the *Loeb-Leopold* case that had just broken. The two who had kidnapped and murdered the Frank boys were very little older than I. They, like me, were Jewish and Southsiders; they were at the end of their academic careers at the University of Chicago, and I was about to begin mine there. The officer, in the simplistic fashion of some police, most have thought that this gave me special competence. We talked for hours, speculating about the reasons for such horrible crimes.

But I was given no food or drink; I was held incommunicado. Suddenly, around midnight, the officer said: "Kid, you can call your father." He also told me, for the first time, that I was being held because a stolen negotiable bond was traced to me. I had deposited one of its interest coupons in my meager savings account. This, the only bond I owned, had been given to me as a graduation gift. Of course, I knew nothing about its being stolen, nor, I learned later, did the person who had given it to me. I explained the situation to my troubled father and he attempted to persuade a judge whom we knew to order my release. The judge was rather annoyed that he was called so late. "Can't your son remain in jail over night?" he asked. Finally, he arranged for my release. The next morning I appeared before another judge. He laughed—I did not know what was funny—and dismissed me; and that was the end, as far as the state was concerned.

I did not know then how many of my constitutional rights had been breached by this outrageous incident, in that day of lesser judicial delicacy. Now I can add up several. I was sure then, as now, that many people, young and old, educated and uneducated, white and black, had been subjected to the same, or worse, treatment. At least I had not been beaten up, and my travail, such as it was, had been relatively brief. With one part of my brain, I had enjoyed it. Then, as now, new experiences intrigued me.

I am sure, too, that, at least in part, I became a lawyer, rather than an architect or journalist, because I wanted to make certain that fundamental rights would be preserved for the people, and that I would have a share in that great task.

For the same reasons I shall never forget the front cover of *The Nation* one day in 1927: "Massachusetts the Murderer." It referred to the execution of Sacco and Vanzetti, "the good shoemaker and the bad fish peddler," after seven excruciating years of uncertainty. No case has ever affected me more deeply. I followed every detail, from the beginning to the tragic end. I read all of the literature, including the controversy between Dean Wigmore and Felix Frankfurter. I associated myself completely with the two Italian immigrants and anarchists, who were charged with robbery and murder. I could not believe they were guilty; I still believe them innocent, after many years of study of the case. This was the most inexcusable miscarriage of justice in the history of the nation. To me Judge Webster Thayer was an obscene bigot, who should have been disqualified from passing judgment. The appeals to the higher courts, special tribunals, and the governor were grossly unfair, pre-determined in their results. The Massachusetts establishment destroyed Sacco and Vanzetti out of fear that these two humble men and the millions who mobilized in their behalf would bring down the walls of the Anglo-Saxon Jericho. With every unfavorable turn of the case, I remained persuaded that their lives would, somehow, be saved. When they were finally killed, I was shaken. I still have not recovered.

So I went to law school.

Law school was an utterly new experience. The methods of teaching and learning were totally different from my undergraduate studies. There was the case-book method that Professor Langdell had introduced at the Harvard Law School many years earlier. In theory, it was the means by which law students were transformed into men and women who were ready for clients and the courts. We did not read text books (they were strictly forbidden) nor listen to lectures. We read the reported cases in the various subjects of our courses, such as contracts, torts, real property, common-law pleading, and discussed them in class under the prodding of our professors, some of whom had never practiced law. Actual cases are not compartmentalized; only the study of law is so broken down for convenience. Bit by bit, case by case, we were supposed to absorb the knowledge and techniques that would make us lawyers. I had not read the essays of that profound student of law, Judge Jerome Frank, and I did not know that the difficulty with the theory of the case method is that it deals with reported cases; that is, the results of appeals from the trial courts and administrative agencies. Frank felt that it would be practically better and pedagogically more sound to deal with law trials and administrative hearings, the real stuff of the daily life of lawyers and litigants since appeals are the exception, rather than the rule. This concept was unknown to me at the time, but I saw it dimly in my more perceptive moments.

The University of Chicago has had a great law school ever since this pursuit was first recognized there in 1906, the year of my birth. The University has looked upon the law as an intellectual discipline as well as a profession; never as a trade or guild. In my day, it would not deign to have the so-called practical courses, such as moot trial and appellate court and brief writing. We had a great faculty, possibly the greatest in the school's history; one equal to Harvard's. It was largely the original faculty, the best legal minds of the day, men whose names are still legendary.

At a law-school smoker, Ernst Freund, one of the founders, told us, proudly, of the history of our school, and rejoiced that the giants were still there. In a moment of superstitition, I shuddered over Freund's statement. Soon afterwards, James Parker Hall, the dean, an authority on constitutional law and my professor in torts, died before he had graded our examination papers. Years later, I met Hall's grandson in Castañer in Puerto Rico, where he was a physician in the Brethren Hospital with Nathan Leopold, whose parole I had procured, acting as technician.

So one by one they all died, including Freund himself. I heard Justice Felix Frankfurter, successor to Freund in encyclopedic knowledge of administrative law, eulogize Freund in moving terms that revealed both the justice and the professor. Physically little, Frankfurter was a giant to emulate; but he was only a

Harvard Law School professor when I began the study of law. It was Frankfurter who advised a young boy that the best preparation for the law was poetry, drama, philosophy, history, reading in general. That was my preparation.

In beginning the contracts course that first day in law school, Frederick Woodward told of Benjamin Cardozo. "He is the model," he said, "for all lawyers and jurists." He then told us, in glowing terms, of the character and attainments of Cardozo, who had overcome the disreputable deeds of his father, an associate of Boss Tweed.

Later, when Cardozo became a United States Supreme Court Justice on, literally, the unanimous recommendation of every law school professor, he appeared at an affair at our law school. It was then that he told us, in his wry way, that the purpose of the law was to preserve the ancestral smell.

We lingered over the peculiar odor of each case thereafter, especially when Cardozo was the one who had written the opinion.

I remember that Walter V. Schaefer, who was at the law school in my day, a year or two ahead of me, spent an inordinate amount of time playing tennis. When he became the greatest justice in the history of the Supreme Court of Illinois, a man of learning and integrity, I commented that, perhaps, tennis courts are better preparation for dispensing justice than law courts. I recalled what Frank Harris had said about the low courts of law and the high courts of justice. Simon Agranat, too, was of my time at the law school, a year or two ahead of me. None of us dreamed that he would become the chief justice of a restored Jewish nation. Since then I have visited with him in Israel, where he is respected for his scholarship and integrity.

I have written generally of our outstanding faculty. I like to recall that Ernst Puttkamer taught both Leopold and myself in criminal law; and many years later sponsored me for membership in the Chicago Literary Club, my favorite club, now a century old. It had numbered Lincoln's son as a member. Puttkamer was not the only law-school professor we had who cherished the arts. I remember going one day to the office of Professor Kenneth Sears. He was so deeply absorbed in a book that I hesitated to intrude, especially when I noticed that he was reading one of Shakespeare's plays. Later Sears and I shared an interest in getting a new constitution for Illinois. Sears wrote and spoke and agitated on the subject for many years, but died before he could see the fruition of his dreams. This was a task that I carried on later.

All through my years at the law school, I was increasingly absorbed in a young woman, almost totally unlike me in training and temperament. This attachment grew out of one of my many extra-curricular jobs.

When I was twenty years old I was employed as a sort of office manager and general factotum at the Star Artcraft, a company controlled by a family connection. It was attempting to produce Christmas cards by a special new process of simulated engraving. I say "attempting to produce" because our mechanical problems were never overcome and, despite great prospects, we eventually went under. During my year of employment, I hired salesmen, composed the syrupy sentiments of our cards, corresponded with customers, and did everything except print the cards. My first problem was with my secretary. She was a lovely young lady, but a total stranger to typing, spelling, and general office routine. I tried to be very patient with her, but each day I found it more difficult. One day she said to me, "Mr. Gertz, I know that my work is very poor." I nodded in agreement, as she went on: "I have a friend who is really good. Would you hire her in my place?" I laughed with delight and in assent. Soon the superior girl arrived. Later I learned that she was not really a friend of my secretary's, but a friend of a friend, who was eager to leave her then employer. I tested her skills; she was quite good, and I hired her immediately. She felt guilty about leaving her employer in the lurch and discussed with me the nature of the excuse she would make.

I enjoyed working with Ceretta Samuels, whom, I soon learned, was called "Nig" by her family and friends, because of her dark complexion and black hair. She was a small woman, graceful, and with a deep and resonant voice. She was given to laughter and friendliness, without being in the least offensive. She was dressed generally in bright colors, like one who had come from a sunny climate and was not reconciled to the coldness of Chicago and its people. Later I learned that she had been born in Lithuania and had come here as a baby with her mother and two older sisters. She had been so ill on board ship that she had almost died. At first glance, she interested one by the quality of strangeness that Bacon said is a necessary part of beauty. There was something almost inexplicably appealing about her, and I found myself attentive to all that she would say, without imagining myself in love with her.

Industrious, she could put aside her work on occasion and chat agreeably. One day she said to me, "Mr. Gertz, may I read something beautiful and moving to you?" She then picked up a copy of D. H. Lawrence's *Sons and Lovers* from her purse and read a passage warmly and thoughtfully.

One Saturday noon (this was a period when the work-week was fuller than today), Ceretta's sister Fae, of whom she had often talked, came to the office, ostensibly to pick up her younger sister. Later I learned that Ceretta had talked so much of me at home, of my intelligence, of the profound books I read, of my kindness, of my other qualities, that Fae wanted to explore my potentialities toward what end I could readily guess.

Soon afterward Ceretta asked me if I would attend her sister's wedding. This I did.

I had been working excessively hard in law school and, after school hours, at the Star Artcraft office. On the very last day of that quarter, I felt ill at ease as I came to the office. I sat at my desk; Ceretta, with her stenographic notebook in her lap, awaited my instructions. Suddenly the room began to revolve. I felt sick; I was afraid that I would keel over. My color changed; I leaned almost helplessly on my desk. Ceretta rushed forward, deeply concerned, eager to do what she could to relieve my distress. Suddenly, in the midst of my personal discomfiture, I realized that I was in love with my little secretary.

Shortly afterward the business collapsed, but Ceretta and I remained close to each other. We had our first real date, a movie followed by hot chocolate and brownies. Being poor, that was all that I could afford. We sat on a step in the stairway of the two-flat building on Congress Street where Ceretta lived, and talked for a long while. Suddenly, she grew vocal in her sadness. "If I were better educated," she said, reprovingly, "you might care for me." I kissed her. "I do care for you," I said, with more feeling than the words suggested. "I do love you." We began to see each other constantly, daily except at examination times. When one of us had to be out of town (I worked several summers at resorts in South Haven and I went to New York to do research on Frank Harris), we wrote daily. It was a long courtship of five years in which I passed from a precocious boyhood to uncertain maturity. A year after my graduation from law school, we were married.

I poured out my soul in conversation and above all in poems and letters, all saved by Ceretta when a flood destroyed so much else in our home. Reading what I wrote forty-five years later, I can sense great gaps in our understanding. There were always separate islands on which we seemed to live. We were so close in every respect and yet so different, so detached. Ceretta was not often given to expressing her love. She would sometimes almost betray herself into telling of her deep feelings. She was more likely to tell others than me of how she felt. When she was gone, many years later, those who were closest to her would tell me of the profundity of her love and admiration for me. I gave excitement to her life, she would say. Yet she would always rebuke me when I was immodest, or inconsiderate, or dogmatic. At the same time she would wonder at my ready acceptance of people whom she found dull. "Does not anybody bore you?" she would ask. Again, she wondered how I could tolerate others whom she found repulsive. "Are all your friends bastards?" she would ask. The truth is that Ceretta was always at war with herself and, therefore, with me. She never became reconciled to her qualities or to mine.

Naturally, I shall have much to say of her in the pages of this book. I have called her "yesterday's glory." She is today's tantalizing memory as well. I try to fathom her motivations, what contributed to her final tragedy. I think that part of the explanation lies in her family, especially that character who was her father. Let me now tell of him in depth, more to gain insight into the lost Ceretta than for his sake alone. Morris Samuels was a folk figure of the kind described by Sholom Aleichem and Isaac Bashevis Singer. Like my father and grandfather, he was a now-vanished type. And he meant much to me, then and in retrospect.

My father-in-law was neither large nor small, neither important nor unimportant. His big shoulders and red hair suggested the physical strength that, indeed, he had until his middle seventies. He used to lift the front half of a steer from the cooler to the counter in his kosher meat market as easily as if it were a squab, and he would be quick to tell of it, as of his other not inconsiderable virtues. His patrons, for the most part plain, Yiddish-speaking matrons, loved Morris Samuels for his sharp tongue and the very masculinity of his bearing, insolence and all. He moved proudly and quickly from spot to spot in his shop, despite his pronounced limp and his preoccupation with many tasks. "Mr. Samuels," a customer would ask, "is the chicken fresh?" "Fresher than you!" he would answer, sharply. "Mr. Samuels," another customer would inquire, "may I have the first cut of the steak?" "If I sell that to you, who will buy the knee meat!" he would demand in answer. A customer might feel the thigh of a hen, inquiringly, and Mr. Samuels would remark, just loud enough for her to hear: "Do you have a better thigh?"

For years I had an intimate view of my father-in-law as butcher. I used to help him before the high holy days—probably the most aesthetic of butcher's assistants since the legendary days of Shakespeare. My most important task, requiring both intellect and manual skill, was the wrapping of the fowl and flesh in brown paper for each customer; then covering the packages with newspapers, after glancing at the ancient texts. (I could never resist reading anything.) One day our simple shop was honored by the unexpected appearance of my friend Peter Pollack, not yet renowned in art circles, who had come to observe his intellectual mentor in action. At the moment, a freshly slaughtered chicken was on the scale and I was about to wrap it, when *rigor mortis* suddenly set in, and the dead chicken jumped from the scale. I jumped in another direction, and Peter gasped in disbelief. Only my father-in-law was self-possessed in the crisis. I am afraid that he might have fired me on the spot, except that he was paying me nothing.

Mr. Samuels always managed to get bargains like that. One day he had a man paint the roof of the barn, and he paid him an entire cherry pie for the work. A rather dull-witted distant cousin of his, who admired him almost rapturously, used to break the monotony of his long hours as a milkman by spending his evenings in the Samuels meat market, working at the hardest tasks as if he were being paid the highest wages.

Mr. Samuels used to display me proudly to his customers, and sometimes he made of my very ineptitude as a butcher a proof of my brains and character. He was singularly undemonstrative and uncommunicative with his five daughters, but he adored his only son and his son-in-law. To Alvin he would feed the best lamb chops, sometimes as many as eight at a sitting, when he begrudged his faithful customers even three or four. To me he gave a watch and a hug when I went on a long journey; to his daughters he would give neither gifts nor kisses. He would grumble, "The mother and her five daughters!" On the boy he lavished a pony and parental pride; on the daughters, work and reproofs.

Morris Samuels fancied himself a singer, a public speaker, a sage, and a musician. He insisted that his son play the violin, although Alvin was completely bereft of musical skill. Poor as I was when I courted the Samuels girl, I used to bribe Alvin not to play the fiddle, in his agonizing way, when I was around. His father would listen impatiently to Alvin's playing and take the instrument into his own hands. Although he had never taken a lesson, he would try to show Alvin how a violin should be played. I cannot truthfully say that his playing was any better, or any worse, than Alvin's.

Mr. Samuels did not think much of America. He talked of our failings constantly. His heart was in the Old Country, and, particularly, in one little Lithuanian village named Luknik, from which he had come at the time of the Russo-Japanese War, when he was already married and the father of three daughters. (The other three children were born here.) Unlike some of his compatriots, he had actually served in the Czar's Army, and had liked it. He was a swaggering cavalryman, and he knew so much about horses that the Army had used him as a purchasing agent, despite its traditional anti-Semitism.

Often Mr. Samuels was too tired after a full day's work in the meat market to do anything except bathe, eat, and go to bed; sometimes eliminating the bath in his fatigue. For amusement he would occasionally go to the Yiddish theater, and thereafter argue with his misguided wife as to the rights and wrongs of the stage situation, with an intensity worthy of the best in the world of make-believe. Often he would play pieces on the handwound gramophone; liturgical music, particularly by Cantor Rosenblatt, was his favorite. He became ecstatic as some ancient chant aroused ancestral yearnings. His idea of a secular masterpiece was an Anglo-Yiddish recording with the refrain: "Shutup! Don't talk! Shut up! Don't talk! *Gewald!* What is it!" I can still hear those words, decades later dinning in my unappreciative ears.

I prefer to think of him in a quieter mood, when he and I would sit alone at the kitchen table, drinking innumerable glasses of tea, into which he had dropped bits of apple. There would then be no boasting, no complaining, only tender conversation between an older man and his young son-in-law.

When our son was born, my father-in-law's joy was unbounded. Although by then it was difficult for him to get around, he used to travel frequently by public transportation from his Garfield Park home to our apartment on the North Side. He would bring with him, invariably, gifts for the little boy, who was going to amount to much, in the eyes of his doting grandfather.

This man, whose heart was so strong, died suddenly, after a brief period of decline. The animation of his red-topped head and semi-humorous voice are with us still. We, too, would like to see that mythical town of Luknik in old Lithuania in order to learn its attraction for an otherwise critical soul. The town, no doubt, has been devastated like so many other towns in the Pale, but it produced more than the armies destroyed—strong men whose heritage lives on in their children in America and in Israel.

four

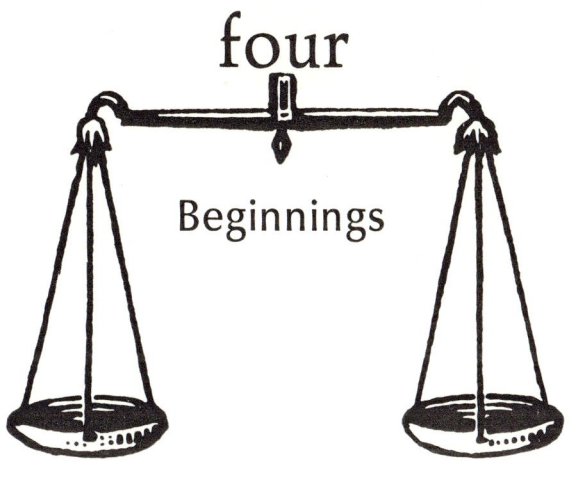

Beginnings

I could not have begun the practice of law at a worse time. I was graduated from law school in June, 1930, less than a year after the stock-market crash of 1929. I took the state bar examination in the summer and was formally admitted before the state Supreme Court in October. It was almost impossible to get placed in any law office. Some of my classmates were never employed, and had to enter private practice like helpless children, tossed into a pool and told to swim to safety. The way to become a lawyer, in the real sense, was to put one's self under the tutelage of an established law firm, at some modest salary, or none. Thus one's baby steps would be supervised and, bit by bit, one would learn how to walk and work with confidence.

Ceretta's sister, Fae, and my brother, Edward, enticed an old friend, Mitchell C. Robin, to interrupt his campaigning for re-election as Clerk of the Probate Court, to explore my possibilities. Normally, when conditions were good, Robin could have placed me by a mere phone call, so eager were many to win the favor of the guardian of the records and employees of so important a public office. But these were most certainly not normal times. It took several months for Robin to succeed by going to his own bailiwick, the Lawndale area. He persuaded his and my brother Edward's friend, the alderman, Jacob M. Arvey, to say that, in a matter of days or a few weeks at most, I could work for his firm, then known as Epstein and Arvey. When I expressed misgivings, Arvey said, good-naturedly, "Hang your hat in my office and begin at once!" This I did, only to discover that he had neglected to tell his partner, Samuel B. Epstein, about his decision, and Mr. Epstein did not like it. He nursed an unexpected grudge, I think, as to the Samuels family. "You're hired only for a month," he told me, brusquely. I remained for fourteen years.

When I was first employed by him, Alderman Arvey was a master-in-chancery, to whom judges handling equity matters, such as foreclosures and accountings, referred cases for reports that might be adopted by such judges as their own decrees. This was a lucrative fee office, doubly welcome in a period of economic stringency. I became Arvey's assistant and worked on his reports. Many masters-in-chancery relied completely on their assistants. Arvey was much too conscientious for that. He insisted upon discussing involved matters with me. Together we would work out decisions. This became too time-consuming for him, as he rose in the political world. He resigned, and Mr. Epstein was named in his place. Mr. Epstein was even more conscientious than Alderman Avery, I found, as I became his assistant.

Many political law firms are simply fronts for men who are only nominally lawyers, and in reality act as professional "fixers" and influence peddlers. But Arvey was not willing to have political hangers-on as his law associates. The result was that he had some of the brightest young men in the profession handling the cases that came in. They gave value to clients when "clout" failed. (Much of the time, even political lawyers depend upon the facts and the law. Besides, what happens when two of them face each other?)

When I was first employed by his firm, I would ask Arvey around election time: "Is there anything I can do, Jack?" He would answer: "Yes, practice law."

For a little while, in 1933, we in Jack Arvey's law office knew a secret, which, fortunately, we did not tell—Jack Arvey was going to be selected by his fellow aldermen as mayor of Chicago, to succeed Anton Cermak. The mayor had been killed by a bullet, intended either for President-elect Roosevelt—or for Cermak. As the council vote was being taken, we huddled anxiously around the office. Then Arvey's secretary came out, in tears, and we learned that Jack was not going to be mayor, after all. Later, we heard that there had been a double-cross, maneuvered by Colonel McCormick, the boss of the *Tribune,* and Edward J. Kelly was named as mayor instead. McCormick had admired Kelly since the days when McCormick had been president, or, as some said, Czar, of the board of the Sanitary District, and Kelly was employed there in a minor capacity.

During the thirties, Arvey's quiet power in the party's inner circles burgeoned as fast as his law practice. As head of the Council's finance committee, he was crucially responsible for restoring the credit of the city, debauched as it had been by Big Bill Thompson and the Depression. His mastery of the municipal budget, and his prestige among his fellow-aldermen, made him indispensable to Mayor Kelly. Then, in 1936, a notable event in local politics occurred, about which Arvey made a decision that has been called the best and worst of his career. Whichever it was at bottom, it saw Arvey accepted as an equal leader of the machine along with Pat Nash and Ed Kelly.

The event was the revolt of Governor Henry Horner against the organization. He had expected to be renominated for governor, and when he was passed over in favor of Herman Bundesen, the highly publicized health commissioner of Chicago, he decided to run anyway. Horner had powerful connections, and his campaign split the party wide open. Like Arvey, he was a Jew, and the matter of loyalty on this basis was invoked. It was put to Arvey that in other ways, too, he was closer to Horner's position than to the machine's.

Arvey made his decision in terms of party loyalty, and committed himself to carrying his ward, still almost wholly Jewish, for the organization and against Horner. Even the neighborhood rabbis failed to change his mind when they called on him as a group, and apparently the rabbis finally voted for Bundesen—he carried the ward by a ratio of ten to one. Elsewhere, Horner triumphed, but Arvey's loyalty led to his acceptance by Nash and Kelly as an equal leader of the party. Subsequently he took the initiative in arranging a reconciliation between these leaders and Horner.

The fact that he was able to do this can be explained by a remarkable anecdote of the campaign. One evening, when they were leaving a nonpolitical meeting, Horner put his arm around Arvey and walked out with him. The alderman felt a little self-conscious, and said: "You know, Governor, I am not with you." To which Horner replied: "I know that you aren't, Jack, but you are one of the few who have never told me they would be with me."

Something more should be said about the old system of references to masters-in-chancery, since it is now abolished in Illinois. Masters-in-chancery would have cases referred to them, nominally by those judges handling equity matters, known as chancellors; but actually by the law firms handling such cases. Some law firms and some chancellors would have favorite masters-in-chancery, because they expected more competent service or better treatment, either in the results or in the fees. Many firms would deliberately spread their cases around, so as to make friends and to speed up matters. Some masters-in-chancery were notorious for the persistence with which they sought references, stepping low, indeed, to get such remunerative legal plums in a lean period. They became wealthy through the fees and often through the interests in real estate that were conveyed in lieu of fees. As the depressed real-estate market rose to inflation levels, property, once almost worthless, became extremely valuable. I handled so many cases that, even if I had been motivated by greed, I would not have been able to concentrate on extracting anything financially rewarding for myself. Others who had less legal ability and a more practical outlook did well, and some showed their gratitude by making substantial charitable and political contributions.

The firm and some clients invested in a strip coal-mining project in an adjoining county, and I was assigned to handle the legal work on virtually a full-time basis. With a participant in the venture, I would go from farmer to farmer in Will County and, on the spot, prepare and have them sign options for land for possible stripping. This is a form of surface mining that requires rather complicated equipment and engineering skill. Once I had to prepare a contract for the purchase of a stripping machine costing hundreds of thousands of dollars, the equivalent, perhaps, of millions today. When I was not doing law work, I would observe the operations, whether in the fields or at the tipples where the coal was stored for shipping. I noticed what I thought were imperfections. A good engineer would slice the earth at such angle as to assure the uncovering of coal without mishap. With us, there were too many slides, as I recall. The earth would collapse, instead of retaining its firmness. This would slow up operations, because of the constant need for corrections.

One day Mr. Epstein drove with me to the scene of our operations. I explained to him what I had observed, adding: "Of course, I am not an engineer." Mr. Epstein listened attentively and then observed conditions for himself. It was apparent that he was in agreement with me. I felt immensely pleased with myself until, about a week later, Mr. Epstein scolded me for not having pointed out the engineering defects earlier! New technical assistance was hired and I felt somewhat reluctant about making further observations.

With the possible exception of the alderman, there was no one in the firm with whom I got along better than John L. McInerney, who had once been Mayor Kelly's closest friend. I learned more about the trial of cases from him than anyone else, particularly cross-examination. He made me understand, for all time, that one does not ask an adverse witness a question unless one is sure as to what he will answer; not what he should answer, but what he will. Good witnesses are trained to destroy the other side on their responses to cross-questioning. Some of the best evidence is kept back on direct examination, so that it may be tossed in the opponent's face, as it were, on cross-examination.

Early in our association, I was working with McInerney on a hotly contested probate matter involving millions of dollars. The preparations lasted for months. Each day I would interview our client or some witness; then I would report to McInerney. His office, unlike mine, was never cluttered. There would be only one sheet at a time on his desk, the sheet on which he might make a note or two as I talked. Finally, the day of the trial arrived. I walked with McInerney to the courtroom, carrying the bulging brief case in the traditional fashion of juniors. He was tall, I of less than medium height; the contrast must have been amusing. We and our opponent answered ready for trial. Then McInerney turned to me and said, "It's your case, Elmer." This was my first knowledge that I was going to try the matter. Had I known earlier, I might have been apprehensive; now I had no time for that. I tried the case, McInerney at my side, occasionally whispering advice, and won it.

Almost on the day I graduated law school, David Belson, the most beloved of my uncles, turned over to me all of his not inconsiderable law business. He was my first personal client. This tangible expression of his confidence in me never faltered, however much he might haggle over fees. There came a time when Uncle Dave wanted me to become his partner in his fairly prosperous electrical goods and sheet-metal business. He was willing that I continue the practice of law if I would devote some time to working with him. But feeling that this would lead to clashes with my cousin, who did not have his father's temperament, I regretfully turned down my uncle. I had this same experience of being asked to participate in their businesses with other clients and, in each instance, I turned down the offers, although in at least one case it would have meant very great prosperity—security in an insecure world. I was determined to remain a lawyer, even if I maintained an amateur standing, financially speaking. True, I had other interests and pursuits, but I remained essentially a lawyer, whatever else I was.

Significantly, one of the very first cases that Uncle Dave turned over to me was a libel action. He had been sued by a former representative who had charged him personally, as well as his corporation, with reflecting upon his reputation. The years have dimmed my recollection of the details of the case. I did not know then that a considerable part of my reputation in later years as a lawyer would derive from my handling of defamation actions. Later, the Chief Motion Judge of the Circuit Court of our county would refer to me, semi-humorously, as the Plaintiff's Bar in libel. At that earlier time I was just another beginning lawyer who was trying to persuade his first client, who happened to be his uncle, that he knew how to handle complicated as well as simple matters.

This was in the period when both the Federal and State courts in Illinois followed the rather complicated practices of the common law, rather than the modern codes. Pleadings were drawn with careful regard for various technical requirements; and it was difficult to obtain the pre-trial discovery, or information, that is a commonplace today. The practice of law then was little different from what it was in the days of bewigged practitioners in the Inns of London.

I filed what was known as a demurrer. This was a technical pleading which, in effect, stated that, assuming everything in the complaint (it was then called a declaration) to be true, it still did not state a cause of action against the defendants. My opponent was a lawyer considerably older than myself and with an established reputation. But I still felt that he had not stated a good case.

When my demurrer came up for hearing before the greatly admired, greatly feared Judge John P. Barnes in the United States District Court, my oppenet did not appear. His clerk had probably failed to enter the matter in his diary—the bane of all lawyers. Very politely, I remarked to Judge Barnes that I would like permission to telephone opposing counsel, as I did not want to take advantage of his absence. This was reckoning without Judge Barnes. He looked me straight in the eye, in his stern manner, and said: "You will proceed at once to argue your demurrer." Judge Barnes was one of the most learned and certainly the firmest man on the Federal bench. He sometimes appeared to be inflexible. I learned later that he would bark more often than he would bite and that he was in reality a kindhearted person, in spite of his rough exterior. He simply expected lawyers to conform to the rules, to be on time, to know what they were doing.

If I thought that arguing my demurrer in the absence of my opponent would be easy, I reckoned without Judge Barnes. He became my opponent. We argued back and forth on my various points for a considerable period of time. He then sustained my demurrer, but gave the other side, the plaintiff, leave to file an amended declaration. Immediately I went to the telephone and called my opponent. I explained that the matter had proceeded, despite my request to communicate with him. He understood, and I then explained patiently the course of my legal argument with Judge Barnes. Somewhat later, the lawyer filed an amended pleading which, in my judgment, did not cure the defects of the original declaration. I filed another demurrer. This time my opponent showed up for the hearing in court and the Judge did not participate in the argument. In a matter of moments, he sustained my demurrer, and this time dismissed the suit.

I had won my first libel action, for the defendants, rather than the plaintiff. This gave me an immediate interest and insight in a unique area of the law that has been subject to both growth and retrogression in Illinois and nationally in my generation. I did much research on defamation and, indeed, on all matters relating to the press and the freedom of expression generally. I read the leading cases. I talked with the lawyers who handled such matters. In the course of the years I found myself often consulted by lawyers and laymen. I helped to make the law, whether I won or lost cases. My opponents referred cases to me. The published reports of my cases in this area afford a guideline to the history and substance of this intriguing part of the law.

five

My First Books

In December, 1931, when I was twenty-five years old, my first book, *Frank Harris: A Study in Black and White,* written in collaboration with Dr. A. I. Tobin, was published. There is so much to be said about it, despite the passage of many years that the temptation is great to say *too* much.

In August, 1931, Frank Harris died in his sleep at Nice, France, and was buried with simple rites in the English Cemetery. No one with knowledge of his stormy career, erratic character, and strange habits would have predicted so peaceful an end. Nor would any unprejudiced person have been too sure then as to Harris' ultimate position in the life and letters of our day.

Not long after his death, the "official" biography of him, written by Dr. A. I. Tobin and myself, was published under modest auspices in Chicago by the young daughter of an old friend of mine.

In England, we entered into a contract with a reputable publisher. At about the date the publication had been scheduled, we received word from our British publisher that he had destroyed the plates of the book, because the widow of Frank Harris had threatened suit (on account of her dislike of our candor). The misadventure in Britain caused the abandonment of plans for French and German editions.

Thus it was that only a small number of readers saw our book. Each of them seemed driven to review it or to mention it. H. G. Wells, G. K. Chesterton, Rebecca West, H. L. Mencken, Ernest Newman, Max Eastman, Louis Adamic, and others were generous in their praise. Rebecca West called it "a great book." Eastman and Adamic listed it among the notable books of the times. Then it was promptly forgotten, except by students of literature and enthusiasts.

I have sometimes wondered if this experience of mine is not a sort of allegory based upon the life of Frank Harris himself. Throughout his long career as editor, author, and man of affairs, he won the verbal tribute of some of the great ones. To them and, above all, to himself he was a man of considerable dimensions. But the world at large was strangely unresponsive when not downright unfriendly. The question always was, Who is Frank Harris? If questions are asked about him today, the first one still is, Who is Frank Harris?

One explained then, one explains today, that he was a man of uncertain origin—born, it appeared, in different places (Galway, Tenby) at different times (1854, 1855, 1856) and of conflicting national stocks (Irish, Welsh, some said Jewish); that he edited *The Fortnightly Review* and the *Saturday Review* in London in their periods of greatness; that he "discovered" or befriended some of the outstanding men of letters, such as Oscar Wilde, Bernard Shaw, H. G. Wells, Max Beerbohm; that he wrote short stories, like "Montes" and "The Miracle of the Stigmata," which George Meredith and others called immortal; that he wrote pen portraits of his contemporaries and studies of

Shakespeare which precipitated flaming controversies; that in his old age, after a life devoted to kicking respectability in the shins, he published an autobiography so outspoken as to shock even the French, who arrested him.

Having recited these and similar facts, or allegations, one waited for the inevitable next question: Why haven't I heard of him?

For almost seventy-five years, individual readers have been discovering Frank Harris, and the likelihood is that for years to come other individual readers will make the same discovery. I once thought that there would come a time when Harris would be universally accepted. In the period when I was held in thrall by him, I used to repeat his own dictum: "We are immortal only when we die."

I no longer believe there will ever be general acceptance of Harris as an authentically great writer. I am no longer even sure that he is a great writer. It seems to me that he is a moment in the fitful life of one who loves literature and all high endeavor. There is a time, generally in youth, when we have actual reverence, and not merely admiration, for those who evoke the image of beauty. For some of us in that mood, Frank Harris is a sort of magic carpet by whose aid we may travel skyward. On others, in the same mood, I realize, he has a totally different effect. To some he is the bloated image of pretense, a mere counterfeit of greatness.

Which is it? I don't pretend to know the answer, despite my book. I still quicken when I see a Harris title on the shelf of a bookshop. I still look for his name in the index of any book dealing with modern writers. Now and then I read a paragraph or two or a page of Harris' own writings and for a fleeting moment that old mood is recaptured.

I have noticed that those who had known Harris were more inclined to write of him after his death than when he was alive. Wells, in his autobiography, had many striking pages about Harris, in contrast with his earlier silence. The biographer of

George Moore assigned to Harris a greater role in Moore's life than the immodest Harris was ever wont to claim. I recall dozens of books with chapters or pages on the man.

He will be remembered, it seems to me, as a somewhat greater Casanova. He had incomparable gifts which he threw away with a peevish disregard for their real worth. He preferred to waste his substance in the wild search in distant fields for the superexcitation that he craved.

Harris wrote his *Contemporary Portraits* because he thought of himself as greater than his contemporaries. More than one of these portraits now affords supreme proof that in his self-centeredness he could be blind to the qualities of those around him. He wrote of Winston Churchill, for example. It is a kindly study, but a smugly patronizing one, without a glimmer of understanding of the manner in which Churchill could stir the imagination of his generation. Harris, who died long before World War II, could not be a prophet of events; but he presumed himself to have spiritual understanding of men. In this he was too often lacking, and most of all in his own self-understanding. That is why *My Life and Loves* is in substance so much less revelatory than the more restrained prose of other autobiographies.

It has always been my passion to study authors in depth—everything by or about them. Then, if they are alive, I have written to them and to those who have known them. This has often resulted in warm and rewarding friendships. Thus, after getting to know Harris through the Little Blue Books, I wrote to him when I was in my first years of college and he an old man. Harris had just written his autobiography and he was no longer a respectable figure in genteel literary circles if he ever was one. He wrote very warm and friendly letters, some of them striking in language and substance. He asked me, a very young man, to do all sorts of errands for him—get publishers to consider his new manuscripts; persuade Colonel Robert R. McCormick, publisher of the *Chicago Tribune,* to employ him as editor of the European edition of that newspaper; confer with Clarence Darrow about defending him from arrest if he should come to America; gather for him books by Negro writers; and much besides. Harris referred me to various friends in New York, two who had gone to prison for marketing his autobiography, several who were running a company that was distributing his writings, others who called him "Master" and were so enraptured about him as to be blind to his faults.

We are on the verge of a great revival of interest in Harris. A major biography of him by Philippa Pullar is about to appear. I have been of great help to her, I believe. Her book builds upon mine, in some respects. Because of the difference in my technique and that of others, it may be of interest to dwell, at some length, on how I went about preparing my Harris book.

Literally, I underscored each statement of fact in Harris' *My Life and Loves* and its sequels and attempted to get proof or disproof for what he claimed, often successfully but sometimes without results. I wrote to all of the universities he was supposed to have attended in the United States, Britain, France, Germany, Greece and elsewhere. I wrote to his fellow-students and associates. I hounded the authorities everywhere for records of passports, visas, travels, residence, education, employment. I wrote to every surviving person whom Harris had included in his *Contemporary Portraits*, and to the authorities on the deceased subjects of his pen portraits. It would be tedious to enumerate all of the many who were taxed by me, because correspondence with the living was then my favorite mode of research, rather than delving into books, periodicals and records. I was then a most persistent and undaunted correspondent. I dragged often illuminating comments out of Bernard Shaw, John Galsworthy, Leonard Merrick, Cunninghame Graham, Augustus John, Lord Alfred Douglas, Winston Churchill, Leon Trotsky, and countless others, known and unknown.

Harris had written a contemporary portrait of Richard Wagner, which Ernest Newman, the greatest of Wagnerian biographers, had pronounced a fake in a series of articles in the *London Times*. I had read and reread Harris' portrait and the

Newman articles and, somehow, felt that the diametrically opposed contentions of the two could be reconciled in what Harris pretentiously used to style a Hegelian synthesis. But how was I to prove this, particularly since I had only a rudimentary knowledge of German? I knew one thing that I definitely counted on; I knew that the Bavaria of the period in question was what we would now call a police state. That meant that records would be kept of the comings and goings of all persons, particularly foreigners like Harris. Perhaps those records would be preserved for half a century. So I wrote to the Munich Commissioner of Police and learned that Harris did in fact reside at the same boarding-house as Wagner—shortly after Wagner had left! This meant to me that Harris learned certain things at first hand—from gossiping with the landlady and other boarders; hence the intimate tone of his portrait, the truth-in-falsehood atmosphere which the generally perceptive Ernest Newman had not seen. I reported my findings to Newman, who was quite delighted. He sent his latest Wagner book, which he inscribed to me as "the sleuth biographer," and wrote an enthusiastic review of my book in the *London Times.*

Harris had written in the third volume of his autobiography about his trips to South Africa before, during, and after the Boer difficulties with Great Britain. He had placed himself, as usual, in the very center of things, in the closest contact with the great Cecil Rhodes, Paul Kreuger, and others. Was he telling the truth? Despite the decades which had elapsed, I found that several of the persons with whom he claimed to have talked were still alive, if old and perhaps feeble. Among them was Chief Justice Kotze of the South Africa Supreme Court. I wrote and waited. Back then came, among other letters, a very long holograph from the Chief Justice. Despite the many years which separated the events from his writing, he had an exact memory for the details. I was excited beyond words. Here was something really good for the book. But almost by the next mail there arrived another message from Chief Justice Kotze, this one frantic in tone. It appeared that when he first wrote to me he had not known about Harris' sexually outspoken *My Life and Loves.* Then he had come across the book. He wanted me to return his letter to him! I thought over the matter and reached a solution, again a Hegelian synthesis, if you will. I wrote the Chief Justice that I would not return his letter, but I would not use it without his permission. So none of it appeared in my Harris biography. The question now is: When, if at all, can I use this material?

Those who have read *My Life and Loves* know that, by way of startling contrast to the lustful episodes of that strangest of all autobiographies, there emerges a luminous portrait of one Byron Smith, a professor of Greek at the University of Kansas, a man who, Harris said, inspired him and illuminated his life as no other person ever did. While still a very young man, Smith died, having never fulfilled his very great promise. Harris mentioned, misspelling her name, the betrothed of Smith, a woman of considerable attainments, whom Harris apparently disliked. My plan to write to her was at first thwarted, because my collaborator told me that she was dead. He wrote a beautiful tribute to her. By one of those curious quirks, I not only learned that she was alive, but we received countless letters from her and other material of biographical as well as sentimental interest. It is a story which some day should be told in full. I learned that others, besides Kate Stephens, who attended the University of Kansas with Harris, were alive. I wrote to all of them, and learned that the Middle-western plains must give vigor and memory to those who reside there; for I received remarkably detailed accounts of distant events, some of which were used in the book, from the surviving students of the early eighteen-seventies.

If no one is a hero to his valet, how much less is he a hero to his private secretary! This I found out when I became an intimate correspondent of Tom Bell, who had been Harris' secretary in his great days in London on the *Saturday Review.* I got to know him through Louis Adamic. Bell went through all three volumes of Harris' autobiography and wrote out for me his comments as to all matters of which he had personal knowledge. He turned over to me his voluminous correspondence with

Harris, some of it "for keeps" and some to copy. He answered my every question and volunteered much besides. He was inspired, largely because of me, to write an article, since published in the now vanished *Bookman,* about his acting as go-between for Harris and Oscar Wilde in connection with the former's forgotten play, *Mr. and Mrs. Daventry.* Inspired further, Bell wrote a book about his relations with Harris and others, a book which is as yet unpublished. Where the manuscript is I do not know. Bell was a linguist, anarchist, man of affairs, and character in his own right. With him as with others, the Harris angle criss-crossed with many others. George Sylvester Viereck, for one, weaved in and out of the story so much that in the end I felt I had to center my researches on him.

Bell and others led me to re-examine Harris' celebrated biography of Oscar Wilde. I heard from Wilde's last surviving son Vivyan Holland; from Robert H. Sherard, a stormy figure of late-nineteenth-century literature, and from many others, including the most controversial figure of Wilde's life, Lord Alfred Douglas, from whom I received innumerable communications, not to say inscribed books and photographs. Proud of his youthful appearance, when he was well past sixty, he sent me a picture of himself in which he looked less than forty. To make sure I would not miss the point, in a covering letter he underscored it! There was much pother by Douglas on minutia and sometimes on basic matters. I learned much about Wilde, Douglas, and Bernard Shaw in the process of learning about Harris.

Wilde's son later wrote an extended attack upon me in his book on his father as a result of Lord Douglas' hounding him for what I had quoted. I could understand the man, despite my being the victim; Lord Douglas had the capacity to make open wounds excessively painful.

On the other hand, Harris always had the capacity to attract earnest young men as his devout admirers, just as, conversely, Viereck used to attract old men. Some of Harris' young men, such as John Middleton Murry, Hugh Kingsmill, and Hesketh

Pearson, became distinguished men of letters. While they were enthralled by Harris, they wrote in extravagant terms in his praise, and when they became disenchanted, they wrote of him in wonder and embarrassment and sometimes bitterness. I corresponded with these men, particularly Kingsmill and Pearson, and watched their rise to fame. Pearson became the very best of the popular biographers. His lives of Shaw and Wilde were so good that I hoped that he would write a book about Harris, already the subject of several lively biographies. Pearson's great friend, Kingsmill, wrote a book about Harris; but, in my judgment, it did justice neither to Kingsmill nor Harris. In their letters to me, Kingsmill, Pearson, and others told of how they fell in and out of love with Harris, the man and the writer. In a sense, I repeated their story in my own life, but I still do not feel as sure as they that nothing by Harris is first-rate, and I have no bitterness about him.

I now recall out of the dim past that when my Harris book was completed it was suggested to me that I ought to publish a little book containing some of the best letters written to me about Harris. I thought it a good idea then, and still think it a good idea. But I have discovered some disquieting things about the nature of the professional writing man. When I wrote to my correspondents for permission to publish their letters to me, some of them asked as a prerequisite for a second look at their letters. When I sent copies to them they almost invariably revised the very life out of their own letters. It was literary mayhem, if not murder. What had been vivid portraiture and uninhibited anecdotage with bright clear phrases became almost dull and unimportant.

The first copy of the book I inscribed to Ceretta, to whom I had been married for four months at the time of publication. She was so much a part of my Harris adventures that Harris' lawyer had called us while we were on our honeymoon to tell us of Harris' death.

A book I wrote about George Sylvester Viereck somewhat after the Harris book was accepted by the Greystone Press, a once-flourishing, now defunct, publishing company. Greystone did not publish my Viereck book; no one did. Yet I still regard it as one of the best studies I have ever done.

And as with Harris, it was, and is, necessary to ask, And who is George Sylvester Viereck? Why should he be the subject of another book when there are already too many books? I should answer these questions; for Viereck meant so very much to me at one time. The answers may help to explain why I was so preoccupied with him.

I met Nikola Tesla, the electronics wizard, through George Sylvester Viereck. I might have written about meeting and corresponding with Dr. Alfred Adler, also through Viereck. And I could have told of sharing the confidences of Colonel Edward M. House, the advisor of President Wilson in World War I, likewise through Viereck. My correspondence with Bernard Shaw came by reason of Viereck, as did my meetings, associations and contacts in varying degrees with Edgar Lee Masters, William Ellery Leonard, Ludwig Lewisohn, Fiorello LaGuardia, Wilhelm Stekel, Johann Plesch, and a host of other writers, artists, scientists, political figures and eccentrics. Viereck, in his day, as journalist and public figure, seemed to know everyone and aroused the unexpected admiration of such varied people as Albert Einstein, Kaiser Wilhelm II, Sigmund Freud, Gerhard Hauptmann, Frank Harris, as well as assorted Nazi leaders.

It is only fair to add that one by one, and sometimes more rapidly, he lost these celebrated friends and many other associates, and he spent several years in an American prison as penalty for his inability to circumvent the foreign agents' registration laws. Freud, himself, once briefly wrote to me that he had "broken off all diplomatic relations" with Viereck, who had been one of his first American popularizers. Bernard Shaw, the great civil libertarian Arthur Garfield Hays, and a few others remained faithful to him. I, myself, had a rather mixed relationship, best described, in one of Viereck's favorite words, as "ambivalent." In Viereck's book, *The Kaiser on Trial,* which I still regard as an important work, as did Shaw, Colonel House and former American Ambassador James Gerard, who wrote introductions to it, Viereck says: "Elmer Gertz has at times goaded, but has always helped me with his criticism." In the more personal inscription in a copy of the book that he gave me, he described me as "friend and antagonist, but more friend than antagonist." It may very well be that Viereck will end up as a mere footnote in literary history, as the father of Peter Viereck, poet, philosopher, conservative historian, and public personality, who seems to become more and more like his father as he tries to escape from him.

I lost many friends when I persisted in being in close touch with Viereck senior. Some of the letters sent to me in condemnation of my forbearance are still unprintable. Even Ceretta wondered about my tolerance. Yet, after he left the Federal prison, she joined me in inviting him to stay at our home during the postwar Republican convention in Chicago and rebuked me for not being more cordial to him.

There were two major threads running through Viereck's life, responsible for his triumphs and his tragedy: the one an attraction for the revolutionary ideas of his generation—relativity, rejuvenation, psychoanalysis, creative evolution, everything except communism (politically he was conservative); and the other, a growing attachment to Germany, even during the Nazi period. He developed a moral obtuseness that was hard to understand in one who was basically generous. Long before he had earned a penny through his Nazi connections—indeed, when Hitler was unknown to the rest of the world or was regarded as a political lunatic with no future—Viereck sensed that the unfunny little funny man was going to influence the course of history prodigiously. In my researches, I found Viereck's first article on Hitler, probably the first that ever appeared in any American publication. It predated the Munich Beer Hall Putsch in the very early 1920's. Viereck had forgotten the article until I called it to his attention; then he constantly referred to it. In it he said—I quote from memory—"If he lives, Adolf Hitler, for better or for worse, will make history." Unfortunately, he lived too long and was the perpetrator of the foulest crimes in history, including, among the lesser offenses, the moral demise of Viereck.

When Viereck went to prison—like Cervantes, Bunyan, Wilde, Verlaine and many other artists before him—he experienced a rebirth of his poetic fertility. I think that the poems he wrote while going through the agonies of confinement are among the best that he ever composed, because they are genuine, deeply human, rather than merely literary. When they are published in full one day they should serve to restore some of his tarnished fame. Viereck wrote me that the poems belong to me; but I have hesitated to act on any assumed proprietory rights.

He wrote a first-rate book about his prison experiences, largely free of self-pity; but he left prison a broken man, living half-heartedly on dried-up dreams.

I wrote an essay on Ludwig Lewisohn, William Ellery Leonard, and Viereck, three highly diverse men who shared some common experiences at the beginning of this century. Viereck's son, Peter, told me that this essay gave him more insight into his father than anything he had ever read.

My Viereck material is a main source of the recently published book on Viereck, covering his activities as a German apologist. Reading Niel Johnson's pages, I lived through the Viereck years and once more I had to ask myself, Were they worthwhile? Is every chapter of one's life to be subject to the same question? This was especially true of my protracted researches and writings on the *Chicago Tribune,* a virtual obsession.

One day during World War II, my friend Arthur J. Goldberg telephoned me. Arthur was then a major in the Office of Strategic Services. "I have something of great interest to tell you," he said, in a mysterious manner. We arranged to breakfast together, and he told me the story, as if recounting an O.S.S. adventure. "I was on the train, going from New York to Chicago," he began, "and a gentleman sat across from me. He seemed eager to converse. 'Where are you from?' he asked me. When I told him, he responded eagerly: 'I am with The Viking

Press. We are about to publish a fascinating book about the *Chicago Tribune*.' Before he could say more, I said: 'Don't tell me who wrote it. I will tell you.' He looked at me, quizzically, and I went on: 'Elmer Gertz is the author.' He smiled in agreement." Arthur paused for a moment. "Congratulations, Elmer," he added. I told him that I had not heard from The Viking Press, although they had had my *Tribune* manuscript for weeks. In the end, they decided not to publish it.

I recall that before I had written a word of the book, when it was simply a project that was mentioned casually to prospective publishers, I had heard from Bennett Cerf, the famous head of Random House. He was much excited about my plans, and asked me to submit an outline and a sample chapter. I did this. The sample chapter dealt with the mysterious slaying of the *Tribune* crime reporter and investigator, Jake Lingle. Cerf became even more enthusiastic. He told me that my book would have tremendous importance for his firm and for me. He was going to Nassau, he said; when he got back, he would enter into a formal contract and I would receive a substantial advance. He returned to New York and had second thoughts. We are about to go to war, he wrote me (this was before the Nazi invasion of Poland in 1939), and we should take to our storm-cellars. When the war is over, he said, it will be an ideal time to publish the book.

I went ahead with my book without going into a storm-cellar. I carried on an enormous amount of research about Joseph Medill, William Bross, Charles Ray, and the other pioneers of the first days of the *Tribune.* One especially intriguing part of my researches was my delving into the careers of McCormick and Patterson as students at Groton and at Yale. I heard from the dearly loved old headmaster Endicott Peabody and the surviving masters, such as Ellery Sedgwick, editor of the *Atlantic Monthly,* and the classmates of the two men, some of whom had very lively and explicit memories. I was able to grasp the basic differences between Patterson and McCormick. A few people within the *Tribune* organization insisted upon turning over material of such intimate nature that I dared not inquire as to the derivations. Later, Wayne Andrews, in his invaluable book, *Battle for Chicago,* wrote: "Above all the author would like to thank Elmer Gertz, who knows more about the *Tribune* than any man living or dead." I was able to write with assurance on such intimate matters as to how Colonel McCormick really regarded his cousin, Captain Patterson (the rumor was that they hated each other); for I had Patterson's own copy of McCormick's book, *The Army of 1918,* in which McCormick had written: "No. 1. To my best friend Joe Patterson—Robert R. McCormick." I knew the inside story of the Paris Edition of the *Tribune* because of the confidences of Farmer Murphy and others who had been connected with that lively journal. I did not know then of Henry Miller's employment there as a proofreader, for *Tropic of Cancer* had only a secret existence at that time.

So pervasive and persistent were my studies that the powers within the Tribune Tower were disturbed. One day John L. McInerney, head of our law firm, chatted with me as we walked down La Salle Street. "I have just heard from Parke Browne [the famous political editor of the *Tribune*]. He expressed surprise that I would let you carry on about the *Tribune.* I told him that it was your business, not mine." McInerney paused for a moment. "I think that you're crazy, Elmer," he went on, with a smile, "but I won't interfere." He then confided in me some interesting *Tribune* information, knowing that I would make use of it.

On another occasion, Jack Arvey talked with me. "When I was at Louis Rose's ranch," he said, "Rose told me that the Colonel was troubled about what you are doing." Rose was the circulation manager of the *Tribune,* successor to his brother-in-law, Max Annenberg. "So far as I am concerned, Elmer," Arvey went on, "you can do as you please."

A bit later the third partner, Samuel B. Epstein, asked me about my book. I told him what McInerney and Arvey had said, and he responded: "If they feel that way, then I have no objections."

To me it made no difference. I would not have yielded to my employers. This was the period when the *Tribune's* reputation among my kind of person was at its lowest. I was determined to complete the book and have it published. Other publishers saw the manuscript and liked it well enough to want to publish it; but, ultimately, each would withdraw. The *Tribune* had the reputation of not taking kindly to those who crossed it. Sensible people did not tangle with it. I was not sensible!

I was beginning to feel that the book would never be published. At this low point, Gwen Glasser, a friend, active in liberal political organizations, suggested to the Union for Democratic Action, predecessor of the ADA, that I ought to be asked to write a long pamphlet about the *Tribune*. The idea met with an enthusiastic response both from the UDA and from myself. In almost record time I completed *The People vs. The Chicago Tribune,* a seventy-two-page production of sprightly text and pictures. It was an instantaneous success and made me feel less badly about the lack of success with the book.

There was a revealing episode involving Harold L. Ickes. One day I received a little package from him, containing a double-column editorial from the trade journal, *Editor and Publisher*, attacking my pamphlet, and two letters, the one a reply to the editorial by Ickes, the other a letter to me in which Ickes said that he was taking the liberty of replying to the editorial on the theory that *Editor and Publisher* could ignore Mr. Gertz but not the Secretary of the Interior. Much to Ickes' surprise and my amusement, the editors wrote to him that I had had my say in the pamphlet and they in the editorial and that was all that there was to it. So much for the freedom of the press!

Why were *Editor and Publisher* and the *Tribune* so exercised over a pamphlet written by a relatively unknown lawyer, thirty-six years old and uninfluential? What I said could be summed up in three paragraphs:

> The *Tribune* and Colonel McCormick are Chicago's problem children: identical twins who snarl, snap and snip peevishly at all who do not share their narrow hates, fears, prejudices and distortions. They gloat over each triumph of reaction, each defeat of a good cause. They have done more to retard progress and to kill hopes than any other forces in the community.

Labor looks on them as its enemies. Racial, religious and national minorities are dubious about them. Educational and cultural institutions are afraid of their sting and rancor. Good men and women expect to be maligned and blackguarded for voicing views or performing deeds displeasing to McCormick and his paper. They take over and soil as many of the people's activities and interests as their greed or acumen encompasses. They are bellowing bullies ready to ruin all that they cannot rule.

And now that we are engaged in a great war, calling for supreme effort, unity, loyalty and understanding, they give lip service to the national cause, while doing everything within their powers to destroy confidence and morale and impede the winning of the war. They will fight Hitler, Hirohito and Company only if they can uproot all liberal causes in the process. They and their self-seeking crowd want to take over totally. They must be stopped in their tracks.

Of course, today the *Tribune* is not the sort of publication it was in 1942, or at any time during the McCormick regime. Today, it is no worse and, in some respects, better than the other papers. It has typographical and illustrative riches; it covers more stories than the other Chicago papers; it does permit those who do not share its views to speak out in its columns; the first page is no longer an extension of the editorial page. Today I could not write my bitter *Tribune* pamphlets—that mentioned, and a summary called The Chicago Tribune—*Poison,* an eight-page pamphlet published by Chicago Citizens' Committee on Press and Radio, an arm of the Chicago labor movement.

Much milder and still of considerable interest is my little work, *Joe Medill's War,* published in 1945. The *Tribune* had labeled World War II as Roosevelt's War. I thought that, with greater accuracy and some irony, I could call the American Civil War of 1861–1865 Joe Medill's War. I gave much of the story of that sad period, some of it little known. My conclusion was more favorable than in *The People vs. The Chicago Tribune.* Writing of Medill and the *Tribune,* I said: ". . . it cannot be denied that, harsh, strident, fanatical although they may have been, they fought, in the large, a good fight for a good cause. They were pillars of strength in a divided and crumbling house and were instruments of purification and restoration in the days that followed the War."

While I was engaged in my *Tribune* researches, *Look* magazine asked me to do an article about Colonel McCormick and Colonel Knox, publishers, respectively, of the *Tribune* and the *Daily News*, and great rivals journalistically and politically. While I was correcting the galleys of the article, which I called "The Morning Colonel and the Evening Colonel," President Roosevelt named the Republican Knox as Secretary of the Navy, and Knox asked me to kill the article as inexpedient. This I did.

My major pamphlet on the *Tribune* was published not long after Marshall Field founded the *Chicago Sun*. While he and his associates were in the midst of assembling a staff, I received a telephone call from Paul Douglas, asking me to have lunch with him. Paul was then combining the careers of maverick Democrat alderman and professor of economics at the University of Chicago. At first he sparred around a bit, telling me that, despite his independent preconceptions, he greatly admired my law associate, Jack Arvey. Then he got to the reason for our meeting. "Marshall Field has asked me to be the political editor of his newspaper," he said, "and I turned him down, as I have other plans." This was prior to his enlisting in the Marines, at fifty, as a private, and later becoming a United States Senator. "Field asked me to suggest someone else for the post," he went on. "I would like to name you." I was startled, but quickly assented and awaited word from Field. It never came, although I met him on many occasions in connection with various community causes.

At the same time, Richard Finnegan, editor of the *Chicago Times* (later merged with the *Sun*), told me that he had suggested to Field that I be hired in an advisory or consultative capacity. I learned that Hal O'Flaherty, managing editor of the *Chicago Daily News*, not then a part of Field Enterprises, had told Field that he ought to hire me in an editorial capacity. I did not even know O'Flaherty, then or later. Others made similar suggestions, but never once did I have any conversations with Field on the subject. When, later, his circulation manager thought it would be a good idea to distribute copies of *The People vs. The Chicago Tribune,* the plan was vetoed.

From the beginning, I did write book reviews for the literary pages of the *Sun* and later the *Sun-Times,* and I still do.

One night I met a rather perky and offhand advertising executive named Leroy Truman Goble. I had been told of his many literary associates. He seemed to have known, rather intimately, almost everyone involved in the Chicago literary renaissance—Harry Hansen, Carl Sandburg, Sherwood Anderson, Floyd Dell, Ben Hecht. He had all sorts of interests and hobbies—books, of course, colonial glassware, masks, pictures. His little home in Ravenswood Manor was a minute museum, packed with everything. In an offhand manner, in our first conversation, the subject of my often-accepted, often-rejected *Tribune* manuscript came up. "It must be pretty bad to have been turned down so often," Goble commented, as if it was the usual thing to speak so frankly, so heartlessly, to a sensitive human being. I was so startled that I said nothing. Somehow, we became great friends, despite this inauspicious start, and ultimately I had the sad task of seeing Goble's estate through probate. Goble confessed that he did not really mean what he had said to me; he had merely wanted to jar me into paying attention to him, just as Nick Matsoukas used to do in our student days at the University of Chicago when he would sit in the front row in the classroom and open a newspaper in the very face of the professor.

I was learning that a successful literary career was even harder to attain than success in the practice of law.

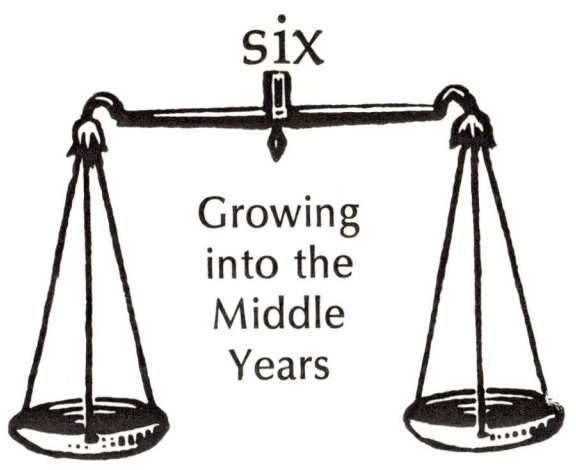

six

Growing into the Middle Years

I have not checked the figures, but I am sure that there must have been over 14,000 lawyers in my community and over 150,000 in the United States, during the 1930's and 1940's—a vast number. I am sure that most of the men and women in my profession were reasonably, if not highly, competent and at least "indifferent honest," in Shakespeare's phrase. Most of them had respectable practices and, unlike the Depression year, 1930, when I was admitted to the bar, they were beginning to earn reasonably good livelihoods from relatives, friends, neighbors and, if lucky, strangers. All these lawyers wanted to win their cases. I wanted to have cases worth winning, cases with substance and meaning beyond fees earned. And I wanted to be a complete citizen, and a writer. I wanted to be erudite without being dull. "Not even a Constitution can prevail against human nature," I had said in one article that I wrote at this time. It was typical of the style that I cultivated. "All law was penal in origin," I said in another article, "a form of licensed revenge in favor of injured parties." In everything I wrote I tried to express views that did credit to my profession, no less than to myself.

And all the while my family and I were growing up.

When Ted was a baby we moved from our little apartment in Austin to a big old-fashioned apartment on Sunnyside Avenue near what was the Clarendon Beach House on the North Side of Chicago. I was self-conscious about the mixed neighborhood. Just a couple of blocks to the north was Wilson Avenue, notorious for prostitution, drinking, and all that was shabby and sodden in the city. South, there were good homes and sober people. To the east there was the built-in land, leading to parks and beaches. Almost from birth, Ted and later Midge had as their closest friends Japanese, black, Jewish, and non-Jewish children. They were truly oblivious to such differences. Intellectually and spiritually, Ceretta and I were free from bigotry, but deep inside us were prejudices against which we constantly and sometimes successfully struggled.

There were very bright and talented boys and girls to stimulate our children. More than thirty-five years later, my son, Ted, and Joel Siegel, son of my office associate and secretary, are still friends, and both are lawyers. As one observed them side by side in their buggies, one could not have been sure what time would bring for them or their families. There was Billy Friedkin, more interested in basketball than the arts—one would never think of him as the future winner of an Oscar for *The French Connection*; there was Phil Kaufman, concerned even as a child about poetry—one could think of him as the producer of way-out *Goldstein*; and Daniel Greenburg, the rather shy son of an artist—one could sense that he would be a humorist and an expert on Jewish mothers. There were others with whom Ted played; he was a leader by reason of courage and imagination. And there would be another boy, from a broken home, polite and deferential, who would stealthily steal from Ceretta's purse and ultimately kill for gain. Another, the son of a prize fighter, would tell, almost eloquently, of his lack of accomplishments, his near illiteracy. All would be welcomed to our home by Ceretta, who shared each child's problems.

These children and others, young and old, friends and strangers, would be attracted by the solid wall in our living room, crammed with books, from floor to ceiling. Visible from the outside, it would suggest something unusual or possibly perverse about the head of the household. No other living room in this mixed area was so obviously occupied by persons to whom words meant so much.

And there was a long and narrow corridor from the living room up front to the dining room in the rear, lined on both sides with paintings and prints, like the wall of a museum. I would look at each picture each day as I walked back and forth from our bedroom to the children's, just as I would glance at each book in the living room, recalling favorite passages. We had little balance in the bank and times were uncertain, but I felt enriched by these things.

I would read constantly to Ted and Midge, and they lived through each word. Midge would howl with glee, as if hearing the words for the first time. Ted would learn about the treedwellers and then act out their lives, by strapping himself to a tree and trying to sleep there through the night. The other children admired his deeds, although they sometimes suspected that his heroism was verbal rather than real.

One holy day, *Yom Kippur,* I believe, Ceretta and I were wakened by a call from her sister, Fae. "What kind of parents are you?" Fae screamed. We learned that Ted, without telling us, had packed a lunch, fixed a pillow in the right place for his sister, and gone with her on a twelve- or thirteen-mile bicycle ride to suburban Winnetka, where Fae and Chuck lived. Midge was a not wholly voluntary passenger. She was kept from tears by Ted's choice profanity.

That vocabulary was like a sailor's. One day, when he was about five or six, I sat down with Ted and reviewed the various four-letter words that he was using. I took up one such word at a time and asked its meaning. Ted did not know what any of the words meant. "Then why do you use them?" I demanded. "They sound so wonderful, Daddy," he replied. No wonder he early developed a talent for poetry.

By now I was so absorbed in community organizations and in my law work that, despite my great love for the children, I was away from them too much, until Ceretta wisely decreed that I had to be home almost every night. This developed a bond that has endured to this day. I discovered that winning cases was less satisfying than retaining the love of my children.

I also began to realize the importance of my Jewish heritage in family life. Though I am opposed to all forms of discrimination, hate, favoritism, I must confess that, in my heart of hearts, I have a very special feeling for mine own, the Jewish people. When now I pick up the daily newspaper and see an article about Israel, I am more likely to read it than anything about other people; if it is good news, I rejoice; if it is bad, I fret. I take pride in the achievements and joys of all Jews everywhere; I am troubled over the sorrows, misdeeds, failures of any Jews anywhere. Skeptical about all religious dogmas, a member now of no synagogue or temple, devoted to the ecumenical spirit that knows no creeds, I get deep emotional comfort from the prayers, prophecies, and liturgy of the Jews. A good cantor chants something special to me; he awakens ancestral yearnings, aspirations, aches, and agonies. On special and solemn occasions, like births, confirmations, death, marriage, the Passover Seder, I share in the ceremonies of my people, without belief or disbelief, scarcely questioning the rituals. They are part of my emotional being, although my mind has rejected them.

No one should underestimate the bitters and sweets of association with one's own people. Even the most cosmopolitan and unfettered individual—and I think of myself as such—must confess, if only to himself, that there really are ties of blood that bind, that Judaism is a mystical cord that draws together men and women of many ages and lands, of varied tongues and cultures, in a kind of Holy Union. Every Jew is the keeper of his kind, and a leader of Jews is a special shepherd of his flock—here at home no less than in Israel and abroad. At the same time, Jews have always embraced others in their midst with gladness of heart. There are Ruths in every generation, and Naomis to welcome them.

One of the most difficult and necessary lessons for a lawyer's family to learn is that the attorney-client relationship is confidential. Both Ceretta and my second wife, Mamie, different in many respects, were alike in their annoyance with me for not revealing professional confidences to them. Other lawyers told their wives everything, they said. Why should not I, especially since my cases were often so interesting? This problem was illustrated for me in an amusing fashion one summer during World War II at a resort whose owner was having an affair with the housekeeper. Ceretta and a friend of hers often speculated as to what was going on, expressing their opinions, in my presence, both as to what was happening and as to what it would lead to. I listened attentively, saying nothing. Suddenly the local newspapers carried stories about the situation. A divorce action was filed by the lady, not by her husband, and I was her attorney. I had been retained during the period when Ceretta and her friend were talking so avidly about the principals, and often mistaken in what they were saying. Both women were piqued about my silence.

Since then, when I have represented friends, they have assumed that I was keeping my wife informed. It comes as a shock to them to learn that if my wife is to know the case, it is through them, not from me.

In the early- or mid-1930's, a New York attorney referred a rather complicated matter to us. He was the advisor and friend of Constance Reed Netcher, the divorced wife of Irving Netcher of the Chicago family that owned the Boston Store, then a leading State Street department store. His mother was Mollie Newberry, a robust woman of Jewish ancestry, who had been celebrated in at least one novel and was still a legend in the city that she had conquered. Constance was one of the three beautiful, imaginative, and headstrong Reed girls, members of an Irish-Catholic family, prominent in the worlds of business and politics. Each girl was married and divorced and unreconciled to the loss of her former life.

We were called because Constance was confronted with an urgent problem. Her younger sister had just died in one of the Chicago suburbs, leaving a twelve-year-old daughter, Muriel Blanche Reno. What was to be done about the estate and the upbringing of the child? I was asked to be administrator of the sister's estate and guardian of her daughter, neither of whom I had ever met. I became virtually a relative and the arbiter of differences. The Arvey firm received the fees, but I was the recipient of the confidences, friendships, and antagonisms. Muriel and I had a very special relationship, almost as if we were parent and child. We shared many happy and some tragic experiences. I won the friendship of Muriel's grandmother after initial hostility, of her estranged father (whose inaction was puzzling), of her aunts, cousins, friends. Young when it began, I grew with it to middle age and beyond. Muriel went from childhood into marriage, motherhood, and maturity. The relationship deepened; it had results that would never have been anticipated when it began. Muriel had an almost ethereal beauty when she was young, and a voice that haunted one. She imbued everything with an unearthly quality.

Since Muriel was Catholic, I felt that I had to educate her in good Catholic schools. I sent her to Sacred Heart Academy in Providence, Rhode Island, where her ancient grand-aunt, Mother Mary Reed, was still active. In extreme old age (she was almost one hundred years old when she died), Mother Reed had the clear handwriting and mental agility of a young woman. She and I would exchange letters about Muriel. Our child needed the attention we bestowed upon her character and spirit, because when school was out she would go with her Aunt Constance to Europe, where the distractions were more prevalent than the rites of the faith.

Muriel developed great literary gifts. When she won national contests, some of my associates would pretend that she was my daughter, not my ward. But her imagination was an exotic one. Influenced, no doubt, by the family vicissitudes, she would create all sorts of strange situations in her rich way which would have troubled old Mother Reed sorely had she known of them.

One day I was called in a panic by the nuns at Sacred Heart. There had been an explosion in the chemistry laboratory and Muriel was badly injured. Her vision was imperiled.

Within hours of hearing the dreadful news, I said to Ceretta: "I am going to see her. If she were our own child, I would be there now, and Muriel deserves the same consideration." I decided that I would first learn the names of the best eye doctors in the East and select one for consultation. Knowledgeable friends suggested Dr. Webb W. Weeks who told me: "I don't really practice any more, but I will take this case." We made an appointment to meet the next morning in New York at the hospital that he designated.

It was difficult getting air transportation in this period and I had to go by train. I met Dr. Weeks at the appointed time and he told me that Muriel would surely lose the sight in both eyes unless he removed one eye. He had developed an artificial eye that functioned cosmetically almost like a natural eye, with seemingly normal movement and appearance. Because there was nothing else to do, I consented to the irrevocable and tragic operation. Dr. Weeks was unbelievably kind. He explained to me that, after the operation, he would have to turn over the postoperative care to his nephew, an opthalmologist of great ability, but he as well as his nephew would keep in touch with me. Very softly, he said that I could conscientiously return to Chicago.

It was the early Fall of 1939. The Nazis had overrun Poland with devastating speed. The universe was in a state of shock, able to converse only about the ominous shadow of coming events. Despite my feverish concern, at this moment I was so numbed by the personal tragedy that the world disaster receded.

I was returning to Chicago, silent in my woe. I sat in the smoking room of the train, hardly thinking of anything except the lovely girl whose life was blighted.

A handsome middle-aged man in a quiet business suit sat alongside of me, his face vaguely familiar. I was unknown to him. But it must have been apparent to the man that I was in pain. In a voice that was both kind and firm, he began to talk with me about the war. He said things that made it apparent at once that he was completely informed about the armies of the world and particularly the armed forces of the Nazis and ourselves. He knew and understood the facts behind the facades.

He said something that shocked me into attention—he had been the judge of the Army war games, held, if I recall correctly, in Louisiana, where an American regiment had been lost in broad daylight. He reminisced, too, of General Pershing in World War I. I asked him if Holland and Belgium could resist if, as anticipated, the Nazis invaded them. "For a couple of days," he replied. There had been wishful articles about the ability of the Low Countries to fight on. Could France hold out if the Western Front became active? I had been persuaded of the strength of the Maginot Line of fortifications. He was skeptical about France's ability to stop the Nazis. I asked him all sorts of questions, and in his quiet, decisive manner he readily gave me answers. I cannot begin to recite all that he said to me; even today it would make fascinating reading. It was apparent that the world, including America, was in a perilous state. Individuals seemed puny, pointless.

I listened spell-bound. It was obvious that the man was in a position of high authority, although he did no boasting. I felt fortunate that I was privy to his confidences. Suddenly, a great peace came over me. I was once more of this world, aware of all that was going on, and grateful that there were compassionate men like the one who had done so much for me, a stranger. I remembered the words of Scripture: "Out of strength comes sweetness."

After some hours, we parted; to the end, neither of us gave his name to the other, and neither asked. A day or two later I picked up the rotogravure section of the *Chicago Daily News* and saw on its cover a picture of my benefactor—General George C. Marshall.

I heard from Dr. Weeks a few times. Over the telephone he explained Muriel's condition in hopeful terms. Then one day I picked up the newspapers and learned that Dr. Weeks was dead. Only at that time did I learn the whole truth. He was in bed dying of cancer, when I first called him. He had cautioned all to say nothing about the fatal condition. He had performed this last operation because something about what I had said to him had moved him. The obituary columns told of a very great physician of international fame. I read columns about him in *The New York Times*. I had my own greater knowledge of a man whom I will never forget.

The Order of the Sacred Heart felt that they had to make amends for Muriel's mishap. They gave her a scholarship to Manhattanville College of the Sacred Heart and this led to yet another by-product of my relationship to Muriel.

Some occurrences are too significant to be described as merely coincidental. There must be some sort of universal law that, at least now and then, there are events in juxtaposition that are intended to be that way by the ironical Master of the Revels in order to show that in due time all good things come to pass.

We had been struggling for years to force the admission of black lawyers to membership in the Chicago Bar Association. Yet, whether we had relatively liberal or conservative presidents, conditions remained the same—black lawyers, even distinguished black lawyers, would be excluded from membership because of their blackness, and for no other reason.

Suddenly, two events occurred at the same time. Mother Dammann, the president of Manhattanville College of the Sacred Heart, had died; and her highly conservative and respectable brother, Francis Dammann, had become the president of the Chicago Bar Association. I did not know Mr. Dammann other than by reputation, but I knew his sister through my ward, Muriel Reno, a student at Manhattanville. I wrote to Mr. Dammann and told him of the circumstances of my knowing his sister and reminded him of her grandeur in resisting students, parents, alumni, and bigots of all kind and continuing to enforce a policy of non-discrimination at the fashionable Catholic girls' college which she headed. She had persisted and prevailed. Young women of all races were admitted to this once all-white institution. "I hope you will forgive me," I wrote, "if I tell you that the greatest memorial to your sister in our community will be the admission of Negroes to membership in the Chicago Bar Association during your term as president." He responded immediately; he was touched by what I had said. "Be patient with me," he wrote, "and I promise you that, while I am president of our Association, Negroes will be admitted to membership on the same terms as whites." He was faithful to his promise. Blacks were admitted; they still are; it is inconceivable that they will ever be denied admission again. Where liberals had failed or faltered, a conservative corporation lawyer had succeeded: because he had the right sister—because I had reminded him of her achievements—because conditions were finally ripe.

seven

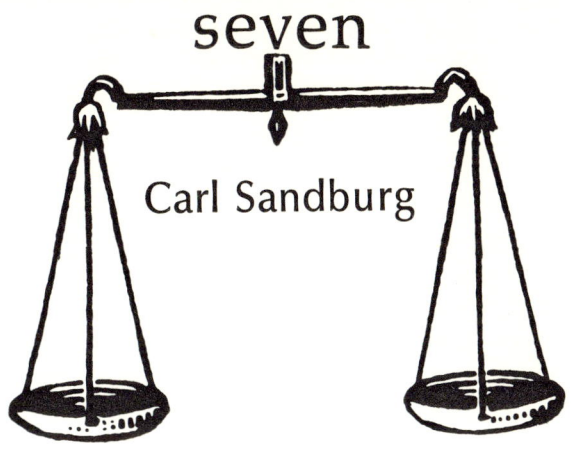

Carl Sandburg

I first met Sandburg when I was an over-eager, tense boy of thirteen or fourteen. An older man had brought me to Sandburg's office at the rickety old *Chicago Daily News* building shortly after the close of World War I. To my boyish mind, the poet had the build and solemnity of an old American Indian. Sandburg talked with me of many things, and never in the manner of one who was simply tolerating a callow kid.

Some years later, when, as director of the Illinois Police Association, I wanted him to act as one of the sponsors of the historical pageant that was going to be staged at the Chicago Fair in 1933, he replied to the long letter I had written to him by penciling on its margin, with characteristic laconic efficiency: "O.K. by me."

Then, largely in the company of Ralph Newman, Civil War student and bookseller, I had many meetings and pleasing adventures with Sandburg. He encouraged me in the writing of a book about the *Chicago Tribune,* and he sought to interest his own publisher in it. There was a Sandburg who was brusque, forgetful, and less than kind. This Sandburg I scarcely knew, but I realized that any meeting with him was unpredictable.

There was more than one visit to Chikaming Goat Farm, the Sandburg home between the writing of *The Prairie Years* and *The War Years.* It jutted out from the crest of a hill in Harbert, Michigan: unpretentious, but suggestive of comfortable living. The visitors climbed the terraced stairway and walked upon the open porch, cluttered with driftwood.

On one occasion, when I was there, a photographer from a now-vanished magazine was in attendance, the latest in a procession of picture publications that had realized the national appeal of the poet, historian, farmer, and American spokesman. Sandburg was cooperative, enthusiastic even. For he always had Lincoln's own love of the camera. The logs and other things on the porch had been placed there by him as an "obstacle course" (in Sandburg's words) for his grandson. Sandburg had the boy go through his tricks while the camera clicked.

He had great accumulations of photographs, newspaper cuttings, off-prints, letters, manuscripts, and memorabilia, running the gamut of his life and generation. He had a decent respect for his own attainments, and spoke of himself neither with boasting nor with undue modesty. He had the same regard for those with whom he had been associated, and only slightly less for the world at large.

He thought, felt, and spoke with subtle nuances. A sentence, a tag of speech, a gesture, a laugh, a moment's revelation, carried meaning for him, and he conveyed it in like manner.

There was talk, for example, of Edgar Lee Masters, the creator of *Spoon River Anthology,* the lawyer who had turned poet, and had warred with his wife and the world. Sandburg had seen Masters in a crowded section of New York, where Masters appeared utterly out of place. "He said to me," Sandburg reported, '"This Country won't be the same after this war. It won't be the same!' I asked him what he meant. 'Those aliens!'

he replied. 'Those aliens!'" Sandburg chuckled and went on to something else.

Man's conquest of the air constantly stirred him during those years of war. At the time of German airborne invasion of Crete, Newman and I visited Sandburg, and he reverted time and time to the amazing event. "Who can talk or write of the Civil War," he asked, "when men descend from the skies today and take over a land?" This day, at Chikaming Goat Farm, the situation had changed. We were conquering Sicily, and from the air. Books on aviation were all over the house. They had been read and pondered over. In talking of President Roosevelt, he said; "I am afraid that this man who so loved his big navy did not really grasp the meaning of Billy Mitchell until after Pearl Harbor."

It has been said that he liked to orate in Swedish. As a matter of fact, he loved the music of all spoken languages. It was always obvious that he enjoyed talking or singing or reading, with or without an audience, and, of course, his voice had a flow and depth seldom equaled even in this nation of orators. There were many people who did not enjoy the extreme slowness of his speech, the care with which he pronounced each syllable and rolled it in his mouth. Still more people were spell-bound by a voice that suggested profundity even when a simple thing was restated.

On one occasion, he read to us at length from the famous "Mrs. Partington," whose drollness delighted America in the months before the Civil War. He relished each malapropism, overstatement, and wry hint. And he read more of his own fables, few of them published, about the strange creatures with quaint names who read books, for good and bad reasons, with good and bad manners. Each time one met him in those years the collection of fables had grown. One expected, in time, a little volume, a poet-philosopher's guide to reading. When I suggested a comparison with Mortimer Adler's famous book on reading, Sandburg sniffed almost contemptuously.

When asked once if he would care to read some sonnets in Swedish, Sandburg declared himself the wrong person to contemplate that verse form in English or in any other language, as he was prejudiced. "Sonnets are like crossword puzzles," he said. "They have to be worked out too mechanically. You say, 'This line is good.' Then you look again and say, 'But, shoot! It don't rhyme!' In all literature there are about six good sonnets.

"There are enough good spokesman for orthodox forms of poetry. I prefer to speak of free verse." He articulated "free" in a tone almost of defiance.

Freedom was no academic word to Sandburg. His appearance, his surroundings, his writings, all showed his instinct for freedom. As it had been wherever he lived, there were thousands of books on the farm scattered in every room and in the barns and sheds. There was an area that he called the Lincoln Room, because the basic material he used in writing *The War Years* was there; but no professional librarian would have approved the arrangement of books in that room, nor elsewhere on the farm. It was not that the house was untidy; it was simply individualistic. I could not help thinking of the contrast with the home of Colonel Edward M. House, where every book was in its place, with a precision that was almost mathematical; no picture on the walls was askew, no piece of furniture was out of line; and the Colonel himself was attired with a care that suggested formal diplomatic dinners.

Again and again the subject of President Roosevelt came up when I visited Sandburg. He gave each of us a rare off-print of his memorable radio talk urging F.D.R.'s re-election in 1940. And he told us that when the President conceived the idea of lend-lease soon after his re-election, Sandburg wrote him: "Thank God, you have the craft and cunning of Thomas Jefferson and Andrew Jackson." Yet Sandburg was slow in favoring American involvement in the war. "I was an interventionist before Carl," his wife said. "He resisted a long time." The two men were, in a sense, friends; at least, to the extent that a President and a poet could communicate when the President had exhausting duties in an unprecedented period of history. Great as was his admiration for Roosevelt, he was not uncritical. He was inclined at moments to the side of Joseph Medill Patterson in the now forgotten, then lively, battle between the *New York Daily News* and the Administration.

"You cannot lump together Joe Patterson and the *Chicago Tribune*," he said, pointedly. "The President has not been entirely fair with Joe Patterson. Joe is still somebody to say 'Hello!' to." Patterson evoked for Sandburg those years when they were both, the rich man and the poor man, fighting for socialism.

Journalism, particularly as practiced in Chicago, was of the greatest interest to Sandburg. The battle between the newly founded *Sun* (now the *Sun-Times*) and the old and snarling *Tribune* called forth many shrewd observations. While not condoning any of the sins of Colonel McCormick's paper, he was critical of the *Sun.* He thought that it was not a part of Chicago, rooted in the lives of people. Marshall Field was struggling to make it a viable institution. Instead of choosing Chicago personalities for the principal roles in the venture, he had turned to other parts of the country. He put Silliman Evans of Tennessee in charge of the paper. It was a mistake to turn over a Northern metropolitan newspaper to a Southerner who was not attuned to the sounds and smells of the city, Sandburg thought. "A Northerner might go South and succeed," he said, "but a Southerner can't go North and run a paper here creditably."

One afternoon in 1942, Sandburg walked into Ralph Newman's Abraham Lincoln Book Shop in Chicago. As usual, I was there. In solemn tones, Sandburg announced that the doctor had forbidden him alcohol—a hard burden for any poet. He handed Newman his card entitling him to special discounts in the purchase of liquors. "I won't need this anymore," he said, sadly. Then he handed Newman a bottle of Scotch and me a bottle of Rye (Hannah & Hoag H & M Maryland Straight Rye Whiskey, 90 proof, quart size), saying: "These are my last two bottles." He turned to the door to leave; then reeled around and took the bottles from us, wrote something in pencil on the labels, handed the bottles back and left. On my bottle, these words appear:

> For Elmer Gertz
> from an alumnus
> Carl Sandburg
> 1942.

Something similar was written on Newman's bottle. But the visible evidence in his case is gone—not that Newman impiously drank it—a servant did, and destroyed the evidence. My bottle remains as the rarest of all Sandburgiana. It may be thought of as Sandburg in the flesh. There are as many rare memorabilia of Sandburg in the spirit.

I have a particularly clear memory of one cold winter night when Sandburg, Ralph Newman, and I were being driven in a car which broke down. This presented no problem. Sandburg got out of the car with us and pushed it to a place of safety. Then we all went into a tavern to warm up. As usual, he engaged in conversation with the waitress, not about poetry or history, but about the tough little things that would interest a barmaid. She could never have suspected that she was talking to a famous poet and historian, a man who, in the judgment of many, deserved a Nobel Prize. On this occasion, he introduced himself as the business agent of some organization, like the steamfitters' union. Newman, genial proprietor of the Abraham Lincoln Book Shop, and I were given other unlikely titles. We did not play our roles with his skill. The waitress must have thought that we just ordinary bums. There was a somewhat similar occasion, when we shared adjoining seats in a barber shop. I overheard Sandburg give the barber a lively account of some of the adventures of my life, none of them true.

Discovering that almost everyone who sits down in a Pullman smoker (this was before the present age of air travel) was an officer of some company or association, Sandburg had cards printed, announcing himself as president of the National Association of Paw Paw Growers. These he would pass out to those who asked, "What's your line?" Enjoying the imaginary distinction, he had letterheads printed for the paper organization and selected a most wonderful board of directors, which included the President of the United States and an assortment of friends such as Ralph Newman and myself. It is doubtful if anyone with whom Sandburg discussed the affairs of the association ever knew it was fictitious.

I was once the center of one of his concentrated attacks. I had written something that had displeased him mightily and Sandburg whacked me with great verbal blows. He had long been brooding about the subject, and when the occasion presented itself he burst forth. Although I was the subject of his fury and thought he was wrong, I felt like a man privileged to observe Jove at work. I could not respond in anger. I listened, protesting mildly at best. Then the storm blew over. Sandburg smiled sweetly. "Forget it," he said; and we remained friends until his death.

In the last decade of his life, Sandburg awakened each morning and found himself more famous; and most Americans rejoiced with him. After many years of sometimes selfless striving and devotion to his high calling, he had arrived in every sense. This went on in a world occupying itself with problems and vexations such as mankind had never known, and yet finding much to marvel about in this striking man. I know of nothing in the history of American letters to compare with the acclaim of Sandburg.

A high point of his life, something that epitomized him, was when he appeared as one of the witnesses in the famous Board hearing that led to the parole of Nathan F. Leopold. Few can ever forget the tall, white-haired, eloquent poet, telling the members of the Parole Board that they had a date with destiny, that they could become historic characters if they had the courage and good sense to free Nathan Leopold. It was clear that they were impressed—deeply moved, in fact.

Sandburg instinctively chose as his great passion the life and legend of Abraham Lincoln, just as the American people have made the man from the prairies of Illinois their principal article of faith. Others have written out of great academic backgrounds and with literary grace. But Sandburg wrote of Lincoln in the manner of common folk. He absorbed him so thoroughly that Lincoln's speech was his speech, Lincoln's posture his posture, Lincoln's thoughts, predilections, and philosophy his; so much so that when he was asked to give his own views of anything, he naturally fell into the Lincoln idiom and would sometimes use the very words of the Great Emancipator. By reflex, he told Lincoln's stories rather than his own. Americans generally thought of Sandburg as soon as Lincoln's name was mentioned. They, Lincoln and Sandburg, seem destined to ride through eternity as spiritual brothers.

It was my privilege to preside at the memorial meeting for him in the Chicago Public Library, when Ralph Newman delivered the principal address. When, somewhat later, the Library marked its centenary, I delivered another address on Sandburg. Meanwhile, his eldest daughter, Margaret, hard at work on a book about her father, had been a week-long guest at our home, and I got new insight into my old friend. I was proud, indeed, when Gene Lovitz and Joseph Haas dedicated their Sandburg biography to me. These things revived my memory of many meetings.

Other writers take inscriptions in books lightly. Sandburg always exercised the greatest care and creativeness in what he wrote on the fly leaves of the books to his friends. There is, for example, a copy of *The American Songbag* inscribed to my children. "Sing often, chilluns, and sing deep," he advised them in his carefully chiseled handwriting.

How will posterity react to Sandburg? Influenced as we must be by recollections of his regal Viking bearing, his speech, his certainties of thought and utterance, we cannot imagine a time when Americans will not cherish that tall, white-haired oracle, Sandburg, strumming on his guitar as he sings the song of

America—young in spirit, as America is young, vibrant, venturesome, always asking, "Where to? What next?," and prepared for everything.

eight

Race, Religion, and the Law

During the two hectic decades of the 1940's and 1950's, I was preoccupied with the National Lawyers Guild, the Decalogue Society of Lawyers, the American Jewish Congress, the Chicago Council against Racial and Religious Discrimination, the Chicago Commission on Human Relations, and, above all, the Public Housing Association, and various related groups. It was not a matter of scattering my efforts and becoming ineffective. These organizations were closely interrelated and highly effective in dealing with race and religion, civil rights, civil liberty, personal freedom. It was as if I were working in one broad, all-encompassing area, the most important one in that harried period of American history when the poor, the blacks, the underprivileged, and the deprived were more restless than ever. Largely because of the impact of a World War, those who had too long been second-class citizens demanded, loudly and irresistibly, that they be heard; that they be permitted to advance to true equality, rather than any counterfeit substitute for what was their due.

I have always been concerned about the public image of my profession and the problems of the practitioner. I belong to a substantial number of the conventional lawyers' groups. I have served nominally, for the most part, on some of the committees of these associations, but was rather active as chairman of the Legal Education Committee of the Chicago Bar Association. I have lectured, in fields of my special competence, and have written articles and reviews for legal journals. But I have always felt that the respectable groups, useful as they often have been, are circumscribed by the conservatism of our craft. My special devotion has been to the more venturesome organizations—for a period of years, before its decline, the National Lawyers Guild, and now, much less actively than I would like, the Chicago Council of Lawyers, and the First Amendment Lawyers' Association. These organizations have sometimes proded the Establishment associations into demonstrating more interest in civil rights, the poor, the deprived, the quality and availability of justice.

To rise to leadership in the respectable groups, one must play a special sort of game, either as a member of one of the larger law firms, allowed time by one's colleagues to participate, or one must do the kind of log-rolling that is extremely distasteful to me.

I have the same quarrel with judicial selection. The worst lawyers are more likely to be placed on the bench than the best. Almost invariably one must be a ward worker, and genuflect before the powers that be in politics, to be considered for the high calling of dispensing justice. The price must be paid throughout one's judicial career. Later I struggled with this problem at the Sixth Illinois Constitutional Convention.

Those of my generation and political persuasion will recall that in the 1930's, the courts, from the United States Supreme Court down, were unwilling to look sympathetically upon the legislative tools created by President Roosevelt to deal with the social and economic dislocations and disasters caused by the stock-market collapse of 1929 and the great disaster of the Depression which followed. The Court struck down laws and practices which they regarded as unconstitutional when judged by their narrow perspectives. It became difficult to cope with the problems of restoring the economy and, meanwhile, feeding, clothing, and sheltering the indigent, then a vast segment, if not a majority, of the population. Roosevelt devised a scheme to pack the highest court with justices more receptive to the new solutions, and almost succeeded. Many of us, including enlightened jurists like Justice Louis Brandeis, feared the long-term consequences of tampering with the basic judicial structure; but we, like the President, felt that the difficulty was that judges, as conservative as the members of the bar associations, would not look at the problems in an unprejudiced fashion. We felt that the constitution viewed realistically, as the great Chief Justice John Marshall had viewed it, in the formative years of the Union, permitted solutions to any problem. The conservatives are not strict constructionalists, as they like to call themselves; they are nonconstructionalists, who want to hug their preconceptions about the basic charter to their bosoms for personal comfort, regardless of the popular necessities.

The National Lawyers Guild grew at this time out of the vision some enlightened lawyers had of a profession that was intended to serve the people, rather than the purses of selfish practitioners. Men and women who had deservedly great reputations nationally and in their communities as liberal crusaders formed a lawyers' organization that would fight for social legislation, enforcement of the Bill of Rights, high standards of judicial and professional conduct. It would protect those in and out of the profession who were fellow-workers in building a genuine democracy. It would goad the established bar associations into showing more concern for popular necessities. It would not supercede these organizations, but supplement them. In its first years, at least, there is no doubt that the National Lawyers Guild had real achievements to its credit. It was a great force, a flaming sword, for the advancement of constitutional rights. It won the respect of many who were not members, including Presidents of the United States, cabinet members, Governors, justices of the Supreme Court, high officials everywhere.

I was a member from the beginning, but not, initially, a leader. There was a chapter of the Lawyers Guild in Chicago, as in other larger cities. Arthur J. Goldberg, William Holly (first judicial appointee here of President Roosevelt), Professor Malcolm Sharp, John Gutknecht, George L. Quilici, and others whom I knew and respected were active in the Chicago chapter and nationally. Shortly after I left the Arvey law firm, I was waited on at my new office by my Arvey associate, George L. Siegel, and a few others. Would I edit a little publication for the Chicago chapter? They would help me, and it was an opportunity to maintain a voice for enlightenment in our profession. I readily agreed and put forth my very best efforts and enthusiasm, converting a mimeographed sheet or two into a printed publication of scope and dimensions. The members liked the new magazine. They contributed to it, some from the battlefields abroad at which they were then serving. Before I could say "Nay," I was drafted to serve as president of the Chicago chapter, while continuing to edit the magazine. I became a national vice-president of the Lawyers Guild. Perhaps I was on the way to becoming national president.

Some years later I left the Lawyers Guild, for reasons that I deemed sufficient. But I did not then, and I do not now, disclaim the organization. I think it rendered great and lasting contributions to our national life. It has an honored place in the history of our profession. I am proud of my own role in it.

The gatherings of the Lawyers Guild in those first flush days were memorable because of the general level of astuteness, dedication, and social drive. Robert Kenny, the national president, was unfailingly amusing and, in his deceptive way, dynamic. Thurgood Marshall was earthy and wise in those days predating his first successes as an advocate for civil rights before the United States Supreme Court and then as a justice of the Court. Wayne Morse, Abe Fortas, Arthur Goldberg, and many others illuminated our meetings and gave us much to ponder over.

There was one member whom I found especially intriguing, because of his combination of good looks, self-assurance, and brains. For a while he had been one of the great driving forces as a highly placed attorney with New Deal agencies; then he had enlisted with John L. Lewis in the epochal struggle for industrial unionism, becoming general counsel of the C.I.O. and one of its intellectual leaders. At each convention, Lee Pressman would gather a small group of us in a private room and discuss the state of the economy, the course of politics, the world at large. I would listen, because Lee did not seem to like interruptions from the ranks. Clore Warne, a hillbilly from the Ozarks who had gone to Los Angeles and become a distinguished lawyer there, was not given to silence. He would contend with Lee, sometimes disagreeing strongly, and Lee would be almost contemptuous in his response. This I did not like, despite my great admiration for Lee's brilliance of mind and speech. One of my most painful memories is of the day when Lee confessed publicly that he was a member of a Communist cell during all of those years. He abandoned all professional activities, and I am not sure what he is doing today. The reaction of the inquisitors to men like Lee Pressman damaged the Lawyers Guild and other groups and individuals that were performing useful public services.

One person in that once-secret cell of Communists who is still active as a lawyer is John Abt. When, as attorney for Nathan Leopold, I was seeking testimonial letters for him from his University of Chicago classmates, I wrote to Abt, not recognizing his identity. Abt replied that he would be glad to help Leopold, but that he feared his name would hurt, rather than help.

After being so active in the Lawyers Guild, why did I cease to be active, why did I resign? The reasons were several. I began to feel that it took too much out of me to keep the organization from falling into the hands of those who might divert it from the course that I thought it ought to follow. This was emphasized for me at the time of the Korean War. Much as I regret any military incursion, I felt that our national policy against a Communist take-over of South Korea was fully justified. Later, as the Cold War led to excessive preoccupation with the containment of other nations, I was less enthusiastic about such adventures; but I am still persuaded that what we did in the Korean War was right at the time and held back aggressive moves for a decade. Too many members of the Lawyers Guild were more preoccupied with foreign affairs than with professional problems or purely domestic matters. They were too prone to act without the kind of mature consideration that was required. A group of us defeated a resolution condemning our involvement in Korea by the narrowest of margins. I feared that this was only a temporary victory, that the radical activists might win the next time and thereafter. I saw no point in consuming myself in the struggle against them. More of value could be accomplished by working with men and women whose motives were not open to suspicion. When I was about to withdraw, the Lawyers Guild was attacked, unfairly I believed, by the House Un-American Activities Committee and the Attorney General. I could not quit when the organization was under fire, lest I appear craven. I waited until I could leave without self-reproach; then I resigned.

During one of the early meetings of the Chicago Commission on Human Relations, I spoke about the numerous ethnic and creedal lawyers' groups in Chicago—more, I am sure, than anywhere else in the country. The Poles, Italians, Bohemians, Greeks, Scandinavians, Lithuanians, Negroes, and others I do not now recall have their own bar associations; the Catholics and Lutherans, also, and the Jews. The latter group, the Decalogue Society of Lawyers, has the largest membership of any such association in the Chicago area, because the Jews, like the Irish, have an affinity for the law. New York City, with the largest Jewish population in the world, has no such organization, probably because the Jews have dominant roles in the over-all bar associations. There was a time when Jews in Chicago had to contend with much anti-Semitism from judges and the bar generally. The Decalogue Society was a reaction against this. It persisted as an organization when the anti-Semitism diminished. In my day, unlike the past, there have been a number of Jewish presidents of the Chicago and Illinois State Bar Associations, and there has been a Jewish president of the American Bar Association for the first time. It may be that, when prejudice vanishes, the ethnic and religious groups will disappear. Meanwhile, lawyers of the Jewish faith, like myself, are confronted with the question as to whether or not to join the Decalogue Society. Many oppose it on principle, feeling that such organizations are divisive. I feel that as long as the association is in being, I want it to be as good as possible. On balance, the Decalogue Society has been worthwhile. It has curtailed all expressions of anti-Semitism in the profession. It has encouraged a spirit of tolerance toward all persons. It has fought for fair employment practices, nondiscrimination in every field, full implementation of the Bill of Rights. It has been helpful to Jewish philanthropies, Jewish cultural and communal activities, generally, and the State of Israel.

When my interest in the Lawyers Guild declined, I began to devote more and more attention to the Decalogue Society. As always, my interest was evidenced by contributions to its publication.

On March 12, 1949, in the presence of almost 1000 persons, three men were given awards by the Decalogue Society of Lawyers. The principal award went to an eloquent and courageous rabbi in the tradition of the Prophets—Stephen S. Wise, one of my personal heroes. The other awards went to Leonard J. Grossman, who had played a role, years earlier, in the tragic Leo Franks case in Georgia, and to me. My personal triumph lay in the coupling of my name with Rabbi Wise's on what he knew was his final appearance in Chicago. Fatally ill, he seemed to lose his feebleness as he rose to deliver his swan song. He said, in a voice that still thrills me in recollection: "I continue to cherish the hope and to point with deepest devoutness in the prayer that the wisdom and statesmanship of the great nations of East and West may yet succeed in averting the most calamitous of all calamities, the most tragic of all tragedies—war between our own and the Soviet Union." This, mind you, was in the period when the Cold War was at its hottest. "After a long life I still believe in one world and one humanity, with freedom under law, with justice and peace for all peoples and races and faiths." He spoke, without manuscript, from his great heart and mind and soul. I knew that I wanted to emulate him more than any living American—even if I had, reluctantly, turned down his request that I become general counsel of the American Jewish Congress, the great organization which he had founded and headed. That same year I turned down offers from the Anti-Defamation League and other Jewish groups. I did not want to become a professional Jew. Devoted as I was to my people, I wanted to serve only as a volunteer.

Fortunately, Rabbi Wise's last great utterance was recorded, and I had the high privilege of presenting a tape of it to his gifted daughter, my friend Judge Justine Wise Polier.

I have had the pleasure, too, of personal and professional dealings with her husband, Shad Polier, a brilliant and strong-willed exemplar of rugged Judaism, and her son, Stephen Wise Tulin, a charming man and gifted lawyer. I knew the lovely wife of the rabbi, Louise Waterman Wise, toward whom he was so courtly and loving. Frail like her husband in those last days, she was a fine woman, who helped sustain a man who carried the very heavy burden of feeling every woe of every man, woman, and child of all races and creeds. I shall never forget Rabbi Wise's cry of anguish as he recalled the millions of Jews who had perished in Hitler's holocaust.

Of all members of the Decalogue Society, I cherished Benjamin Weintroub most. He attracted my attention by his overwhelming appearance. You knew, at once, that his ancestors had not come over on the Mayflower. His English was somewhat formal in the manner of one who had been brought up on another language. Soon you forgot everything about him except his intense interest in the best in people, literature, and the arts. The law was an afterthought to him.

I was one of the those who for many years spent every Friday night with him and a group of congenial spirits. It was our Sabbath services, much less ritualistic than anything in any Temple and far more spiritual, too, even when we were swallowing hastily the delicious morsels that his wife, Ruth, prepared for us. The best in the world of letters was of momentous importance to us. We were concerned, too, about war and politics. A particular source of much heat and occasional light was the Soviet Union. We were divided into three camps on that subject: those who still had confidence in Russia as a beacon of hope; those who were utterly dismayed by its activities here and elsewhere; and those, like myself, who still wanted to be shown. (Alas, I have been shown too well.)

In a world of stereotypes, clichés, identical products, Ben was a real individual. There was no one quite like him. I have been fortunate enough in my life to know many men of distinction and fame, some of great gifts. No one was more of a personality than Ben Weintroub. No one achieved more in his carefully selected sphere than did Ben. Some men choose the world as their oyster. Ben was more modest. He wanted to influence and, above all, to help those whom he liked.

When you looked around Ben, especially at the time of his famous New Year's Eve parties, you sensed his broad range of interests. You saw poets and poetasters, novelists, painters, printers, journalists, actors, musicians, English-speaking people, and polyglots. The rooms were crowded and yet there was something intimate. You could go from group to group and absorb much, little segments of the big Ben.

The world has a distant and unreal and somewhat unfriendly spirit since Ben has gone.

The American Jewish Congress, under the inspiration of Rabbi Wise and Dr. Alexander Pekelis, created what was called the Commission on Law and Social Action, on which I was, for years, one of the few Chicago members; the other members were the outstanding fighters for constitutional rights. The concept was a simple one, but it had a profound effect. Dr. Pekelis believed that progress could come only if the courts, legislative bodies, public officials and agencies generally were constantly pressured. There had to be test suits, legislative proposals, administrative action, carefully researched, vigorously and resourcefully carried out; and, since the blacks were the principal victims of constitutional deprivations, organizations basically concerned with matters Jewish had to concentrate on winning victories for the blacks. The theory was that, if achievements were registered for the blacks, the Jews and all others would gain. There were some who resisted this emphasis on fighting for the blacks, because Jews are not exempt from prejudices and narrow vision. But Jews, and particularly the leaders of the American Jewish Congress, were in the forefront of the struggle for civil rights, at least until the wave of separatism, advocated by some black extremists.

Dr. Pekelis was a very remarkable man, one of the most original social thinkers and legal scholars I have ever known. He had been a refugee, successively, from the authoritarian nations —Russia, Germany, Italy. In each country he had become a leader of the bar before fleeing. Then he came to the United States and before long his views were quoted in opinions of our Supreme Court. He and I became good friends by instinct.

One day I arranged a discussion for him in Chicago, in which other civil-rights spokesmen were to participate. First, he had to attend a conference of the Religious Zionists in Europe, as I recall—his daring thoughts were combined with quasi-orthodoxy in religion. Flying back to the States in order to keep his appointment in Chicago, his plane crashed over the River Shannon in Ireland, and a brilliant life was snuffed out. There is no limit to what he might have achieved. Now he is hardly a memory. As I taught evidence in law school years later, a leading case, involving his fatal accident, recalled him to me most poignantly. The facts adduced at the trial indicated that the crash was due to culpable negligence on the part of the airline.

The commission created by Dr. Pekelis survives as a working arm of the American Jewish Congress. It is not likely to be superceded while the Congress endures.

During my terms as president of the Greater Chicago Council of the American Jewish Congress, I urged that we give a special award to Bell & Howell and its president, Charles H. Percy, ostensibly for their courage in sponsoring a series of television programs on public issues. This was prior to Percy's having run for any public office. I encountered some unexpected opposition, but, in the end, prevailed. I had in mind more than praise for good works. The Congress, in league with similar organizations, had been giving leadership for years to a drive to persuade the Illinois General Assembly to pass fair employment practices legislation. We repeatedly failed because we could not pressure any Republican legislators, other than black ones, to join with us. It was my plan to seize upon the award luncheon as an opportunity to persuade Percy to obtain the necessary Republican votes. I found him a bright, far-seeing, and charming man, and I had no difficulty in firing him with the ambition to deliver enough votes to assure passage of our bill. "There won't be many votes from my Party," he said, "but I promise enough to turn the tide." And he kept his word and Illinois, at last, had some sort of F.E.P.C., not as good as we wanted, but good enough as a start. Percy then loaned one of the top officials of Bell & Howell to the governor to act as the first chairman of the Commission. Because Charles Gray tried to do an honest job, a hostile Republican legislature made life miserable for him and, ultimately, he was glad to leave Illinois to undertake other responsibilities. While he was with the Commission, he was sensitive to criticism. At first he took some of my suggestions for the improvement of the Commission as a personal affront. When the Motorola Corporation, led by a Republican Party fundraiser, sought to impede the operations of the Commission and to invalidate the law, Gray had little confidence that the Attorney General would wholeheartedly support the Commission. One day, when I was out of town, I received a long-distance telephone call from Gray: "Would I represent the

Commission in resisting Motorola?" Without inquiring about details, including compensation, I immediately said, "Yes." Gray told me that the Commission was unanimous in seeking my services. I put in much effort and the law was sustained by the Illinois Supreme Court, while it gave Motorola a victory on some technical points.

My experience with Percy, who later became a distinguished United States Senator, illustrated for me the fortuitous nature of much accomplishment. A budget, a staff, persistent lobbying, much public support produced no F.E.P.C. A conversation with a man on the way up was the magical element that brought about success.

When I see persons of all races, colors, creeds, and national origins working in banks, department stores, all places where they were previously barred, I rejoice that, in some measure, I helped to bring it about.

Because of my efforts to secure nondiscrimination in housing in the years prior to the outlawing of restrictive covenants by the Supreme Court, the American Jewish Congress asked me to write a pamphlet entitled *American Ghettos,* published in February, 1947. In it I expressed the essence of what I had learned about housing conditions in America. It was largely what I had incorporated in my brief for the American Jewish Congress in the then notorious case of *McCormick vs. Green,* fought out in the Illinois courts. I designated housing as "America's most critical domestic problem" and said that the principal obstacle to the achievement of decent housing for all people in all communities was the deep-rooted and all-pervasive prejudice. My studies had convinced me that as many as four-fifths of the population had hostility toward some group or other, especially Negroes, Latins, Jews, and orientals. The acute housing shortage, following the war, had only aggravated the tenseness of the situation and had led to outbreaks of violence. I told of the many forms of housing discrimination—increased costs for vacant lots, construction, mortgage loans; of the withholding of building permits and the refusal to extend utilities on technical grounds.

"But," I said, "by far the most prevalent and most effective device for achieving segregation in housing is the racial restrictive covenant." I described the nature and terms of such discriminatory agreements. The ingenuity and technical competence of lawyers, real-estate operators, and virtually every skilled person in the white communities had gone into these documents. They had succeeded where racial zoning by statute and ordinance, held unconstitutional as far back as 1917, had failed.

I told of how segregation-minded property owners would band together as soon as there was a threat of "infiltration." The respectables would join in as a matter of course. They might pray for peace and the brotherhood of men on Sunday mornings, but the rest of the time they would be as concerned as the most virulent bigot in preventing "encroachments" by human beings who did not "belong" to the accepted group.

Suddenly, as I wrote, there was a rash of suits everywhere in the effort to set aside these unconscionable covenants.

I illsutrated the situation by dwelling on the special situation that existed in Chicago, where the Negro population had expanded tremendously, but was still crowded into the same near South Side area of less than five miles square. The area had a population density at least five times greater than the white area. It was clear that, even if the Negro population did not grow, which was improbable, at least five more square miles were required for decent living. "Translated into human terms," I wrote, "the statistics yield a picture of indescribable filth, grossly inadequate shelter at exorbitant rentals, inadequate educational, recreational, and health service." The death rate was double that in the city as a whole. Illegitimacy was more than doubled, juvenile delinquency eight times worse than the rest of the city. For every disease the ratio was far greater where the Negroes lived in excessively crowded structures. Diphtheria, for example, was 600 percent greater than the city average. Fires were almost nine times more prevalent than elsewhere.

It was found, I said, that when the congestion was reduced, death, disease, delinquency, all of the distressing incidents were greatly reduced. In short, society paid a very high price for its mistreatment of the Negroes, as well as other ethnic groups, and that price included social tension, festering hatreds, and public violence.

I narrated case histories of violence in Chicago, Detroit, Los Angeles, Minneapolis, and elsewhere in the United States, arising out of the effort to secure better housing for Negroes, Niseis and other non-Establishment groups. Returning veterans fared no better than others.

"Discrimination in housing," I said, "is part of the general pattern of prejudice which runs through every aspect of our social and economic life. Like all prejudice it seeks to clothe itself in rational garb." There is solemn prating about the decline in property values when the unwanted people intrude. I showed that such decline is only temporary at worst, induced by panic peddling, but in the long run there is no decline. I pointed out that the National Association of Real Estate Boards and the Federal Housing Administration, no friends of minority groups, established that Negro housing was a good investment, Negro mortgages as good as or better risks than white's, Negro tenants and home buyers as good as white ones. Yet, the effect of restrictions was to permit any white person, however undesirable, to buy and occupy property, and no Negro, whether philanthropist or philosopher, to do likewise.

I told of the increasing drive to rid the nation of the disaster-breeding covenants, not as yet successful in the States. It was felt, I said, that Chicago would be the ideal ground for winning a decisive victory over the restrictive covenant. Over twenty cases were pending as my pamphlet appeared. In a Chicago case brought by the National Association for the Advancement of Colored People, in which I was one of the attorneys, one colored woman, when asked her race by the attorney seeking to uphold the covenant, replied: "The human race." Asked her color, she replied: "Natural color."

In that case I had prepared and filed an *amicus curiae* brief on behalf of the American Jewish Congress. On May 17, 1946,

Judge John McGoorty had given us leave to file the brief, the first time such intervention was permitted by an Illinois Court.

The Chicago case was lost. But the language of the judge in upholding the restrictive covenant gave promise of future victories. A defeat is sometimes the harbinger of victory.

I concluded my pamphlet with these prophetic words:

"The fight in the courts and in the legislatures to end discrimination in employment, in education and in housing is, in the last resort, part and parcel of democratic education. When people learn that the law forbids discrimination, they will eventually learn not to discriminate at all. When the practice of discrimination disappears the roots of the prejudice of which it was an expression will eventually wither and die."

This was my faith even in the face of defeats and setbacks.

McCormick vs. Green did not exhaust my efforts in the courts against restrictive covenants. When Loring B. Moore, the dignified and distinguished counsel in Illinois of the N.A.A.C.P., suffered a heart attack, I was asked to take over for him, at least temporarily, in connection with the case of *Tovey vs. Levy,* which was expected to go ultimately to the United States Supreme Court as the great constitutional test case in that area. The Master in Chancery referred to my efforts as special counsel in his report, saying that my arguments "were predicated upon a plea for justice based upon enlightened and liberal principles rather than upon an application of the set principles of established law." Apparently, he believed that "enlightened and liberal principles" were no part of the law.

Judge Robert E. Crowe, who succeeded to the case after another judge had upheld the restrictive covenant, felt constrained by this opinion. "If I had the authority to set aside the ruling of my fellow judge in this identical case, I would do so," he said. "It is with great reluctance that I sign the decree upholding the restrictive covenant in this case." He declared himself as outraged over the state of the law.

To me, as I reflected upon Judge Crowe's words, it was difficult to think of him as the State's Attorney who had so savagely though unsuccessfully fought for the death penalty to be imposed upon Richard Loeb and Nathan F. Leopold, Jr. I then held no brief for Leopold—my effort to free him from his long imprisonment was in the future and unforeseeable—but then, as now, I found capital punishment hateful. Concerned as I was with achieving justice for all people, regardless of race, color, or creed, I was determined to rid my country of all vestiges of savagery, including the death penalty. In its application I found that, as in other areas, the poor and the blacks were especially discriminated against.

Finally, *Tovey vs. Levy* reached the Supreme Court of Illinois and, on November 18, 1948, that court handed down an opinion reversing the lower court's decree and finding that racial covenants constituted State action which is prohibited by the equal-rights clause of the fourteenth amendment of the United States Constitution. Of course, I rejoiced both in the result and that I had had some role in achieving it. The Illinois Supreme Court had been preceded by the United States Supreme Court in the famous case of *Shelley vs. Kraemer,* which settled the matter for all time. Now all that remained was the implementation of the court victory. The struggle is still going on and at times it seems a hopeless one to those less optimistic than myself.

nine

"Mr. Housing"

Housing was my main preoccupation, professionally and as a citizen, for a decade. There was a time when the post office would actually deliver to me mail addressed to "Mr. Housing."

All of my life I have been absorbed in architecture—the habitations, work places, and cathedrals of men. After high school, the interest lay dormant until it was reawakened by Milton Shufro, assistant executive secretary of the Chicago Housing Authority, in the early 1940's. A complaint had been made about some aspect of public housing, and I replied publicly. Shufro got in touch with me, and set the facts before me rather persuasively. I was immediately impressed by this bright and articulate man. I learned that he had a multiplicity of responsibilities imposed upon him by a most remarkable woman, Elizabeth Wood, who was in charge of the growing number of public-housing projects in Chicago. Miss Wood, tall, almost beautiful in appearance, at once confiding and reserved in manner, had several completely devoted top assistants, all of them men. Later, when I read a novel that she had written in the days when she was a professor of English at Vassar College, I had glimpses into her inner life, which encompassed love and a great range of emotional subtleties. She seemed to tread lightly, when stepping on toes, as in her determination to minimize discrimination in the city's housing projects. She was the heart, the very soul, of the public-housing movement in our community; and Shufro quickly brought me within her orbit. I became one of her most devoted followers.

Shufro's role was to create an atmosphere that would be helpful to Miss Wood's housing agency. This included winning the support of the chief executive officer of Chicago, Mayor Edward J. Kelly, a tough unsentimental politician.

One morning, during the period following World War II, I was called by Kelly—would I visit with him in his city-hall office? The mayor immediately plunged into a discussion of the housing situation; now agreeing, now disagreeing with me, now throwing questions, or simply listening. Suddenly, he leaned forward and: "Gertz, I don't care how much hell you raise. Step on my toes, step on the governor's toes, do anything you please, as long as it will produce housing." A few days later, he named me to his Emergency Housing Committee, of which I subsequently became legislative chairman.

I always felt that Kelly, despite any other failings, was deeply interested in providing better living conditions for all, including the blacks. How else account for the magnificent aid he gave Elizabeth Wood, executive secretary of the Chicago Housing Authority during its greatest days? In Kelly's time, the politicians did not dare touch Elizabeth Wood or the Housing Authority. Both were free, by Kelly's orders, from all interference from those who looked upon the projects as legitimate patronage and plunder sources.

Once I told the mayor that some aldermen in the better areas of the far Northwest Side of Chicago were objecting to veterans' housing projects in their wards; they feared an influx of blacks.

Kelly said, "Tell them that I told you to tell them to go to hell." He paused for a moment, and added, "I'll tell them myself." Thereupon, he picked up the telephone and laid down the law.

The veterans' housing projects, and all other public-housing projects, were approved without a battle during Kelly's time, in contrast to the situation which developed later when it took desperate struggles to achieve any part of the program.

Shufro and Miss Wood worked on the five commissioners of the Housing Authority, who set policy and gave directives. Appointed by the mayor, with the approval of the City Council and the State Housing Board, the commissioners had to be something of a cross-section of the community.

The task set for themselves by Shufro and Miss Wood was the creation of a citizens' organization that would exert pressure, if need be, on the commissioners, the politicians, the media, and the public. I figured in the plans, and readily became a part of them. A diverse group of us met with Shufro and others from the Housing Authority and then formed an organization, at first under a rather clumsy name, changed in time to the Public Housing Association. I recognized how potent we were in certain influential circles when Cardinal Stritch, never known as a radical among churchmen of the Chicago archdiocese, gave a substantial contribution to the Public Housing Association, out of his personal funds. Later, in a book about the Chicago housing situation, the learned authors wrote, to my amusement: "The Association was financed mainly by a few believers in the cause of public housing, among them Gertz and the elder Marshall Field, the publisher of the *Sun-Times*." It was the one and only time that my name was coupled, in financial matters, with a multi-mullionaire. I often talked with Field about housing and he assured me that he read every release that emanated from our organization. I think that we had other attentive readers as well, some in rival groups and among our foes.

During my decade in housing, besides being the President of the Public Housing Association, I was chairman of the Veterans' Housing Committee, a working group of many organizations and individuals involved in the fight for dwellings, and was the leader of other housing groups. The experiences were as frustrating as they were fascinating, as disappointing as they were fulfilling.

The war resulted in shortages of essential housing materials, manpower, financial, and legislative tools. Nothing could be done quickly or with assurance. There were delays on top of delays. Expediters were needed, and expediters for the expediters. There was a period of years when nothing would succeed.

In the closing days of the administration of Mayor Kelly, his Emergency Housing Committee agreed upon a program and prepared to present it to a civic assembly to be convened in the City Council Chambers. The program had been formulated by me, as legislative chairman; the general chairman of the committee, James C. Downs, Jr., a powerful force in the community, had taken the floor to oppose it in some basic respects; but when the vote had resulted in my favor, he accepted the program and declared himself as willing to defend it in the public meeting.

Meanwhile, the mayor-elect, Martin H. Kennelly, was sunning himself in Asheville, North Carolina, and was constantly being interviewed by the press. Some articles in the newspapers quoted him as favoring a housing program different from the one that we had formulated. Jim Downs said to me that, since our program and our committee had been repudiated by the new mayor, it was our duty to call off the public meeting and to resign. I dissented vigorously, because I felt that the housing crisis was too acute to permit delay; and I was supported by my associates. Accordingly, the meeting was held and the program unveiled.

Then Mayor Kennelly returned to the city, and within hours, as I recall, he summoned Elizabeth Wood, Downs, Ferd Kramer of the Metropolitan Housing Council, and myself to his office. "You are to be my housing advisers," he said to us.

Whatever the mayor's own ideas may have been, he gradually ceased to decide what his housing committee did, although everyone was polite, even deferential. This was the pattern throughout his administration; he talked and others took over.

I favored the immediate construction of low-income housing; the committee program, as the chairman, Holman Pettibone, frankly stated, was for a long-range urban-development program—the heart of the city, the downtown area, was to be restored for the big State Street merchants. I still believe that the program that we adopted and carried through the legislature was a good one and is helping to remake Chicago, but it was slow moving. It never had the drive for immediate action that the times called for. In that respect, it was quite typical of Martin H. Kennelly, a good man, a true gentlemen, with integrity, with a civic conscience, but essentially unable to cope with the politicians, the business community, or the public. Nobody in the city hall ever looked more the executive type, but, by comparison with either his predecessor, Kelly, or his successor, Daley, he was a mere novice.

Kennelly believed that Chicago was a council-governed city, whatever that meant. He would not presume to dictate to the council what it should do. Held in check by Kelly, it ran away with the driver during Kennelly's time, going hither and thither, with the mayor having little more control than if he were an outsider, and, indeed, he was; for Kennelly eschewed politics, too. He was no longer master in his own household. A wise man named Truman once said, if you will not ride the tiger, it will ride you. That's what happened to Kennelly. He was ridden by the tiger. With all the good faith in the world, and he had plenty of it, the real rulers of the city asserted themselves in time and dismissed him; and, whatever their motivation, they were right.

When my old college friend, Alderman Archibald Carey, proposed an ordinance to forbid racial discrimination in connection with all publicly aided housing, the City Council fought his proposal bitterly; and, strange to say, it was opposed, too, on the grounds of expediency, by the liberal press. The mayor and others opined that housing was more important at the moment than civil rights, with the result that we got neither. Kennelly and his supporters did not realize that it is never expedient to surrender principle, and that one surrender leads inevitably to another.

Mayor Kennelly had said, over and over again, that Elizabeth Wood, the great woman who directed the Housing Authority, would be safe during his administration. When the aldermen began yammering about her, because of her advanced views and her refusal to surrender control to them, he, unlike Kelly, failed to stand up for her, and she was forced out. The mayor soon lost the ability to stand up for, or to, anybody.

Some problems have not been solved to this day, despite our best efforts. They are summed up in the struggle in Chicago in 1949, during Kennelly's time, for suitable housing sites. My colleagues and I, inspired by the creative thinking of Elizabeth Wood, reasoned that housing projects would become human jungles and destructive forces if they were largely confined to the black ghettos. These areas were already the most densely populated. They had more poverty, disease, delinquency than other parts of the city. There was no vacant land in these areas. If more housing projects were built there, they would have to be high-rise structures, people piled on top of people. They would be like feeble fortresses, soon overcome by the forces around them. We urged that the projects should be built in the outskirts of the city, where land was plentiful. They should be garden projects—single family dwellings or rowhouses, with ample space for human beings, rather than rodents. There should be facilities for civilized living. In that way the ghetto vices would be eliminated, and the whole community would gain. It seemed simple enough to us, but not to the aldermen, reflecting the prejudices of their people.

We tried every means at our disposal to persuade the aldermen to go along with us, but all were in vain. The specter of blacks in their neighborhoods overcame all else. So the cities subsidized their own destruction—more crowding of the inner city, more high-rise monstrosities, more crime, disease, delinquency. And since the whites fled to the suburbs in large numbers, the tax base of the city was undermined at the very time when financial needs were greatest.

I remember a meeting with Joseph Gill, the elderly leader of the Democratic Party, who had a philosopher's wisdom behind his practical veneer. We voiced our desire for a decent housing program for Chicago. He listened respectfully, agreeing with much that we said in theory, but declaring that it would not work here and now. "I know," he said, "that one day there will be complete integration, intermarriage, amalgamation of the races, and it will be good. But not now. It will have to come in its time."

With the same assurance, Holman D. Pettibone, chairman of Mayor Kennelly's Committee for Housing Action, warned me of the consequence of impatience in racial matters when he returned from a conference in Springfield with the Governor and a group of legislative leaders. "We have worked out a good practical program for housing and neighborhood redevelopment," he told me early one morning, within hours of his return to Chicago and before the entire committee had met to consider the program. Apparently, he feared my reactions. "We have said nothing about nondiscrimination in the proposed program," he continued. "If you raise that point, it will kill our chances of getting anything through the General Assembly." I promised nothing. I said that I would think about it.

I did think about Holman Pettibone, president for a long time of the Chicago Title and Trust Company, a company that had to be considered in connection with almost every real-estate transaction, because it had the one complete set of property records. I had been consulted, several years previously, by several Jewish organizations that felt, for good reasons, that the title company was discriminatory against Jews in its hiring and promotion practices. I led a small delegation that called upon Mr. Pettibone to discuss the matter. Before I could say what was on my mind, he interpolated: "Mr. Gertz, if you are going to tell us to hire Negroes, you had better save your breath. We will not hire them." I responded: "Mr. Pettibone, we are here only to discuss discrimination against our own people, although we disagree with your policies on the Negroes as well." Mr. Pettibone made a not-very-good attempt to prove that his company was fair to Jews. "We would hire more Jews," he said, "but they are not attracted by our relatively low wages." We left, dissatisfied. It is only fair to add that almost immediately more Jews were hired and more upgraded and, ironically, wartime shortages in the labor market caused the Chicago Title and Trust Company to hire blacks, despite Mr. Pettibone's prior dogmatic stand. Now he and I were considering discrimination in another context.

Very soon the committee met. I was troubled in spirit. I did not want to kill a much-needed legislative program. At the same time I did not want to give comfort to the bigots. Before I could speak up, John Yancey, a black Catholic, a member of our committee and not usually assertive, moved to amend the proposed program by adding a section forbidding racial and religious discrimination in connection with any project supported, in whole or in part, by public funds. I promptly seconded the motion. Mr. Pettibone said nothing. And the motion was carried. It did not defeat the legislation. The program was approved as thus amended. Illinois thus became the first state to provide in this fashion for nondiscrimination, long before the United States Supreme Court outlawed racial restrictive housing covenants in the landmark *Shelley* case.

I acted as lawyer for a group of printers in their efforts to build a new community. Many of them were employees of Marshall Field, who took paternal interest in them. One day Field asked me if I would object to Ward Farnsworth's assisting me in our efforts. He would pay for Farnsworth's work. Farnsworth was a very well-known realtor, a resident of the fashionable Libertyville area near Lake Forest, and the trustee of Field's own estate. Of course, I agreed to the arrangement. Thereafter, for a period of months, I saw Farnsworth every day. We would look at parcels of land; we would discuss the many problems involved in a complicated venture. We took to each other almost instantly. We became dear friends. Farnsworth would frequently report to

Field. He apparently reported favorably on my abilities to Field, now subtly, now more directly. One day he said to me, "Elmer, I think that you ought to be Marshall Field's personal attorney." Later he declared that he was going to make certain of this. As he left for New York at this time, he said: "I have arranged a meeting at the Chicago Club to take place upon my return. You will be there and various Field officials." The day before the momentous meeting, he took a Pullman bedroom in New York for the return train trip to Chicago, and in his sleep passed away. That was the last of my representation of Field. How different my life would have been had Farnsworth not died! Certainly, there would have been no *Leopold* or *Ruby* cases, no representation of Henry Miller, nothing of that dramatic nature. Speculation is futile. One must accept one's destiny, knowing that, like one's skin, it belongs to one. Anything else does not fit.

ten

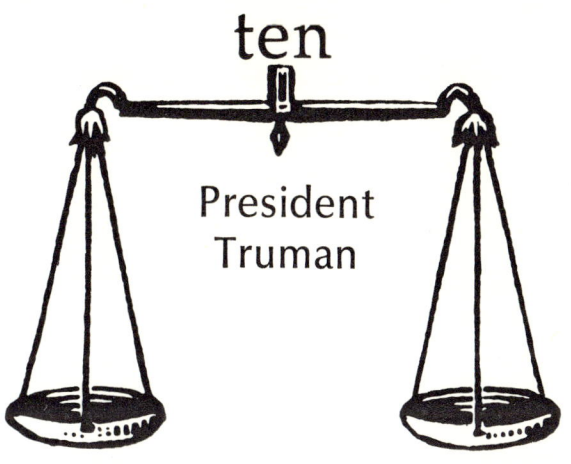

President Truman

In the summer of 1944, my friend Robert W. Kenny was in Chicago as the chairman of the rules commitee of the Democratic National Convention; I gave a luncheon in his honor. Bob had been a Superior Court judge and was then the Attorney General of California. It was assumed that he had a very bright future ahead of him and that it might include, as suggested by Carey McWilliams, the White House. Hence, his heading the most important committee at a convention that was destined to make history.

Everyone knew that Roosevelt would receive a fourth-term nomination because of the continuing war; and many people feared that he would not live to complete his term. It was assumed that the Vice President would soon become the President. There were important elements within the Democratic Party who were determined that the then Vice President, Henry A. Wallace, to them the voice of revolution, would not be renominated. F.D.R., himself, was cognizant of the struggle against Wallace; and he might well have feared that it could imperil his own chances. At the same time, Wallace had a devoted, not to say fanatical, group of supporters; he could not easily be brushed aside, even by Roosevelt.

We thought of this situation as we awaited the arrival of Kenny. A friend of mine and Wallace's hurried into the room to consult with me. He asked: "Would you tell Kenny that Wallace wants him to make one of the seconding speeches?" Then he pleaded: "Do what you can to persuade him to agree."

Kenny arrived, his usual humorous self. His quips were a delightful combination of whimsy and perceptiveness. As we sat together, I told him of Wallace's request. To my surprise, he did not give an immediate answer. "Let me think about it," he said. Toward the end of the luncheon, Bob turned to me and mused, "Some people are so strongly, so unreasonably, for Wallace that they hurt Roosevelt and would harm the Democratic Party." He became silent again. In the end, he did not second the Wallace nomination; instead, Helen Gahagan Douglas, then a Congresswoman from California, later a friend of ours, seconded the nomination, as the hosannahs for the great advocate of the common man went on.

Aided by the dubious maneuvering of Roosevelt and the activities of the big-city bosses like Chicago's Mayor Kelly, Senator Harry S Truman replaced Wallace as the Vice-Presidential candidate. The Democratic ticket was elected in the fall. In a few months, Roosevelt was dead; and Truman, hardly prepared for the overwhelming responsibility, had succeeded him.

When Truman spoke over the radio, after succeeding to the high office, I was ready to weep again, as I had when Roosevelt died. The contrast with Roosevelt was so dismal. I am afraid that none of us gave Truman credit for any qualities, so enthralled were we by the voice, personality, and accomplishments of his predecessor.

Truman began inviting the resignations of members of Roosevelt's cabinet, some of whom were dear to us. Changes of all kinds began taking place. Truman was, indeed, a man of movement. I remember attending a dinner in Washington where almost every top official of the government, except Truman, was in attendance. Bob Kenny was the master of ceremonies. He brought down the house by his reference to "Hairbreadth Harry."

By the time of the 1948 convention, there was serious doubt that Truman should get the nomination; there was a certainty that he would be defeated for election. Many suggested that the haloed Eisenhower would be a good replacement. Wallace became the inspired nominee of the so-called Progressive Party (George McGovern, a young man, was for him); a State's Rights Party was formed in the South to oppose both Wallace and Truman.

In those catastrophic circumstances, there were maneuverings to replace Truman with Justice William O. Douglas. Douglas, himself, was not a party to such conspiratorial steps—he has always had affection and admiration for Truman, as I know at first hand. A friend of his, now a federal judge, came to me and said: "You are close to Robert Kenny, who is one of the prime leaders in the Wallace movement"—four years had made that amazing difference in Kenny's attitude—"why don't you suggest to Kenny that he help to get Wallace out of the race as part of a deal to substitute Douglas for Truman?"

It seemed to me a good idea; I broached it to Kenny. He took to it with enthusiasm. "If Douglas is substituted for Truman," he said, "I am confident I could get Wallace to withdraw."

As everyone knows, Truman remained in the race, and Wallace did not withdraw, nor did the Southern secessionists. It was taken for granted everywhere that Thomas E. Dewey would be the next President of the United States. His term was a short one—no longer than a premature headline in the *Chicago Tribune* and one or two other newspapers.

It was at that moment that I, who had once been so critical of Truman, suddenly discovered that I was blind to his very great qualities and that the fault was entirely mine.

I have talked with many people about Truman. I carried on extensive correspondence with him and with his associates. I have probed deeply into his public and private life.

One could always speak to the former President without inhibition. I could ask him questions that you would not ordinarily put to a person in his position. One day, I asked, "To which members of your cabinet did you feel closest?" He replied instantly, "Marshall, Acheson, and Snyder." "Why?" I asked. "Because they were on the firing line with me." I then asked: "To which Supreme Court justices did you feel closest?" I expected him to say Fred Vinson and Tom Clark; instead, he answered, "Douglas and Minton." Soon enough I had tangible evidence of Douglas' regard for him. When I wrote to Justice Douglas about a dinner for Truman I was organizing, he said that he would attend, and, indeed, he did, making a very warm and revealing little talk that night.

I felt completely at ease in discussing my children with Truman. I told him that Ted had called me from college one day to say, "Dad, my allowance is too large; reduce it." "You need never worry about Ted," Truman told me; and then later, when Ted was admitted to practice before the Illinois bar on the very day of Truman's birthday, Truman wrote a letter of congratulation in which he told Ted that he would do well if he emulated his father. He did gracious little things by instinct. Once when he was in the hospital, my wife and I wired flowers to him with our wishes for his recovery. As soon as he left the hospital, he wrote more than the usual thank-you letter. Knowing that we could not have seen the flowers sent in our names, he described them in detail, something that few people would have thought of doing.

It has been said that many an Englishman loves a lord—and many an American, too. There are people everywhere who count it as one of the great memories of their lives that they saw—not "Shelley plain," as Browning had phrased it—but some pinchbeck patrician who was dubbed a knight by a royal Philistine because of his proficiency in selling soaps. The greatest of all poets had an ingrained snobbishness that caused him to sing the praises of generations of kings and their courtiers through half of his immortal dramas.

In these United States we have snobs, too, who dote on dowagers, tinseled tyrants, the highly placed and, above all, the high-priced. But the prevailing mood is that every man is as good as the next one, and that no President is above the people who put him in office by their votes and can remove him in the same way. Only occasionally, as in the case of Chester A. Arthur (with his valet, French chef, dainty dishes and foppish clothes), have we had Presidents who put on airs and forgot that every American, even a President, has only one vote. Other Presidents in our day have suffered for the excesses that come with power.

The man who reminds us most that our truest leaders are just plain Americans was the thirty-third President of the United States. All of his life, and no less so when he was in the White House, Truman shared the common experiences of his neighbors, as family man and father, farmer, soldier, merchant and politician; and in his simple, effortless fashion he remained of the people. It would have been unthinkable for him to imagine that he had been transformed so as to rise above his fellows.

Three of us saw him in his customary surroundings as he worked in his modest office in Kansas City. The name "Harry S Truman," and that alone, appeared on the door. There was a plain and unpretentious woman in the simple anteroom, who acted as receptionist, telephone operator, and general assistant. When she announced us, Truman himself came out to beckon us into his office. He grasped our hands, exchanged a pleasant greeting, and in a moment made us feel completely at ease. We conversed of big and little things. He talked simply, candidly, colloquially, without affectation. He did not talk down to us. We did not talk up to him. We were a representative group of American citizens, voicing our views in a friendly and unafraid manner. We were symbols, we could not help feeling, of the natural greatness of the nation at its best, where it is easier to be with a President than with a petty bureaucrat in some far-off land.

There is a further detail in connection with our visit to Truman's Kansas City office that was of special significance. The three visitors—Judge Henry L. Burman, Bernard Sokol, and I—were all Jews, deeply interested in matters Jewish. We were there on a mission for a Jewish group. Around Truman's office were all sorts of items of Jewish interest—a bust of Chaim Weitzman, first President of Israel, an Israeli flag, pictures of Truman's great friend and wartime buddy Eddie Jacobson, and the like. His research assistant, Francis Heller, was in and out of the office. The kind of posturing person accustomed to saying, "Some of my best friends are Jewish," would have called our attention to such items, subtly or directly, but not Truman. We talked for a long while, and he never said anything about what was before our very eyes.

Much later, when we had become friends, and I had just returned from a trip to Israel and had sent him pictures of a village in Israel bearing his name, Truman did write generally of a plan he had in mind for the Middle East that he said would discuss with me later. He opined that no one in authority—it was the Eisenhower period—would ever ask him about his plan, and, alas, we never had the opportunity to discuss it, either.

At the time of the dinner honoring Truman, he treated everyone who was close to him in any capacity as a friend. The newspapermen and photographers, who kept after us throughout his stay in Chicago, took more than professional delight in being with him, and he reciprocated.

He had the deepest respect for the office he had once held and, out of it, he felt that he still had to conduct himself so as not to demean it in any way. I noticed, for one thing, that he would not permit himself to be photographed with a whisky glass in his hand.

The Trumans, a friend or two, and I spent hours in their suite in relaxed conversation, mostly in political reminiscence. Mrs. Truman, who was rather reserved in public, was voluble in private conversation. I was gratified and instructed to observe her intimate knowledge of the details of practical politics from the ward level up.

If I had been inclined to be nervous during the dinner, the demeanor of the former President would have reassured me. Sitting next to me, he conversed in the most amiable manner, speaking words of comfort and encouragement throughout the evening, intermixed with sly and wise comments on all subjects. I noticed that he ate with a considerable appetite. I inquired if the necessity to make a speech lessened his intake of food. No, it had no effect. It was just another task to be performed as it came along. He took a few moments to glance through his manuscript and made emendations here and there. He commented on President Eisenhower—"He will make Grant seem like a statesman." I suggested that Roosevelt had served too long as President. He agreed. But when I said that, perhaps, the country would have been better off if Willkie had won in 1940, he dissented strongly. I told him of what Alf Landon had written to me of Truman—"I have long admired his frankness in dealing with the American people and in facing the most difficult foreign situation he inherited. I believe the future historians, with access to public papers that are now not available, will rank Mr. Truman as one of our great Presidents in that field." He commented, quickly, with a laugh, "I almost wish Landon had gotten more votes in 1936." As the dining part of the evening neared its end, he said: "Come with me. I always go to the men's room before making a speech."

A few weeks before the Democratic Convention in 1956, I received a letter from Truman, telling me that he was going to occupy his usual suite at the Blackstone Hotel in Chicago and that he expected me to visit him. A committed Democrat in those days, I was still highly dubious about the chances of unseating President Eisenhower. I felt that, because of health problems, Eisenhower ought not to run, and that, even if he ran, I would prefer his being replaced by Adlai Stevenson, who seemed almost too good, too articulate, and too intelligent for the rough and tumble of American politics. I remembered that Truman had said to me, as we walked and talked together about a year earlier, "It's too bad that Adlai is not more of a human being." It was true and regrettable, but I felt that he had other superb qualities which the country needed. As the Convention neared, Truman, never greatly enamored of Stevenson, had plans to thwart his renomination by the Party. Truman and Eleanor Roosevelt were in different camps, she a staunch supporter of Stevenson, although the two differed in so many respects. Mrs. Roosevelt, an aristocrat in birth and upbringing, was, with Truman, the great friend of the common man, whose century this was supposed to be. Stevenson remained an aristocrat even when he voiced the aspirations of all good Democrats.

Shortly after the delegates assembled in Chicago, I went to the Blackstone Hotel in order to see Truman. The passageways of his floor were closely guarded. At a glance, I assumed that it would be impossible to see him, and I left. After all, the former President had many tasks to perform and I, unconnected and uninfluential in the political world, could be of no service to him. He had simply been polite when he had invited me.

Instead, I went across the street to the Hilton Hotel, where many delegations and leaders had their headquarters. I wandered to one of the upper floors of the hotel and looked around in an almost desultory fashion. Suddenly, I saw a large group of reporters and photographers heading rapidly in the direction of what I soon learned was Speaker Rayburn's suite. The door opened and I stepped out of the way of the horde and observed what was going on. Truman was just leaving Rayburn's quarters, and the press was pursuing him. Reputed to have bad eyesight, he yet noticed me, left the line, and walked up to me. Putting his arm around me, he said: "Elmer, why have I not seen you earlier?" So a former President of the United States could be interested in a man in the ranks. I smiled happily, as I sensed the curiosity of the press. Who could this man be who interested the still-very-newsworthy Mr. Truman? I had not then achieved my own measure of fame as Nathan Leopold's attorney and my efforts as "Mr. Housing" were no longer remembered.

Later I heard Truman speak at a well-attended press conference in favor of Averill Harriman, whose candidacy never really got off the ground. Truman was eloquent and persuasive, but not persuasive enough.

I was present at the Convention at its high tide, the race between Senators Estes Kefauver and John F. Kennedy for the Vice Presidency, after Stevenson, nominated for the Presidency again, instead of making his own choice for the second place, had turned to the delegates to make their own decision. It was a see-saw race with now one and then the other in the lead. I never saw press correspondents so personally involved. All of them seemed to be pulling for personable young Kennedy. The publisher, John Knight, and I seemed to be the only uninvolved persons in the press section. We were not acquainted, but we looked at each other knowingly, as excited reporters, some of them Irish and all looking for great news, stood on their desks and cheered as the tide seemed to turn toward Kennedy. It was not to be, but his defeat at the 1956 Convention opened the doors of opportunity for him at the 1960 Convention, which he won handily. Neither Truman nor Mrs. Roosevelt were excessively pleased with the young candidate. The former First Lady would have wished the nomination again upon the battle-weary Stevenson. Truman again had other ideas.

I was present at the groundbreaking ceremonies in Independence for the Truman Library. It was in purely Masonic form, with the apron and trowel and ritual and special dialogue of the great fraternal order.

I was present when the Truman Library first opened in Independence. There was a luncheon that day for all who had come to Independence, at the Mormon tabernacle— Independence being the center for those Mormons who do not recognize the headship of the Salt Lake City Church. Later, a number of guests, including Ceretta and myself, were invited to the Truman home for cocktails. The home was almost excessively modest in appearance, inside and out. Herbert Hoover, Eleanor Roosevelt, Chief Justice Warren, Sam Rayburn, and many other Americans of great attainment mingled with those lacking their luster. The Trumans were equally gracious to all. Not for one moment did I observe any sign of special treatment for the mighty. Ceretta was in the last months of her life and showed signs of fatigue. Regretfully, we, therefore, said goodby to our hosts and were about to leave. The former President insisted upon walking the two of us out of the house and through the grounds to the front gate, where he spoke consolingly to Ceretta and bade us farewell as if we alone were his guests—not Hoover or Mrs. Roosevelt or anyone else. It was that quality in Truman that won for him the loyalty of so many people, myself among them. I suspect that it did not matter to us whether he was right or wrong; what mattered was that he was so much a friend.

I think that this accounted for the increasing devotion to him even on the part of Republicans like Barry Goldwater and others on the right. Truman was Mr. Democrat, but he was even more the embodiment of some fundamental American traits. Many who are still unreconciled to Roosevelt speak warmly of Truman.

I have received in all more than a hundred letters from Truman, all of them in the candid vein for which the late President was renowned. One can create a faithful impression of him from sentences taken almost at random from these letters: ". . . I have had so many busts made that I am about ready to swear off. It is quite a nuisance to have a fellow ogle you and sight measurements with his thumb while you wonder what the Sam Hill he's going to come up with. This is not a reflection on sculptors, because that is the way they have to work." ". . . You must not let yourself be disturbed by MacArthur's spasm in *Life* Magazine. If you will read it carefully, you will find that his attacks did nothing to offset the veracity of my statements. I think he made a mistake in writing that article, and I cannot say truthfully that I am sorry he did it." ". . . The atitude of the magazine about which you wrote me is consistent. They lie about a person and find out it is too much trouble to tell the truth but I wouldn't worry about it because they have been doing that to me for forty years." So I might go on with letter after letter from this perky and proud President who did not believe in polite deceptions.

In my quest for understanding of President Truman, I obtained copies of his more important State of the Union messages, his vetoes, his speeches, his books, and articles, almost everything under his name that was available. Often he inscribed these things for me in his generous manner. I purchased innumerable books dealing, directly or indirectly, with his Administration, his life, his personality. I got memorabilia of all kinds, including pictures, campaign buttons, coins, postage stamps. It is amazing what a rich variety of material can be found about public figures, particularly popular Presidents. One of my best finds was a history of Truman's World War I regiment, published in 1920, when memories were still fresh and legends had not been created. At that time no one could dream that Captain Truman would become Mr. President. This regimental history documented what had been reported—that Truman was an exceedingly good military officer under fire and in Army camp.

Truman once wrote to me that, from my material about him, one could write the history of his Administration. I had material that he did not have. Some things I sent to the Library in original or photostatic form; others I selfishly kept as reminders of the man I had come to admire so deeply.

Years later I came to know Bert Maybee, who had served under Truman in the war. The two had remained friends and retained a standard mode of address. Even when President, Truman was still Captain to Maybee, and the latter was Private to the Captain. Maybee was Truman's dentist when I met him. One day, in recent years, according to what Dr. Maybee told me at the time, Truman and Mrs. Truman visited Maybee's office professionally. Maybee examined Truman's teeth carefully. "Captain," he said, "this tooth [indicating it] and that [indicating it] need immediate attention." "Private Maybee," replied Truman, "I have made note of what you have said." Bess Truman interjected: "Harry, as long as we are here and we have someone to drive us home, why don't you have the work done that Bert suggests?" Truman remained silent. His wife suddenly changed the subject: "Harry, you have not shaved properly. You have a beard like an old man!" Truman retorted firmly: "Bess, have you anything else to say before we leave?" With that characteristic anecdote, I may close this remembrance of a justly loved man.

eleven

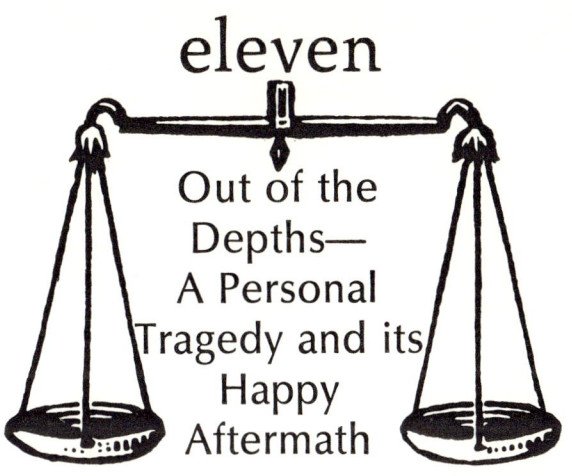

Out of the Depths—
A Personal Tragedy and its Happy Aftermath

Those who saw Ceretta in her happier days, when she was an incomparable mime and could laugh at herself, would never have suspected that she was often on the verge of tragedy. She had a discontentment with herself, with me, and the world. I admired Ceretta's aspirations and gifts. I thought that there were barriers, but they were created by those dark forces within her.

Ceretta pursued the dance with passion, especially Spanish dancing; but gradually she recognized her lack of agility. She turned to other efforts at self-fulfillment, and I encouraged her. Child guidance became her new interest. She fell strongly under the influence of Dr. Rudolph Dreikurs, the associate of the great Viennese psychiatrist, Alfred Adler, whom I knew. She was an active participant in the various Adlerian groups, devoting hours to learning and helping. In a limited way, I tried to be a part of these endeavors. Of course, she applied what she learned in our own family life.

During Ceretta's last decade of life, there were long periods of happiness, when the shadows receded. We went with the children to various parts of the United States and Mexico, almost delirious in our joy over new experiences.

My law practice took a better turn, because of a case involving a partnership dispute, and we bought a new house in a better part of the city. Ceretta found great delight in furnishing our new home. Ted and I took to gardening. Ceretta began attending classes at the Art Institute; she cultivated a new group of friends, some advanced in years; she studied the art of flower arrangement.

Then we looked forward joyfully to our impending twenty-fifth anniversary. We were going to go to Europe for the first time. Never were we happier. The shadows seemed, indeed, to recede in a reawakening of our love.

It was at that time, in February, 1956, that the great disaster of our lives occurred. Ceretta was badly injured while being driven to the child-guidance sessions in an Evanston school. She was in traction because of a severely fractured leg and arm and other grave injuries, which refused to heal. She needed more bone grafting, plastic surgery, constant attention. There were more than a score of physicians in every specialty attending her. Her spirits, at first high and courageous, withered and died. She became utterly cheerless. More than once, after midnight, she would telephone me from the hospital, imploring me to be with her. Of course, I rushed to her side. I learned later that our daughter Midge was so disturbed that she vomited for hours. She neglected classes, friends, everything to console her mother, as did Ted.

After months, Ceretta came home, still mending. We thought that the cheerful surroundings would heal her. We thought my manifold activities would interest her. But hepatitis set in and she was back in the hospital. The new disaster utterly depressed all of us. More than fifteen years later, it is still too painful to recall.

We tried to be cheerful for her sake, but our efforts were transparent. There was an air of doom around us.

How did I survive the agony of Ceretta's last months of life? Our children, then and always, were incomparable, far more concerned about their parents than themselves. Midge shows her deep affection by kisses, caresses, inquiries, constant attentiveness. She will tease me, make humorous reports as to what I say or do, mimic my mannerisms, show pride and devotion with every glance. She resented anything that reflected in the slightest degree upon anything in which I was involved.

Ted was more philosophical. He participated in many of my activities. He attended the Leopold parole hearing. He shared my confidences on other matters, professional, financial, personal. He and I spoke as man to man. Womanly and bright, Midge remained the daughter, rather than the equal.

It was fortunate for me, too, that I was so deeply involved in the Leopold case all through Ceretta's illness. On the night before the parole hearing, Ted and I went to a motel near Statesville, so that I would be free, temporarily, of obsessive fear about Ceretta. Busy, I could live without the dread of what was to come, but it was always in the back of my mind.

Other matters kept my interest. While the Leopold case was going on, I taught real property law for one quarter at the downtown center of the University of Chicago.

I read constantly. I wrote reviews and articles. I engaged in a multiplicity of professional and communal tasks. But the gnawing apprehension continued.

One night I was about to go out for a walk. Ceretta called down from her bed, "Elmer, please come upstairs and stay with me." She was in an almost ominously calm state. In her agony, she had sometimes been accusatory and difficult. Now she said to me, in a quiet manner: "Elmer, no matter what happens, never rebuke yourself. Nobody could have been a better husband than you. I want you to know how grateful I am and how much I have loved you." Foolishly, I permitted myself the hope that all would be well. We talked quietly until she dozed off, and I felt more content than in a long while.

The next morning when I awoke, I asked Ceretta how she felt. To my dismay, she sighed a sad response. Reluctantly, I went to the office.

Fortunately, Ted was at home that day. He telephoned me toward noon. "I can't arouse Mother," he said. He seemed to be in a daze. I instructed him to call our doctor and I said that I would be home at once. I virtually flew in my automobile. Ceretta, still in a coma, was moved temporarily to one hospital and then to the Michael Reese Hospital. My brother George and a corps of physicians were summoned. They worked with her around the clock. For a few hours, they expressed some hope; then the reports were unceasingly bleak, despite the use of a kidney washing machine. She lingered in a coma for six days.

For the first two or three nights the hospital permitted us to sleep in chairs in the lobby. Then, very gently, we were persuaded to take rooms at a nearby motel. Relatives and friends kept vigil with us. I knew the situation was hopeless, yet permitted myself to hope. Scarcely ever did I leave Ceretta's room. I stared at her living corpse. I ruminated about the sometimes cheerful past and the gloomy present. By sheer will power, I forced myself to read Harry Barnard's book on Senator Couzens, which I had promised to review for the *Daily News*. I wrote a review, a good one, I think. On the surface, I was calm and resigned. One night my brother George said that the children and I should spend that night in his home. When we were resting there, he summoned his courage and said, "Elmer, I did not want you to be in the hospital, because it is unlikely that Ceretta will survive the night." Somehow, this shocked me. Of course, I knew that she was dying, but I did not face up to it completely until that moment. I cried inconsolably and, gradually, I was restored to peace. I fell asleep, dreamless, and awakened early. Very quietly, George said to me, "Ceretta is gone."

Midge became a woman instantly. She insisted upon choosing the dress and other attire in which her mother would be buried. She and Ted were so eager that I be spared unnecessary anguish that they suppressed their own grief. In Ted's case the reaction was all the worse when it did come.

I was so busy at first I had little time to brood, but soon I did little more than dwell upon my departed wife. We had known each other for more than thirty years and had been married for over twenty-five years. I went through her pictures and papers and mementos, and such items only magnified my obsessive grief. There were our letters, the children's school papers, Ted's poems and drawings, dance programs, combs that La Argentina had given her, the family constitution in Ted's handwriting, signed by each of us, evidencing the nonauthoritarian spirit in which we conducted ourselves. Everything suggested pathos and joys. I fear my conversation was confined to our life together—not that anyone was annoyed. Although her end was tragic, people tended to recall her humor, her zest, her devotion, her many interests. I knew how very much she was moved by Shelley's threnody on Keats, and I was determined to quote from it on her tombstone, altering a word: "She has outsoared the shadow of our night." I was in a sort of twilight zone myself, not really part of this world.

So months went by, outwardly of extraordinary interest, inwardly slow, frustrating, painful. I lacked the spirit that had once characterized me. My children and Ceretta's sisters observed this with anguish. They began to insist that I had to go out with women. I was reluctant to do so. Ceretta's image would come before me. My first date was not promising. Then I ran into Lillian, whom I had known when our sons had attended the University of Illinois, before Ted's transfer to Chicago. I had been president and Lillian vice-president of the parents' group at the fraternity. We had rescued it from financial disaster. Then her husband had died suddenly. She was a little, lovely woman, who radiated excitement. She was more than ten years my junior. I became infatuated with her. We were so different from each other, that I knew that we would be divorced almost before we were married. I could not reason; I could only devour her with my passionate looks. I began to drink more than I should in order to keep up with her. She loved dancing and I loathed it, but I took lessons diligently. We went everywhere like youngsters. One day her son, Fred, asked her where she had gone with me. She listed all the places where we had been that day, and Fred commented: "Now I know where Ted gets his energy!" I owed much to Lillian. She drew me from my obsession with the dead. She recalled me to life.

Everyone assumed that we would be married; everyone, including her mother, encouraged us. But Lillian, sensibly, drew back, despite saying: "I know that one day I will think myself a fool for not grabbing you." She told me of her affection, of her admiration, and of her reservations. I loved and feared her. I began to see that I had to draw away. On impulse, I had friends arrange other dates for me. Ten nights in a row I went out with every sort of woman—divorced, widowed, unwed, bright, sometimes joyous, all eager for male company. In some respects it was a sad period, but it had a climax that was both amusing and thrilling. My cousin, Marvin Gertz, and his wife arranged a blind date for me, my first blind date. It did not excite me. I said to Ted, "I don't think I will keep this date." "Why not?" he inquired. "She is a school teacher . . ." I replied. The wise young man commented: "What have you got to lose?"

So, on March 28, 1959, I met Mamie, the most vital and enthralling woman I have ever known. She was bigger than Ceretta or Lillian, and I had thought that I liked only little women. She was uninhibited, and I thought I liked reserve. From first meeting, I began to forget Lillian. I began to laugh more. I became more vital in every respect. Yet I did not see Mamie at first as much as I wanted to, because I had arranged other dates and I thought it was wrong to break them. I would call Mamie every day while I was dating others—foolish me.

One day my brother Robert and his wife invited us to Sunday brunch. My sister Bernice was there, too. Impishly, I said, "Mamie, I don't like your first name and, to tell the truth, your last name either." (It was Friedman.) Quickly, she responded: "If you don't like them, change them." And I changed her last name within three months of our first meeting. I grew to like her first name. At first we were going to marry in the fall, then in August, then in July; finally, on June 21, 1959, our children and Mamie's mother went with us to the rabbi's study and we were married. We felt like young lovers. We still feel that way.

It is now almost fifteen years since we met. We are together almost constantly, and I cannot imagine a world without Mamie.

Shortly after Mamie and I were married, our housekeeper, Betty, announced that Mamie had been selected for me by Ceretta; that the first Mrs. Gertz approved in every respect. I am sure that she did.

Mamie was the instant love of Ceretta's family. They accepted her as if she were their flesh and blood. The years have only accentuated the closeness. Once Esther, the youngest sister, said to me; "I sometimes wonder about how my boys will fare when I am gone; then I think of Mamie. While she is around, they will be all right."

Still the shadow of Ceretta hovered over me. I would awake at moments in anguish, as I dreamed of the sadness of her last months of life. I could not help making comparisons and dwelling on what might have been. Mamie did not resent this. She understood the ties of the past and tried to share them.

Mamie formed an imaginary Happiness Club, consisting of those who had won contentment in second marriage. She was always looking for recruits, as a born marriage broker. Those of our friends who had lost their spouses and then remarried happily were members of the club.

Thus I came out of the depths. There was a quickening of my creative faculties. I wrote and published more books and articles.

I entered into great new projects. In a sense, I became a new man. Mamie shared each moment with me. She could listen to my innumerable speeches and read my every word, and all would be fresh and wonderful to her. This bred great self-confidence on my part, greater attainment, greater joy. My natural optimism was accentuated. I was Pollyanna grown up.

twelve

A Literary Boom

It was in 1963, I believe, around the time of our victory in the *Tropic of Cancer* litigation, that my old friend, Max Siegel, suggested that I do an autobiographical volume about my more celebrated cases. He felt certain that he could market it. I said that I was eager to write such a book if it were commissioned by a good publisher and I received a substantial advance. Max had been a well-regarded bookseller in our community, knowing everyone in the book trade. It was easy for him to progress from the sale of books at retail to becoming an author's agent. Our city had few, if any, literary agents and there were many prospects for their services. Very early, Max succeeded in selling manuscripts for both Dr. Preston Bradley, the most esteemed and long-lived of our clergymen, and Kupcinet ("Kup"), the best-known newspaper columnist in the city. He soon persuaded Follett, a local firm, best known for its school bookstores, reference works, and juveniles, to enter into a contract with me.

Follett was trying, at the time, to develop its trade-book department and, apparently, thought that a book by me would have some built-in popularity. Louis Zara had just become trade-book editor at Follett's, and he was delighted to work with me. He asked me if I wanted a ghost-writer or editor and I turned him down at once. I said that it was either going to be my personal book, or it would not be published. We agreed, tentatively, upon a title for the book—*A Handful of Cases.* Later, it became *A Handful of Clients,* which I still regard as an excellent title. I have practiced law on a retail, an individual, basis, rather than wholesale. Each case is one that I treasure.

Gladys Fuller was my secretary at the time, the ablest and most conscientious secretary that I have ever had. I went through the files of my most important cases with her, particularly the Leopold case, pointing out the more important letters and other documentation, and she photostated this material for me. She and Mamie photostated innumerable newspaper clippings. Then all of the vast mass of material was arranged in chronological order in loose-leaf notebooks, and I brooded over the material. I saw at once that this material did not cover the entire story. There were gaps in the documentation. There always are. I prepared a working list of everything I wanted to cover. I wrote out or dictated sections without regard to chronological order; then I pieced it all together, did much revising, and then sent on the manuscript, hopefully, to Zara. In its initial form, the manuscript contained some material unconnected with my law cases—recollections of Frank Harris, Carl Sandburg, and others who had played roles in my life. Zara, wisely, eliminated everything unconnected with my cases. He retained my pen portrait of Henry Miller, but thrust it into the middle of my account of the *Tropic of Cancer* litigation.

Of course, much of the book dealt with my most famous case—the freeing of Nathan Leopold. Other big segments concerned the *Compulsion* case and the *Tropic of Cancer* litigation, and the copyright infringement case that I handled for Otto Eisenschiml (which I called "Litigating the Civil War," because it concerned the piracy of Eisenschiml's books on the death of Lincoln). The concluding chapter concerned the narcotics-conspiracy case involving three police officers, represented by me, and an assortment of alleged drug peddlers, mostly blacks, represented by others. I tried to write with a dual purpose in mind—to give those legally trained an adequate account of celebrated litigation, and to interest laymen, completely unfamiliar with the technicalities of our craft.

There is a passage in this book that is an essential part of my autobiography and I must quote it at length:

> The law can be—it has been—a very profitable pursuit for the ambitious. It can be—it has been—the gateway to financial security, as well as to eminence in politics, government, business, commercial affairs and even philanthropy. As a result of what they learned, or perhaps as a result of what they did not learn too well, some men come to the acquisition of vast blocks of real estate and sizable holdings in commercial and industrial enterprise. The law is rich in manifold legitimate opportunities, and every man who practices it will find for himself the avenues that will permit his own self-development and aggrandizement.
>
> Perhaps my confession here reveals some perverse chemistry in my own psyche. But I have never been able to regard the law simply as a means of earning a livelihood or of amassing a fortune. I have sought a competence, yes, because I have needed that to make independent living and independent thinking possible. For the rest, I have looked upon the law as a way of enabling me to live a more useful life as an informed citizen and member of my community. I suspect that this view has made many of my colleagues think that I am intent upon maintaining a sort of amateur standing in my profession. Fortunately, the record, as we lawyers like to say, will show otherwise. . . .
>
> So the law has come to mean more to me than the lawbooks. It means to me life under strains and stresses and life confronted by powerful challenges. Now I understand the word "liberty"; I have fought to win it for other human beings. Now, too, I understand "the pursuit of happiness"; I have done my best to make it available to others.

In a sober mood I once said that there are only two things wrong with the practice of law—clients and no clients. But clients have made it possible for me to learn something of tactics and strategy, without which no courtroom lawyer is worth his salt, and without clients I should, frankly, have become nothing. It is about some of my clients and their unusual cases that I decided to tell my story. Not because I wish to be a writer—I shall always regard myself proudly as a lawyer—but because from this handful of cases others may come to understand better how fortunate we all are that we are privileged to live in a society where a system of justice prevails.

In my day I have drafted countless real estate sale contracts, bills of sale, leases, releases, partnership agreements and dissolutions, wills and a multiplicity of other documents, sometimes simple and conventional, at other times intricate and a test of one's skill in the use of language. These have often represented a useful expenditure of time, and have won the gratitude of clients, but they are not, except superficially, what I mean by the law.

I have filed, or defended, foreclosure suits, accounting suits, divorce actions, adoption proceedings, naturalization petitions, anti-trust suits, almost everything in the vast realm of litigation; and I have never been certain in advance where any of these cases would lead me. A partnership accounting suit might cloak a rich family history worthy of the Tolstoy who wrote *Anna Karenina*. Behind a contest over a will there might be a chronicle worthy of a Charles Dickens, another *Bleak House*. Legal formalities reveal, as well as conceal, everything that is human and sometimes also, what is almost inhuman.

There is another quintessential passage in the introduction:

The lawyer has been privileged to study the age-old machinery for regulating the relations of men. He has developed skill in the use of the technical tools employed by the courts in arriving at results—the disposition of cases, civil and criminal. He knows the virtues as well as the limitations of our legal system. If he has a sense of dedication, if he is a philosopher as well as a craftsman, he will think and act beyond the exigencies of the moment. He will try to learn what can be done by him in a particular case and in all cases, so that the low courts of law may become, in the words of a philosopher, the high courts of justice. Then, the courts will become increasingly the means for making this a world safe for humanity, rather than for special interests alone. . . .

Law, then, has meanings far beyond any courtroom and any conflict. It can be a humanized instrument to help achieve a more viable, more sensible, world.

From the Spring of 1964 until Jack Ruby's death on January 3, 1967, I was part of the national team of lawyers who worked, successfully, toward setting aside the death sentence imposed upon the man who had slain Oswald, President Kennedy's assassin. Within days of Ruby's death, I received a very remarkable and persuasive letter from Dwight Follett, head of the firm that had published *A Handful of Clients.* Dwight declared, in rather exigent terms, that I had performed a considerable public service during the protracted proceedings and that I now owed it to history to tell the true story of the case before the fictionalists took over completely. He said that he would regard it as an honor if his firm were privileged to publish my book. Although I regretted that Louis Zara was no longer editor-in-chief at Follett, it was relatively easy to negotiate a contract for the book and to get to work on it.

The book was called *Moment of Madness: The People vs. Jack Ruby.* I had not known what to call it, until I enlisted the aid of my creative son-in-law, Henry R. Hechtman. He came up with a title that captured the essence of the story.

I elicited and won the assistance of many persons who had been connected with me in the handling of the case or had been part of the story in some other phase of it. I was pleased, indeed, that Joe Tonahill, one of Belli's associates in the original trial, whom we had fought so bitterly for so long, was enthusiastic about the book and sent inscribed copies to numerous friends and members of his family. I was even more pleased that Judge Louis Holland, who had succeeded Judge Joe Brown in presiding over the case, liked the book and respected me. Most of all, I was pleased that Professor Jon R. Waltz, of Northwestern University

School of Law, was highly enthusiastic and expressed his views in a very remarkable preface. Professor Waltz, one of the brightest and most candid of men in our community, had had mixed reactions to *A Handful of Clients,* chiefly with respect to Nathan Leopold, and he had collaborated with Professor John Kaplan in the writing of an earlier book on the Ruby trial, which some thought had pre-empted the field. Waltz said in his preface:

> I have a theory, or perhaps it is only an opinion, about the law and lawyers and their power to get at facts fairly and adequately. It is that the purposes and the actual workings, and the flaws, of our legal truth-determining machinery can best be demonstrated not in all-encompassing treatises . . . but rather in knowledgeable and close dissections of particular litigated cases. . . . And the same theory impels me to say that the book in your hand by Elmer Gertz, focusing principally on the post-trial proceedings in the Ruby case, is an important and useful effort. . . . Elmer Gertz . . . has written with substantial objectivity from a unique fund of knowledge about a case that strikes me as being of genuine importance to all who care about the law in the United States. . . . I know of no book . . . that so fully illuminates what for most non-lawyers has remained an almost total mystery, the criminal law's procedures following trial, conviction and sentence.

I liked, too, Professor Waltz's reference to me as "something of a cross between Don Quixote and an ethical Clarence Darrow," although my good friend Arthur Weinberg, the most devoted of Darrow's admirers, took umbrage at what he regarded as a gratuitous slur at his idol.

In my book, I tried to tell the whole story of the Ruby case—the personalities, the legal involvements, the solutions to the various problems, the reasons for all that happened. I tried to be fair to Ruby himself, out of a sense of compassion and of loyalty to the family and the facts. I think that I struck the proper note at the very outset when I wrote:

> Jack Ruby's manliness has been belittled by many persons, and his stature in the community in which he lived has been

ridiculed. At the end of his life, after the trial and the appeal, he was indeed a shrunken shell of the person he had been. But when he was taken into custody on that November day in 1963, he was still the bouncy, buoyant Jack Ruby of the Carousel Club. He had been, in his own terms, something of a success, and he was not without friends. Within a very short time of the shooting of Lee Harvey Oswald, five of his friends and acquaintances called five different attorneys to represent him, and all of these attorneys appeared at the jail prepared to act in his behalf. Perhaps they came in the hope of notoriety; perhaps they saw cash in the venture; but in any event they came.

The arrival (and departure) of these men foretokened much that was to happen in the case, for from first to last, even to death and beyond, the spectacle was provided in scenes by attorneys, and the chief actor was gradually edged offstage.

Step by step I retraced, critically, the whole sad, mad story from the crime to the selection of counsel to the first bail hearing to the second bail hearing, and on and on, step by step, to the trial itself. I told, for the first time, of the intimate fact-crammed reports by R. B. Denson, the Dallas investigator, largely ignored by Melvin Belli. I analyzed the vast amount of publicity occasioned by the Presidential assassination and its aftermath and how it affected Ruby. One of my conclusions really spelled out the whole tragic story:

> If there is going to be any villain in this piece, however, it must be the public, or if not the public, then that intangible quirk of the mind that caused Pandora to loose on the world all its woes. For the people's curiosity has been converted by the press into "the right to know," and that has often become "the right to intrude." The press, radio, and television know one and only one objective, and in pursuit of it their representatives flocked to Dallas. The sheer force of their presence is seldom, if ever, felt in most communities, and with it the Dallas authorities were entirely unprepared to cope. The result was pandemonium and disaster.

Inevitably, Belli felt that these things made a change of venue imperative. He tried, unsuccessfully, to persuade Judge Brown, who would not forego his hours of glory. There were problems in the jury selection, compounded by the community prejudice and the fact that the members of the panel had witnessed the slaying of Oswald on their televisions. The impact of this first television-recorded killing could not be eradicated or diminished.

Because Kaplan and Waltz had done so well in their book, *The Trial of Jack Ruby,* I made only a quick survey of the original trial, passing on to later proceedings. Still, my account was twenty-five pages in length. I then retraced part of the story and did what no other writer had done. I analyzed in great depth the testimony of the Dallas police officers, not alone at the trial, but before the Warren Commission and in statements to the Police Department. This was material unknown to Belli, concealed from him, in fact. It demonstrated that the police testimony should not have been received in evidence and, if received, not believed by the jury. I said:

> If one were to sum up the meaning of all the conflicting testimony of the Dallas police officers, one would have to say that these men acted and spoke in the traditional manner of police officers in every part of the country. Objective truth was much less important to them than the official story of what had occurred. This does not mean that they were prevaricators or completely dishonest. Men in authority, and men out of authority, too, have the habit of suiting their words to the desired end. They respond to the suggestions of their superiors and mentors; they say what they think is wanted or required by the circumstances. This is unfortunate, but human. It is the basic justification for the guidelines laid down by the courts for the admission or exclusion of statements allegedly made by accused persons. As this narrative proceeds, we shall deal in depth with what the United States Supreme Court said in three historic cases that followed the Ruby death verdict. They will serve to explain and justify the ultimate result of all our maneuvering.

I narrated in my book much that cannot be found elsewhere. The courts and judges, who had been hostile to Ruby and ourselves, his "foreign" attorneys, ultimately saw the light, as we focused on the law and the facts. We won a reversal of the death sentence, the grant of a new trial in less hostile circumstance, and much praise. As we prepared for the new trial, Ruby died. In a sense, as I tell, I was the discoverer of his fatal malady, and I helped tape, under the very noses of the authorities, the historical death-bed statement by Ruby. I am still moved as I think of Ruby's funeral in Chicago:

> There was symbolism in the bearing of Jack Ruby to his final resting place. The pallbearers were the husband of his favorite, his youngest sister, Eileen; a childhood companion, Joe Kellman; and four of the lawyers who had participated in the case that had now come to so dramatic an end—Michael Levin, the boyhood friend of the family; Phil Burleson, the one attorney who had stayed with the case from the beginning; William Kunstler, who had ignored his many commitments to be on hand; and myself. As I accompanied the flag-draped coffin (for Jack had earned the right by his honorable, if undistinguished, wartime service), my thoughts encompassed every step of the way we had gone. I saw how fragile our grip on reality might become, given the stress of emotional events. I saw a vindication of our great American judicial system, in which an impoverished nobody can receive justice, despite the primitive forces that impede the way. Those gathered about the coffin were diverse men united in the one aim of bearing a fellow being to the grave in peace and dignity. Dust to dust. Nothing else mattered or had meaning, neither sins nor virtues, greatness or littleness. This is the common end of the great and the humble, the slain Presidents and of their avengers.

By way of farewell to Ruby the man and his travails, I said:

> The long vigil was over. A kind of immortality had come to a little man and his little family.

Then, much to the unexplained annoyance of Louis Zara, I devoted a chapter to disposing of the conspiracy theories of demonologists like Mark Lane, and drew parallels between the assassinations of Lincoln and Kennedy and their aftermaths. I am glad that I added this material to my book. I still agree with what I said in closing the subject:

> He who would make much of a conspiracy in the death of President Kennedy would do well to reflect on this brief recital of the all-too-similar circumstances of the death of Abraham Lincoln. Events are not well ordered, the truth is not always knowable. And what is known is known provisionally, with some quantum of doubt appearing inconspicuously in the next phrasing. John F. Kennedy is dead; Lee Harvey Oswald is dead, and Jack L. Ruby is dead. These are certainties. That there is tragedy here is well established, but that there was or is a conspiracy will remain, in my opinion, beyond proof, for there are and ever will be in our midst individuals who disarrange history by their actions in a moment of madness.

To mark Henry Miller's seventy-fifth birthday, *Syntheses,* an international review of the arts, published in Paris and Brussels, decided to devote an entire double issue to him. There were articles, long and short, by Pierre Lesdain, Anaïs Nin, Joseph Delteil, Brassaï, George Simenon, Antoine Denat, Osamu Okumura, and others from lands as distant and distinct from each other as France, Holland, India, and Japan, so widely and favorably known had Henry Miller become in his late years. Appropriately I wrote, in English, under the title, "Mon client, Henry Miller." I was glad to learn from the editor's comment that I am *"grand défenseur de la liberté d'expression."* It is good to know this in any language, especially in the language of Voltaire.

After the appearance of my Ruby book and after my writing a foreword to his book, *Tropic of Cancer on Trial,* Professor Earl R. Hutchison asked me to write an essay for a study of the press. The book was published in 1970 by Wiley-Interscience, a division of John Wiley & Sons, under the title, *Mass Media and the Law—Freedom and Restraint.*

My essay, about twenty pages in length, was entitled, significantly, "A Lawyer 'Uses' the Press." It appeared in a section of the book which propounded the question: "Will Rules Solve the

Problem?" My answer is a qualified "No." My thesis was simply stated:

> If press excesses have created, at times, the atmosphere making a fair trial and due process of law difficult, if not impossible, then press silence has on many occasions resulted in unjust results. It does no good to pardon an Evans in England, posthumously, after he has been hanged for a murder he did not commit. It would have been much better for there to have been the vigilance and outcry that might have prevented the grossly wrong result. . . .
>
> The press people are shrewd and cynical and they know when they are being used. They resent pushers. They use the would-be users. They reject what is useless, despite the importunities and devices of the publicity-seekers. If they sense that one is essentially in good faith, and that what one seeks from them is legitimate and newsworthy, they are often cooperative. United in a good cause, a lawyer and his cohorts of the press can accomplish a good deal in the quest for justice or in undoing an improper result. They must be a team; neither must be taken advantage of; confidences must be exchanged mutually, and not doled out in a one-sided fashion, begrudgingly or selectively. On very few occasions has my confidence been betrayed by any good reporter; on no occasion have I knowingly harmed any one of the press with whom I have worked. . . .

Writing, as I often did, of Henry Miller in the decade of the 1960's and later, he was continually under my observation. We corresponded; we visited; I read the increasing volume of material about him that appeared. A few changes in him were patent. He was much less interested in book writing than earlier; it was clear that he preferred painting—perhaps because it led to less strain; perhaps because there was more serious interest in him as a water colorist; perhaps because he felt less like an amateur and more like a dedicated professional. He corresponded much less than earlier. Where once he was prolific in his communications with friends, now he was sparing of himself. A few lines would take the place of the long letters he used to write. He tried to rest more; he was less accessible to people.

He was concerned more about his health than earlier. Certain physical activities were curtailed—not ping-pong, to be sure, or swimming in his over-heated pool in his lovely Pacific Palisades home. There was a kind of mellowness in him that became more apparent with the passage of time. He was deeply concerned about his two younger children, Val and Tony. Like other parents in this distressing Vietnam period, he did not want Tony to shed his or other blood. I would hear long conversations between Henry and his young son on every occasion that I was with him.

He could be aroused into activity when the welfare of a prisoner was involved, particularly one under sentence of death. He corresponded with William Witherspoon, long under sentence in Illinois until spared by the United States Supreme Court in a landmark decision. When, earlier, I had sought commutation of the death sentence, he sent me a magnificent letter, to be filed with the governor and the Pardon Board. He encouraged Witherspoon to paint, as a result of which I have Witherspoon's first effort in that field.

To one prisoner, who shall be nameless because of the change in his circumstances, he was especially helpful, for this remarkable bank robber and barber developed a great interest in literature. He read everything by Miller avidly and with understanding. Miller persuaded Anaïs Nin and other friends, myself included, to correspond with the fascinating prisoner. Miller visited him in the penitentiary, going many miles out of his way; hired attorneys for the man, and spent substantial sums in his behalf. Later, at least in part by reason of Henry's efforts, the man was released and, at Henry's request, I kept a friendly eye on him, since he was to reside in the Chicago area during his parole. He visited Henry and his friends; he lived an exemplary life; all of which cast an unexpected light upon the author of *Tropic of Cancer*. One can understand why Thomas Moore, the Miller bibliographer, said that Henry made a man of him; or why clergymen have found spiritual quality in his writings.

To anyone who had seen Henry Miller scrounging in his early surroundings in the Villa Seurat in Paris, his habitation today in a lovely upper-middle-class area of Pacific Palisades in California must seem luxurious, indeed. It is not a villa or chalet that the Rockefellers or Vanderbilts or Harrimans might choose, but any artist in America would find it wholly suitable. Lacking the wild grandeur of Big Sur, which Henry has often celebrated so lyrically, it is more than sufficient in a stage of life when creature comforts are more important than when one is young. The house is unmistakably his in its furnishings and appurtenances, in its warm glow and distinct aura. One could visualize him in every part of it. The furniture is comfortable and uncluttered. The principal items in the living room are the little piano and several sofas, easy chairs and desks, the many books with a firm sign, *Achtung!* in tone, indicating that they belong there and are not part of a circulating library. Above all, there are simply framed pictures and memorabilia of all kinds on the walls— Henry's water colors, handwritten outlines of books, a few items by his friends and others. There is comfort, let us repeat, in an easy to reach fashion. Adjoining this room, there is Henry's great delight, a big space with a huge ping-pong table, a well-stocked bar (the kitchen beyond it), pictures and posters and other things on the walls and even on the ceiling. And beyond this there is the big outdoor swimming pool, heated so well that the bills are enormous. The first floor contains the ample bedroom, a den and, most striking of all, the toilets— adorned with pictures, paintings, legends and graffiti of all appropriate and inappropriate kinds, inducing extended visits and much conversation. And upstairs there are more bedrooms and other facilities. Henry goes easily from one part of the house to another—now answering a few letters at his desk, now playing the piano, now reading, browsing, meditating, never hurried, never feeling that this day must be crammed with activities. If he feels like it, which is often enough, he will leave word that he is not to be disturbed by telephone calls. He might nap. He might swim. Until arthritis began to bother him, he might ride a bicycle into the lovely neighborhoods of Pacific Palisades, whistling a quiet tune.

On one wall of Miller's home is a wholly characteristic outline of a projected book, in his own unusually clear and beautiful handwriting, scarcely changed by the years. It is to be, if it is ever written, a book about people and places and his interrelationships with them. The title, apparently, is to be *Where Am I? What Am I Doing?* Good Miller questions, these, with true Miller answers. There must be over a hundred names on the list, some self-explanatory, some with a phrase or two to denote their meaning for him. Of course, I found the early reference to Chicago intriguing:

> Chez Elmer Gertz
> Rattner's stained glass window in
> Loop Synagogue.

How well I remember Henry's week-long stay "Chez Elmer Gertz," the very words he placed on a water color, more carefully done than most—almost tight in its composition, in fact—that he gave to us. The stay meant, not alone a visit to "Rattner's stained glass window in Loop Synagogue." It meant a trip to the largely abandoned Stock Yards, the ghostly quality of which, in its twilight, delighted Miller. It meant long bouts of conversation. It meant the strengthening of the bonds of affection between us: Henry, Mamie, and myself. Henry was as frank as he was friendly, not frank in the sense of using four-letter words—they were surprisingly rare—but frank in letting us know exactly what he thought of all that came up for discussion, and little was omitted.

So, in the latest visit to his home in Pacific Palisades, I read, with mounting fascination, Henry's entries upon the framed outline on his wall. Just as he had referred to the Chicago Loop Synagogue in the first column, he referred to it again in the third, the last, column under the heading, "Synagogues":

Prague, Toledo, Seville, Loop—Chicago. Two succeeding entries are underscored and starred:

Venice—near suicide!
Verona—my town! (Caliger family)

He notes Minden (Hanover), the home of his father's ancestors, and Bremen, his mother's ancestors; but he makes note as well of "the town where Eleanore Duse was born!" One can pause long hours over this unusual outline or souvenir of a rich life. The book will probably not be written. Perhaps, it was never intended to be written. It is characteristic of much that is in Henry Miller's home that fits him like a warm and comfortable glove.

The series of novels, called *The Rosy Crucifixion*—indeed, virtually all that Miller ever wrote—was fully outlined by him on large sheets, long before he had put down one word in definitive form. That is the Teutonic martinent in Miller, a taskmaster not generally reckoned with by those, including himself, who only see what Miller himself has described as "Joey the Clown." He is that, too, a true clown, but to no lesser extent, I believe, he is the disciplined technician of what is seemingly an undisciplined style of writing and living. "I am the opposite of what I seem"—this might be his motto.

I remember when Mamie and I first met Miller's Japanese wife, Hoki, in the very entrance of his home in Pacific Palisades. With almost Oriental ceremony, Henry recounted for us Hoki's great virtues, ending: "I want you to meet my fifth and last wife, Hoki." With a twinkle in her eye, Hoki responded: "You know better than that, Henry. You will have two or three more wives!" Only for a moment were any of us speechless at this unexpected candor and plausible prophecy. Henry has infinite capacity for loving his wives and mistresses. His marriages and liaisons do not end with hate. He has retained almost tender regard for all of his women, except for his first wife. This was dramatically illustrated for me, a lawyer, when Henry was in my office in

Chicago, following a trip to Europe. His pockets bulged with royalty checks; the total must have been several thousands of dollars. Gone were his lean days! I was aghast. I explained to him the legal consequences of such neglect—the risk of loss, such as through the closing of accounts—was on the one who failed to make an immediate deposit. I recalled to him, all too poignantly, what had happened during the Great Depression when banks closed suddenly and almost daily, spreading financial ruin. "Let Gladys [my ever-efficient secretary] send the checks to your bank for deposit," I pleaded. "I'll send them to June," he replied. "She will take care of them." Not long previously, he had been divorced from June. He still regarded her as his trusted friend. He still cherished her Israeli artist brother-in-law, Bezalel Schatz, as flesh of his flesh. Similar stories could be told of his relations with the other women in his life, save, again, the first wife. If Henry believed in elaborate marriage ceremonials, it would not surprise me if Hoki were bridesmaid for her successor or successors.

I first heard Hoki's name somewhat earlier when Henry was concerned about her remaining in the States. She was an entertainer, a gifted pianist and singer, on temporary visit from her native Japan. She would have to leave the country unless her status were changed. Henry consulted with me and I with an associate in Washington, specializing in immigration matters. We were in the midst of solving the problems when Henry took a short-cut. He married Hoki and, as his wife, she could remain here.

Even when the marital status was precarious, Henry retained his faith in Hoki. He had always wanted to go to the Orient, particularly to China and Japan. He believed that his facial appearance bore indisputable evidence of Oriental escapades by his seafaring forebears. Somehow, he could never go—even when he was offered free trips by travel agencies. His excuses were good, but they never really persuaded me. He had great admiration for several Japanese writers and artists and sent us books by his favorites. Henry's writings were very popular in

Japan, and that fascinating and perceptive country was beginning to show great interest in his water colors, which have a kind of Japanese quality. Exhibits were arranged in the leading cities. Henry sent me the very elaborate programs of these exhibits. Since he could not go there to receive the acclaim in person, he sent Hoki, instead, and had her pocket the very considerable sums that his paintings fetched. As I recall, virtually all were sold.

Henry has an enormous interest in Jewish liturgical music. He has a large collection of recordings by the best known cantors and plays them frequently. He seems to cultivate Jewish friends and associations. He turns to Jews for legal, accounting, dental, and medical help. One of his wives was at least partly Jewish, another with Jewish family connections. Perles, Fraenkel, Lowenfels, and others who were associated with him during his fruitful *Tropic of Cancer* period, and friends of later years were Jewish. He toured the country with the Jewish artist Rattner, to whom he is devoted as to a brother. As I have narrated, when he visited with me in Chicago, he insisted that we had to spend some time in meditation before Rattner's windows in the Loop Synagogue before we did anything else. Yet some people persist in thinking that there is an anti-Jewish streak in him, because of a few ambiguous passages in his writings. He tried to answer these critics in his Big Sur book; but they will persist.

I have a very large collection of books, inscribed and uninscribed, by and about Henry Miller, thanks largely to Henry. For a period of time he had his publishers, here and abroad, send me all editions of all books by him as they appeared. I have books in English, Italian, French, German, Danish, Norwegian, Hebrew, Russian, Finnish, Japanese, Korean, and many other languages, illustrated and plain books, well printed and simple ones, big and small ones, hardcovered and paperbacked, limited and popular editions. The variety is dazzling. Increasingly, beautifully printed books with his water colors appear, here and abroad, with texts in various languages. Having seen Henry paint, largely in my home, I am intrigued by the quality of his work. At first glance, his paintings are simple, sometimes primitive, but they often have a subtlety that is not immediately apparent. One acquaintance of mine, a distinguished law professor, Philip Kurland, insists that Henry Miller is the greatest water colorist of our day.

I had occasion to learn at first hand the appeal of his paintings. During one financially flush period, he found it advantageous to make gifts of his work to public institutions, so that he might take tax credits. He asked me to take care of the matter for him. I wrote to universities, art museums and other such institutions throughout the country, inquiring if they would like gifts of Henry Miller's paintings. Some replied with great excitement. I received a long-distance telephone call from the nuns at a Catholic girls' school in California. They were almost delirious over the opportunity to own some of the paintings. This joy was almost invariably the reaction. Now and then, some respectable institution was reserved and negative in response.

My experiences with inducing friends to read Henry's books were revealing of them as well as Miller. Those I admired most seemed to grasp readily the inner music and meanings of his most explicit writings. My friends, Melvyn and Helen Douglas, were absorbed in my defense of Miller in the courts, just as they were when I tried to get Leopold out of prison. I sent them *Tropic of Cancer* and they were enchanted. On the other hand, Nathan Leopold, singularly lacking in aesthetic feelings, despite his extraordinary intelligence, was unimpressed. He had a prison inmate's view of the four-letter words and sexual explicitness. Miller had more charity toward Leopold than the latter toward him. There were blunt, honest men of another generation, like Carl Sandburg, who could not abide Miller. Still, Carl was impressed by my understanding of Frank Harris, despite the verbal frankness of that literary buccaneer. I am always aware that tastes in literature, as in politics, are matters of chemistry. One cannot argue with anyone's genes. Mine naturally absorbed Miller, as they had Harris.

I sometimes think I could write a fair critique of almost any creative person by analyzing the kind of inscriptions he habitually writes in the books he gives to friends. I could tell whether he is generous of spirit, uninhibited, extravagant, or uptight, mincing, or grudging. It seems to me that Carl Sandburg's inscriptions, to which I have already referred, show the care with which he carved out what he had to say in making presentations. Not only is his script beautiful, a work of art, but there is a measured quality, the giving of one's due, in the words used, nothing light and ill-considered. There were sometimes similar and sometimes dissimilar qualities in Frank Harris, George Sylvester Viereck, Lloyd Lewis, and other writers I have known. When I pick up a book of theirs that they had sent to me, they come to life again, not only by reason of the contents of their writings, dedicated to the whole world, but even more through the intimate phrasing, intended for me alone.

Thus, Henry Miller's inscriptions say much of the sort of large-spirited person that he is. I pick up several of his volumes and, as I read what he penned in them for me, the warmth and extravagance and gratitude of the man is irresistible. When we were about to win the *Tropic of Cancer* case, it was to be expected that he would say overly kind things: "For Elmer Gertz—A lover of freedom, truth and justice, a lover of books and a peerless barrister. May Heaven protect him ever! In gratitude and admiration—Henry Miller—2/21/62—on the eve of the great decision, 'Victory.'" And when I saw him in Minneapolis in the company of the incomparable Eddie Schwartz, founder of the unique Henry Miller Literary Society, which did so much to establish his reputation, he gave us copies of *Stand Still Like the Hummingbird* and wrote in mine: "For Elmer Gertz—one of the most amazing men I have ever met—and so gentle, modest, humble withal . . ." Whether or not these words are true does not matter in the least. It is, rather, the revelation of spirit that counts, just as when he insisted, publicly, that I ought to be named to the United States Supreme Court—an impossible dream, of course, but one that does credit to an utterly devoted friend. I should add that, as Henry knew, one of my friends, Arthur J. Goldberg, who was a justice of the highest court, had great admiration for the water colors of Miller; Arthur's wife,

Dorothy, had arranged an exhibition in Washington while Miller, the writer, was still held in disesteem in some circles. One day, shortly after Arthur was named to the court, we ran into each other at a meeting of the American Bar Association. Greeting each other like old friends, Arthur said: "I understand, Elmer, that you are the attorney in some obscenity cases." "Yes, Arthur," I replied, "and we had better not discuss them." Then we both blushed at what might have been an embarrassment.

So I could go through each of the many books Henry has presented to me; for instance, *Tropic of Capricorn,* in which he wrote: " . . . And let's hope he does not have to defend this one—though he *could* defend anything! . . ." Fortunately, we did not have to defend "this one," nor *Sexus,* nor *Quiet Days in Clichy,* nor other outspoken volumes by Miller; the *Tropic of Cancer* litigation had exhausted the censors, apparently. I would have felt certain that we would encounter difficulties with these uninhibited works. *Sexus* is at least as explicit as the *Tropics.*

And in one of my favorite little-known Miller works, *The Books in My Life,* in which he reminisces of the books he has read and re-read, he promised to write a sequel, to which he referred in presenting the volume to me: "For my very dear friend Elmer Gertz, who could probably do a better job with the promised sequel than I . . ." Henry always insisted that I recalled his writings better than he did, a form of poetic truth.

Great as was his devotion to me, he was equally devoted to Mamie. Almost with regret, he repeatedly defeated her in ping pong when he neared his eightieth birthday. He was kind enough to say that he had to move around, bestir himself, to defeat her, while he could stand in one place in defeating others. His physical adeptness into his old age was marvelous to behold. It was if to teach us that having violated at least one of the Ten Commandments and many of the rules of the respectables, he had earned the serenity and strength that he was enjoying.

He would talk to Mamie of Isaac Bashevis Singer, whom he greatly admired. To make certain that Mamie would become acquainted with this modern master, he presented her with a copy of *The Family Moskat,* Singer's first novel, I believe. On the first free page he wrote, characteristically: "For Mamie—to read at her leisure (preferably on an ocean voyage). I don't know whether we should be happy or sad over the disappearance of the 'shtetel'. Long live Singer and the characters he has created. And to *you*, and *all you* have created—blessings on this day of Purim. Henry. 3/17/65. Erin go bragh for St. Patrick's day!!!"

Somewhat later, Mamie attended a lecture by Singer at a North Shore Temple and proudly showed him her copy of his novel with Henry's inscription. Smiling, Singer wrote on the next free page: "To a friend of my friend with good wishes. I. B. Singer."

Thus, the confraternity of the faithful and creative.

Miller professes to dislike the conventional celebrations of Christmas and birthdays, but he can be very sentimental and endearing when unobserved!

I do not pretend to have drawn a full portrait of Henry Miller in these pages, although I visualize one. I have written of him in some depth in *A Handful of Clients* and in the other writings to which I have already referred. These things may add up to a picture not without its value. Here is only a series of snapshots and quick views of a man who has deeply interested me for a dozen years. He is a man and artist who stands apart. He cannot be epitomized in snap phrases. One must let time speak out in his behalf.

thirteen

Litigating for and against the Police

There had been disorders at the Civic Center in downtown Chicago in the Spring of 1968 during the holding of a peace demonstration. The police had reacted badly, beating up bystanders and arresting participants, as if in preparation for their even worse reaction during the Democratic Convention that summer. A committee of leading citizens—the Sparling Commission—examined both situations in depth and issued reports as to the causes and cures; the cause was lack of respect for first-amendment rights, the cure, respect for them. I was counsel for the committee in 1968 and 1969 and influential in the writing of its reports.

Work on the Sparling Commission was only a small part of my effort to combat police lawlessness. I may have filed more cases in the Federal and State courts for violation of civil rights than any other lawyer in my day.

There was, for example, the case of a young black man. Early one morning he had been awakened in his parents' home, where he lived while going to high school. Two policemen wanted to know if he would accompany them to the police station for questioning. He was not involved, they said, but he could be helpful. Having nothing to hide, as he believed, he went with them. For many months he was detained, at the police station and then at the Cook County Jail. He told a story that is almost commonplace in big city ghettos. He was kept from food, drink, and toilet facilities. He could not call his parents. He was not informed of his rights. He was threatened and beaten up. When he was thoroughly exhausted, he was harassed into signing a confession that he had acted as a lookout in connection with the burglarizing and murder of an old lady. Notwithstanding the extorted confession, a jury was not persuaded of his guilt. It was what is called a hung jury, discharged finally because it was unable to agree upon a verdict. Then the United States Supreme Court handed down one of its landmark decisions on coerced in-custody statements, and the charge against the boy was *nolle prossed,* and he was released from the County Jail after having been detained for eighteen months!

It was then that the parents and grandmother came to me and asked to file a suit because of the violation of his civil rights. He was in a sorry state, they said, because of his terrifying experience, a physical and emotional wreck, unable to secure proper employment, unable to concentrate on school work. With many misgivings, I filed a suit in the Federal court. These cases involve much preparation and are seldom successful. There were the added handicaps in this instance of a grandmother filled with religious fanaticism and a mother who placed too high a monetary valuation upon a suit that was a gamble at best.

Our troubles were manifold. The trial judge struck some of the most forceful passages of our complaint and would not permit evidence in support of them. He hobbled our efforts at the trial. He would not give the jury the instructions that we sought, instructions that would have placed the case in its proper context. I tried to retrieve lost ground by an effective closing argument, but, in the end, the jury chose to believe the several white police officers, rather than the black boy and his black witnesses. We appealed the adverse result. So persuaded was I of the rightness of our cause that I advanced several hundreds of dollars in costs. We filed only the pertinent parts of the record because the costs for the entire record would be too great. We argued before a panel of the United States Court of Appeals, and we won; that is, the lower court was reversed and the case sent back for re-trial. The opinion of the appeals court, written by Judge Otto Kerner, was a model of enlightenment. It told exactly what could be alleged in a civil-rights complaint, what evidence could be offered, what instructions given to a jury. It was a guide to procedure in a civil-rights case involving the police. We tried the case again and lost. We appealed and again won a reversal. The city took the case to the United States Supreme Court which declined to intervene.

In one short period of time, I was consulted separately by two sets of parents who had been shattered by the same tragic experience. In each instance, a son, coincidentally each nineteen years old, was shot to death by a policeman. The Wagner boy was killed while he faced the police with his hands in the air; the Nelson boy was shot in the back while fleeing from a policeman who had previously made threats against him.

Some foolishly believe that such things happen only to black boys, as if this makes the rank deed defensible. Both the Wagner and Nelson boys were white, just as were others I have represented in similar cases. The police may react more brutally against the blacks, the Latins, the poor, but they have been known to mistreat as distinguished a jurist as Judge John Dempsey. The vice of police brutality is flagrant, inexcusable, epidemic, and dangerous. It must be eradicated if we are to achieve the sort of world in which we profess to believe.

We were able to get judgments in both cases—a modest amount, in connection with the police slaying of the Wagner boy, by agreement of the city. The case came up before the famous Judge Julius Hoffman and, after the usual arm-twisting, the consent judgment resulted.

There is at least one unfair aspect of such judgments. Payment is deferred until the city appropriates funds for such purpose, and this is often long delayed, when the need on the part of the judgment holder may be immediate and great. There are insiders who traffic in judgments against the city and purchase them from the highly pressed parties at substantial discounts. I think that a government ought to pay its obligations immediately. I think that it ought not to be able to escape liability for the misdeeds of its employees, as it often does, by claiming that they were willful and wanton in their actions. Citizens are entitled to protection and quick redress, regardless of technicalities.

I hope that nobody assumes that I am invariably hostile to the police. Those who have read my book *A Handful of Clients* know that I successfully defended three police officers when they were charged by the Federal government with being part of a narcotics conspiracy. I also defended them successfully before the police board when charges against them were preferred, and later I obtained back salaries for them—in all, complete exoneration and restoration of all rights.

Thus I learn again and again how police, too, are the victims of a harsh code. Fortunately, more than once I had satisfying results. One notorious officer was distinguished for his scrapes with his superiors, arising from his advocacy of what many would describe as an extreme rightist line. In the period of Senator Joseph McCarthy, he was a McCarthyite. I loathed what he stood for, but I firmly believed in his freedom of expression. One day his exchange of words with a lady, whom he is supposed to have called "Fatty," was given as an excuse for his dismissal. I defended him before the police board and saved his job. He continued his crusades, though in more moderate form than in the past. He kept me posted about his activities by occasional letters, leaflets, and pronouncements.

Daniel Gallagher, my clerk when I was with the Arvey firm and then the attorney for a police organization, sent a unique case to me, involving a traffic officer named Fred Magee. In an unsuccessful attempt to entrap Magee, his superiors used an electronic device to overhear his conversations. There was no basis for their action, not even justifiable suspicion. I brought a suit against the superintendent of police and others to punish and prevent such unwarranted prying into Magee's activities. But the court said the department could do this. Thus, at least one police officer learned that eavesdropping can work against law-enforcement officers as well as against mere civilians.

Gladwin Madel, another police officer, found himself in another sort of situation. His beat was in the black ghetto, a tough assignment. The owners of the Blue Flame Lounge, against whom he had pressed charges of violating the laws preventing the sale of liquor to minors, attempted to frame him for bribery in a rather elaborate manner. He was brought before the police board, and this, of course, required the hiring of an attorney and much effort and expense before he was acquitted. In the process, his health and his standing on the force suffered greatly. The Blue Flame Lounge owners, Roy and Lillie Marshall, did not stop with their unsuccessful effort to get Madel off the police force by charging him with extortion. They repeated their story to the editors of a crusading community newspaper, who published it under the heading: "Police Shakedown Tavern Owner." I filed a libel action against the Marshalls, the newspaper and its editors—this before *The New York Times vs. Sullivan* case and its progeny, which limited recovery in libel actions brought by public officials and public figures or where public issues are involved. In a bench trial, Judge William V. Daly found that Marshall's testimony was "contradictory, incredible and unworthy of belief" and that he "was activated by actual malice." The court, therefore, assessed damages against him. As to the editors and their publication, Judge Daly found that since Madel "is a policeman and as such is a public official, although of the lowest rank and least amount of responsibility," recovery would not be had against them, because actual malice was not proved.

One could multiply the details of the heartbreak endured by law-enforcement officers. Perhaps their reactions to the public are simply reflexes. At any rate, I have been for and against the police in many situations. I am both sympathetic and critical. I think conditions can be improved if a real effort is made. The law and order excesses are not the answer; they are, if anything, the causes of the trouble.

fourteen

Writing a New Constitution for Illinois

At 1:00 A.M. one day in June, 1969, my telephone rang. Alderman Seymour Simon was on the line. Seymour was an old friend, a man of great intelligence and tremendous energy. He had once been President of the Cook County Board and was on the way to becoming either governor of Illinois or mayor of Chicago, when, suddenly, he found himself denied renomination. Since then, with at least part of his energies, he has thought of what he could do to make life unpleasant for the Democratic power structure which had betrayed him. He became a part-time insurgent.

What was it now?

"Elmer," he said, peremptorily, "you must become a candidate for delegate to the Constitutional Convention."

"Why?" I asked.

He answered: "Both parties have nominated such incompetents in this district that it is a disgrace."

Mamie advised me not to run. I told her of my dread that, in a period of distorted preoccupation with law and order, the Bill of Rights was likely to be weakened by a constitutional convention. "I ought to be around," I said, "to see to it that our present Bill of Rights, a good one, is preserved."

A few days after his first call, Seymour telephoned again. He pressed me for an answer. "How do I know," I asked, "if there will be support for me? Where will the funds come for my campaign if I should choose to run?" Seymour said that he would raise whatever was required and he would demonstrate that there was an insistent demand that I be a candidate by calling a meeting of leading citizens at a home in the ward. "The best and most influential people will persuade you that you ought to run."

That Sunday, just a few days before the filing deadline, I was in my home with my family. We were about to have dinner. It was raining rather hard. I commented, "I don't think many people are out getting signatures for my nominating petitions in this weather." At that moment, our doorbell rang and Mamie answered it. There was a young man in the company of a young woman. They had several filled-in petitions in their hands, one of two of them spotted with rain drops. The young man was a medical student named Marc Slutsky; the young woman was his date. Mamie was her usual enthusiastic self. "You must have dinner with us," she said to the two young people, whom we did not know. All through the dinner, we talked about politics. Marc had been very active in the inspiring Eugene McCarthy campaign and was deeply committed to playing a role in public affairs. He was going to be a doctor, perhaps practicing forensic medicine, but he was not going to forego his duties as a citizen. For a young man, he had amazing knowledge and dedication. He seemed to know everyone in independent and liberal politics in Chicago. By the time dinner was over, Marc had committed himself to running any office that might be set up for me. Thus I had at least one worker, in addition to those that might be produced by Simon.

Early in the campaign I learned what too many candidates for public office have to contend with—the great need for funds, in order to pay for a staff, literature, telephones, all of the essentials for winning support. It is degrading, depressing, and dangerous; it accounts for some who are, in a sense, bought and paid for. I would not have run myself if I had not been assured by Alderman Simon that he would see to it that I had sufficient money. He did raise a considerable amount, but not all that was required if there was to be a chance for success. Unlike other candidates, I did not have any paid staff (except for one secretary whose compensation was provided through Simon). My total outlay, I understand, was considerably less than that of any other independent candidate in the city. But I had to swallow my intense dislike of personal fund appeals and send out letters of solicitation. This brought in the bulk of the money that was required in my campaign.

Ethnic, racial, and religious considerations are much too important in American politics, even in the election of delegates to a constitutional convention. My district had very few non-Caucasians. With my record of struggling for the rights of minority groups, this was a disadvantage. The district had many Jews, especially in my immediate area of residence, and this was helpful. My name was familiar to my co-religionists for a variety of reasons, some of them quite good. When I walked up and down the major thoroughfares, I was quickly recognized and warmly greeted. One of our major opponents was John Geocaris, a member of one of the better-known Greek families of the city. "Greektown" had moved from the old Halsted and Blue Island area to my district. There were many establishments and thousands of persons that proclaimed their Greek ties. Geocaris' own cousin, State Senator James Loukas, was in my corner and strongly opposing him, because Loukas felt that Geocaris had betrayed him in a recent bitter political contest. Loukas and his charming wife, Helen, helped give me acceptance among the Greeks. I like to think that a stronger factor in my Greek support came through my dear friend, Harry Mark Petrakis, a very wonderful writer and the son of a renowned Greek Orthodox priest. Harry wrote to the Greek press in my support; my literature showed pictures of us standing side by side. He walked through the streets with me.

My wife, Mamie, played a unique role in the campaign and later at the convention. A public school teacher for more than thirty-two years, she had spent the last of those years at the Boone School in our ward. There she had been an inspired harnesser of the energies of the brighter fourth-grade students. I used to be deeply interested and often amused when Mamie would tell me of these students. With her wonderful power of mimicry, many of the boys and girls were familiar to me by name, voice, and manner. Now and then we would have some of them over to our home.

When I got into the race, I found that one of my great reservoirs of strength was derived from these students, many of whom were now in high school and some in college. They rallied around Mamie and me with tremendous enthusiasm.

Mamie worked like a legion during the campaign, never sparing herself. She distributed literature, hung posters, worked precincts, chauffeured me and countless others. It was difficult to say who was more energetic, Mamie or me. During the early part of the campaign, Mamie was sometimes discouraged and tired, but as we got past the primary and well into the pre-election period she was tireless. I sometimes found it necessary to rest, but she never did. My two campaign managers, Marc Slutsky and later Morris Dyner, leaned upon her; so did everyone else. She fed, pampered, and encouraged all of us.

Of course, to jump ahead of the story, Mamie came down to Springfield in the early days of the convention, but she had to miss some sessions due to her school commitments. She soon decided that there was nothing more important than being with me in Springfield, which can be a very lonely city, even when one is surrounded by multitudes. She resigned as a school teacher and spent the rest of the nine months of the convention with me. At the end, she was the only nonmember to receive recognition by the delegates and staff. She was named as the Jewish Mother of the convention. One delegate, having domestic difficulties, survived only through daily counseling by Mamie. Others had their socks laundered by her. She sewed on buttons. She did big and little chores for all, regardless of party labels. She attended more sessions than some of the delegates. Up front in the visitor's gallery, the delegates used to enjoy observing her crocheting and listening. She distributed literature to visitors and explained to them what was going on. The guards told me that their work was done for them by my wife. She absorbed the pros and cons of all of the controversies and did not always agree with me. While I was fighting on the floor for a continuation of the system of cumulative voting for the lower house of the legislature, she told me that she was persuaded that single-member districts were better. Delegates and their spouses confided in her. She was part of the fun and serious work every day. I don't think that I will soon forget the sight of Jeanette Mullen, one of the delegates, and Mamie skipping down the streets at night while mere males had difficulty in keeping up with them. Her signature does not appear, like mine, at the end of the new Constitution, but it is written large, if invisibly, in the pages of the document.

Finally, primary day, September 23, 1969, arrived, and, before too many hours of the evening had gone by, the results were known. I was fourth and thus survived for the final election.

I learned later that my dearest friends, my family, and observers generally felt very sorry for me. I had made a good showing, but it was utterly unlikely that I would prevail in the end. Fortunately, I did not hear their rumblings and I was surprisingly calm and confident about the ultimate result. I was shaken a bit when Marc Slutsky, my young manager, told me, in no uncertain terms, that if I were to have any chance of prevailing, we would have to raise some thousands of dollars immediately. I replied in an almost icy tone: "Marc, I am not going to raise any such amount of money and we are going to win." Every now and then I have certainty about a result, whether in a law case or in some other endeavor, and almost never is the result other than anticipated by me. I have a kind of inner appraisal machine that seems to function better than public opinion polls.

Around this stage of the campaign, one of my friendly opponents, Jack DeMichaels, had said to me, in his usual cocksure manner: "Elmer, you have done pretty well, but you are not going to win because John Geocaris and I are going to increase the number of our votes by 50 percent." He then added, "You have all of the endorsements and we have the precinct captains." In the end, DeMichaels was accurate in his projection of the 50 percent increase in the votes cast for himself and Geocaris, but Ronald Smith and I had about 175 percent increase in our votes.

Throughout the weeks between the primary and the election, Ron and I worked very closely and we schooled our associates to show a spirit of collaboration. I impressed upon those who were enthusiastically pro-Gertz, but not so staunchly for Smith, that if Smith went down I would go down, as well. "Of course, I don't mind having more votes than Smith, but he must have more than the two Democratic candidates," I said.

Shortly after the campaign was over, the ward lines of Chicago were redrawn because of the "one man–one vote" requirement. This was the cause of much fancy pencil work by the political leaders, who wanted to retain circles of influence while fulfilling the constitutional requirements of equal population, compactness, and contiguity. When the tentative ward lines first became known, I found myself in Simon's 40th ward, rather than the 50th ward, in which I had resided for twenty years. Seymour telephoned me—one of his customary late-hour calls. Would I serve on the executive committee of the ward (a small group of six, as I recall)? In gratitude for what he had done for me and because I thought it would be an interesting experience, at least initially, I said that I would serve. This time I had no hesitancy. A few days later, the ward lines were changed again, and I was back in my old ward, and on no executive committee.

At one point in the campaign, I was told that much would depend upon the impression I made upon the ladies of St. Hilary's Roman Catholic Parish. I met with a large group of the ladies and their husbands in a home in the area. I was asked the usual questions about support for parochial schools out of public funds. I expressed my sympathy for the problems of Catholic parents, but declared that I could not constitutionally support parochiaid and I explained my viewpoint as carefully as I could, concealing nothing for the sake of placating my Catholic audience. In the end, I was applauded loudly, and an official of a large downtown bank spoke enthusiastically in my favor. When the votes were counted, it was clear that I had won in this area. My integrity and candor apparently cost me few votes.

Charles Nicodemus, political editor of the *Chicago Daily News,* summed up the story of the Gertz-Smith victory under the title, "How Daley Lost—On Party Turf." He began his double-column article by declaring, "Hell hath not many furies like Seymour Simon scorned," and he recited the well-known details of how Simon had once been ousted from the political mountain tops by a cabal and had been sniping at Daley since then. ". . . The stunning victory by Gertz and his running mate, independent Ron Smith," he wrote, "has given fresh encouragement to independents city wide, who have been energized by the demonstration that the machine can be beaten, even on strong Democratic organization turf." He predicted that the Daley organization would be further bedeviled by ambitious, talented independents, which would cause the organization to put up better candidates. Nicodemus told of how I had finished fourth in the primary, with the regular Democratic "spear-carriers" finishing one and two. Then, he said, "Gertz finished on top, after a model campaign that is likely to be widely imitated, where possible, in other independent efforts." "Thanks to . . . the elderly Gertz's strong ability to attract youngsters by the flock, City Hall was vanquished."

The nine delegates known as independents met several times between our election and the convention recess following the election of Samuel W. Witwer as president of the convention. Our aim was to discuss means of exerting influence at the convention, initially wth respect to the selection of committee chairmen and vice chairmen and, ultimately, as to our roles in the drafting of a supportable new constitution. In some respects, it was a trying experience for me, and, later, when we continued to meet during the course of the convention, it became more frustrating. I did not know all of my independent colleagues prior to our sharing the experience of confounding the party organizations.

I was the oldest in the group and, perhaps for that reason, sometimes on the defensive. I remember the assurance with which the group discussed possible committee chairmanships. No, I would not be chairman of the Bill of Rights Committee, Dawn Netch said, seconded by others. The Democrats would see to it that someone like Malcolm Kamin would be named, because of the family reputation for liberalism and Malcolm's willingness to be a faithful part of the regular Democratic organization. On the conversation went, often to my annoyance. No, it would not be this; yes, it would be that. Then I spoke out: "The only ones in our group having a chance to be selected for high committee posts by Witwer are Peter Tomei, Dawn Netch and myself." I told why. At that time I did not know Witwer. I had had my first friendly conversations with him during the early days of the convention, really during the pre-session orientation. I had learned from his friend and mine, Louis Ancel, that he had been very happy to hear the news, on election night, that I had won. I talked with Ancel about the possibility of my becoming chairman of the Bill of Rights Committee, the sole assignment to which I aspired. Ancel was the only one with whom I talked, other than the group of independents. He said that no one was better qualified than I for the post, and he would tell Witwer so. I have no doubt that my ultimate appointment came through this means, reinforced by the other inquiries that Witwer made in the black community and elsewhere. There were counter-influences, too. The *Chicago Tribune* let its opposition be known.

In the end, either in committee or on the floor of the convention, we came up, despite my misgivings, with an almost completely satisfactory Preamble and Bill of Rights. We set the goal in the Preamble: the elimination of poverty and inequality; legal, social and economic justice; and opportunity for the fullest development of the individual. Thomas Kelleghan squealed that this was socialism and revolution, but the majority thought it inspiring. We added equal protection of the laws to the due-process section. We provided for security against unreasonable invasions of privacy and interceptions of communications by eavesdropping devices or other means. We declared that all criminal penalties were to be determined, not only according to the seriousness of the offense, but with the objective of restoring the offender to useful citizenship. We mandated the right to a remedy and justice for all injuries and wrongs. Before the United States Supreme Court ruled in that area, we greatly eased the consequences of being fined in criminal cases. We added far-reaching self-enforcing provisions against discrimination in employment and property, far beyond anything in any State constitution.

Many declared that we had written the very best Bill of Rights. Senator Charles H. Percy proclaimed that opinion in the *Congressional Record,* and others, including convention President Witwer, were equally enthusiastic. Some who opposed the new charter as a whole were enthusiastic about what we had done in our area.

I regard the experience as the most rewarding of my life. If you are interested in the what, why, and how details, you may want to read my book *For the First Hours of Tomorrow: The New Illinois Bill of Rights.*[1]

---

[1] *For the First Hours of Tomorrow: The New Illinois Bill of Rights,* University of Illinois Press, 1972.

Until I saw our committee work-product through the convention on first reading, I was determined to act with caution and circumspection on the floor when other articles of the constitution were debated. This policy bore dividends. It created good will for myself and the committee, where earlier we were terrible and raucous examples for all to observe. Frank Cicero said that our committee attracted more attention than the State Capitol and the Lincoln Tomb, only a slight overstatement. Delegates flocked to view Father Lawlor's fetus in a bottle on his desk, his exhibit against abortion. A pile of thick sticks and clubs were placed near our meeting place, with the legend: "Debate material for Bill of Rights Committee." When one delegate was married, a shotgun was placed on his desk, with the words: "Gift from the Bill of Rights Committee." Some wondered if we would ever come through with anything worth considering. Then we confounded the convention and ourselves with superlative results, still talked about when the delegates gather.

I learned from the example of others. A poll taken near the start of the convention indicated that one delegate, more than anyone else, commanded the respect of his fellows for leadership qualities. By the end of the convention, as his committee floundered, no one any longer thought of him as a leader. Another committee chairman was so busy creating acrimony on the floor that all residue of good will vanished.

The delegates generally were of a high order of intelligence and dedication, far superior to most legislators. Close attachments were formed, regardless of political labels. The fifteen women were an attractive group, not merely in appearance, but more in their determination to achieve results. The fifteen blacks, largely dominated by the Daley organization, did not achieve their full potential, although several were outstanding. The younger delegates showed qualities that indicated that they were going to play substantial roles in government.

The constitution we wrote was not perfect; that would have been a sure recipe for failure. It was the result of realistic compromises between men and women who wanted to succeed, if the price was not too high. Often it appeared that some in the convention wanted us to toss aside all of our hard work and acknowledge failure.

Paul Elward was a fascinating example of the Chicago Democratic contingent. No one worked harder than he, day and night, and he did not smoke, drink, or philander. I once remarked that that was Paul's difficulty, and, with rare humor, he laughed. One day he would come up to me, happily—I had spoken or voted as he wished—and say, "You can join our caucus." The next day, angered over something I had said, he would snap: "You have insulted me!" On at least one occasion, we were co-sponsors of an amendment that did not pass.

I tried not to be dogmatic in my independence. Out of compassion, I refused to vote with the Republicans and independents to expel a young Democrat who had probably violated the electoral statute in one or more respects, reasoning that if I could battle for the life of a murderer I could do no less for another fallible human being. Thomas McCracken, a Democratic leader, had tears in his eyes when he thanked me. Once or twice I was asked by Thomas Lyons, the spokesman for the Democrats, to take the floor for them because my views on revenue and local government happened to conform to theirs. Without sacrificing my principles, I was able to maintain the respect of my opponents. By the end of the convention, I was welcomed by all camps. Republicans wanted me to be a judicial candidate on their ticket.

The convention was rather evenly split between Republicans and Democrats, with the Cook County Democrats well organized and the Downstate Republicans owing allegiance to no one. We in the independent ranks were Democrats unafraid of the party dictators. We could exert influence only as long as the professionals in both parties did not join forces against us. We soon found that we could win recruits, not among the Cook County regular Democrats, but from the Downstate Democrats, free and enlightened souls like those who would remember that they were in Springfield to perform creative work, and not to act as party hacks. It was from the Republican ranks, regardless of geography, that we could garner other needed votes in good government situations. Thus, as the convention neared its end, we were the recognized leaders of a coalition that could win on some basic issues. I truly believe that the convention was saved because of us. Despite the partisans, it produced a document worth voting for. By the time of the referendum, the regular Democrats felt that they had to accept what we had brought forth; the home rule and revenue provisions were enough to make the charter salable; those things to which they were opposed, like merit-judicial selection and a single-member district system for legislative elections, were in separate submissions, and not in the main body of the proposed constitution. They could vote against some of the separate submissions while voting for the package.

The black delegates were a great disappointment to me, because I expected too much of them. The difficulty was that they had placed all of their eggs in the Democratic basket and, except for Leonard Foster, who was temperamental and erratic, and, of course, Albert Raby, they were unwilling to go along with the independents or others who, in the long run, were likely to be more helpful to them than the regular Democratic organization. Some of them recognized this.

Once I took the train back to Chicago with one of the black delegates and we had a long and intimate conversation. At the beginning I was assured by him of the virtues of the regular Democrats and that it was certainly in the best interests of the blacks to go along with them. I argued the matter in as reasonable and unemotional a manner as I could muster, but, whatever I said, there was a reply to it. Then, suddenly, my friend turned to me and said with a smile: "Elmer, you know I am a humbug. I agree with you completely, but this is not the time to say so publicly. One day we will be working together on the issues and the candidates." I could not help admiring this sudden burst of candor. Somewhat later this black delegate was double-crossed by the regular organization. A political plum that was promised to him was given to another. He ran nonetheless and was soundly trounced. I have not since discussed the racial aspects of politics with him.

On the matter of judicial selection, all of the black delegates, excepting Foster and Raby, were deeply committed to the elective system because of their fear that any method of merit selection would make it difficult for minority groups to be adequately represented on the bench. They were almost beyond the reach of reason on this.

I can illustrate how some of the blacks took the matter of judicial selection by my relations with Odas Nicholson, the secretary of the convention and a very brilliant and hard-working woman. On the first day of the convention, she had said: "Mr. Gertz, you don't know me, but as a young woman I was Mr. Dickerson's secretary. [Earl Dickerson was one of the outstanding leaders of the black community with whom I had years of joint effort in the period when white advocates of nondiscrimination were much rarer than today.] I admire you more than anyone at the convention." Yet, before the debate on judicial selection was at an end, Miss Nicholson and I engaged in very sharp and angry talk with each other. Later our good relations were restored, but it took very careful effort on my part to heal the breach. Miss Nicholson was that member of the judicial committee who fought most unyieldingly for the views of the Democratic organization on judicial selection. But she and virtually all of the other blacks deserted the organization Democrats on the issues of capital punishment and abortion.

A constitutional convention, I found, is like a post-graduate course in political science and the law. The defect of many State charters is that they are really statutory codes, rather than general guidelines. Cluttered up with detail, they soon become obsolete and unworkable. It was our task to cut from the 1870 constitution everything that did not properly belong in a constitution. We did throw out more than 4000 words. It would have been better if we could have excised more. For example, I believed with Dawn Netch that the best revenue article would be one which simply declared, in one generalized sentence, that the legislature has the right to raise revenue. Such an article would have caused the new charter to go down to inevitable defeat. We had to spell out limitations on the income tax, on the personal property tax, and in other areas, in order to make the document palatable.

There were other areas in which we had to question ourselves. Should a constitution have limitations upon corporations in general and banks in particular, as did the 1870 constitution? Most of us felt that these were legislative matters, rather than constitutional. We were able to chip away here and there, but not entirely. Some items of a statutory nature remained in the document, but fewer than in the 1870 constitution and fewer than in most State charters.

Ideally, a constitution should be succinct, simply written, a general guide to government. We wanted to shorten the ballot by making fewer elective offices constitutionally necessary. Only to a very limited degree did we succeed in this area. But we did provide for municipal home rule on a wide scale. We created a finance article that might eliminate the worst defects in governmental spending. We created an electoral board that could make the voting process fairer, more uniform, and less corrupt. We provided for a State board of education. We declared a right to a healthful environment. I suppose I could list fifty or more innovations and improvements, large and small.

From the viewpoint of old-line politicians, the most important matter before the convention was the manner in which judges would be chosen, whether by election in the first instance and retention votes thereafter, or by some form of merit selection. In a time when ordinary patronage jobs are not as important as they once were, it is still vital to political organizations to have some rewards for those who do work in the wards. Many, if not most, of these people are lawyers, whose principal aim in life and their reason for hard work in politics is the possibility of becoming judges. In a city like Chicago, there are no real elections for judges, in the sense of a choice being presented to the voters. The political organizations select, from among the faithful, the most deserving in a political sense, and they are presented to the voters, who accept their qualifications on faith, since they have no real opportunity to vote for anyone else. This has resulted in a judiciary which many people regard as incompetent, inefficient, lacking judicial temperament and skill, and possibly corrupt. The feeling among leaders of the bar, the press, and informed citizens has been that, in order to elevate judicial standards, it will be necessary that judges be selected on the basis of competence, rather than political allegiance. There was division on the judiciary committee and throughout the convention as to which method of choice would be placed in the new constitution. Some seemed to feel that all of the judges should be screened through a selection commission, chosen in some fair manner. Others felt that perhaps Appellate and Supreme Court justices might be selected in that manner. Now one group, now the other, was dominant on the judiciary committee and in the convention.

A closely divided committee finally recommended merit selection, and was resisted vigorously by the minority, led by several Daley stalwarts. On so-called first reading, a form of merit selection won, with the choice given to the voters in a separate submission to retain elections. On second reading, those who wanted the election of judges prevailed, and the alternative of merit selection was placed in a separate submission. Governor Ogilvie was with us in favoring merit selection, but he did not control the Republican delegates in the manner that Mayor Daley controlled almost all of the Chicago contingent. Those of us who were pledged to secure a better method of judicial selection were troubled. Would we be able to do anything on third and final reading, so that at the very least we would give a choice to those who voted on the new constitution?

Another basic issue dividing the convention was the manner in which members of the House of Representatives of the General Assembly would be chosen. Illinois had a unique system of cumulative voting, the legacy of the old Czar of the *Tribune,*

Joseph Medill. It provided for the election of three representatives from each district. One could give all three of one's votes to one of the candidates, or one and a half votes to two of them, or one vote to each of the three candidates. Thus, minority groups, through the proper use of cumulative voting, could select a certain number of representatives. It meant that Democrats and Republicans would agree as to whether there would be two candidates or one from the respective parties in each district. The result would not be arbitrary. It would depend upon the relative voting strength. This would not harm independents, because in the primary they could concentrate on one candidate in the district and, by the bullet vote (three for one candidate), stand an excellent chance of his being nominated.

There were many people at the convention, particularly downstaters and one or two of the Chicago Democrats, who felt that it was much better to have single-member districts, which would necessarily be smaller in size, and thus the voters would get acquainted with their one representative, instead of their interest being diffused by the three representatives selected from each larger district.

Many of us, including myself, felt that, despite any failings, the system then in effect was better than the single-member system. Many of those who favored the kind of merit selection of judges that we wanted were at the same time in favor of single-member districts. Thus, on the first and second readings, there was a flip-flop on the method of election, and the matter would not be decided finally until the third and last reading.

It appeared to our group that the only hope for a good result was a package deal whereby in the body of the proposed constitution the method of determining representatives and judges would not be included; that, instead, the voters would be given a choice, by separate submissions, as to what they preferred in each instance. This sort of arrangement would create a firm alliance between good government people with strong differences of opinion.

One Friday night toward the end of the convention, a group of us independents and some others who could be styled leaders of the better elements in the convention, had dinner together. We were joined by two or three of the officials of the Illinois League of Women Voters and Mary Lee Leahy's husband, Andy. Elbert Smith voiced the feeling of several of those present when he said, sadly: "This convention has some of the finest men and women I have ever known—intelligent, dedicated, determined. Yet we are going to present a new constitution scarcely superior to the old one. I, for one, cannot say with assurance that it is worth supporting." We discussed the matter back and forth. I suspect that most of those present were in agreement with Elbert. As is often the case, I was somewhat more optimistic.

The next night the same group of us had dinner together. This time Elbert spoke with great enthusiasm: "We now have a constitution worth supporting. We can fight for it."

What had happened in the intervening twenty-four hours to cause such a shift in the thinking of Vice President Smith?

Early Saturday morning, we arrived early at the convention, and were all in our places when the president opened the deliberations. The Democratic leadership, except for Paul Elward, were not there. Apparently, the night's festivities had gotten them down. They had won victories the previous days that caused them to lower their guard. This morning, we had the votes to bring about the kind of arrangement that would save the situation, in our estimation. Where election of judges was, by the last vote, in the body of the constitution, we now placed the choice of election or merit selection on the outside in separate submission, so that we could fight for our viewpoint in the open forum of the ballot. And where there had been contention as to the manner of selecting representatives in the General Assembly, we now had the two choices set up for separate submission to the voters. When, later in the day, the Democratic stalwarts and their allies arrived at the convention, they tried to regain the advantages that they had lost. They literally ranted and shouted and tried every kind of maneuvering, all in vain. We had finally overcome them, and we remained in control. The combination of independents, Republicans, and downstate Democrats had, in our judgment, rescued the situation, and Elbert Smith and all of us could rejoice.

The Democrats never gave up until the very end of the convention. I remember that, on the last working day before the ceremonial closing, they tried to prolong the session. Since I felt that there was nothing to gain by further debate and the risk of a change in positions, I moved for adjournment, without consulting my colleagues. The Daley Democrats insisted upon a roll call, an extraordinary turn on a motion for adjournment. I resisted efforts to delay the vote. The roll call was the most exciting event of this last day, and we won. We now adjourned until the following day when everything would be wrapped up formally.

After the convention was adjourned, the *Chicago Daily News* published a lengthy editorial in which it named a relatively small number of delegates as those most responsible for the success of the convention. In this small number, seven (myself included) of the nine individuals in our independent group were named, and the other two might well have been named. This was confirmation of our potency.

Difficult as it is to write a constitution with the multiplicity of modern-age problems that are largely without solution, it is infinitely more difficult to persuade the voters to adopt any constitution that is offered to them. The history of such submissions in recent years is that, almost without exception, they are defeated, sometimes overwhelmingly. The last Illinois constitution that was offered to the people of the state fifty years ago was defeated by a fantastically high percentage. The defeats have come where excellent documents have been tendered. Sometimes the cause is only one or two bad articles, as when in New York the framers of the new constitution changed the provisions which forbade public aid to parochial schools. Now and then a constitution has been adopted by a very narrow vote. In one of the larger middle-western states, only 5000 votes determined the favorable result.

We had a formidable task before us in view of the fact that large segments of organized labor were on record in opposition to the new constitution. They had opposed calling the convention, in the first instance. At the same time, there were many people influenced by extreme reactionaries, largely led by the John Birch Society, which opposed the document because they regarded it as radical.

There were others who feared the revenue article, and it did not matter to them that any revenue article presents dangers. Some people felt that, because of a decision handed down by the State Supreme Court during the period that we were in session, there was not the same need as earlier for a new revenue article.

The piling up of opposition to this segment or that could add up to a majority against the document. But we won.

There is now in print a series of seven huge books, thousands of pages in length—the complete, and I mean complete, transcript of the proceedings of the Sixth Illinois Constitutional Convention, every word of what every person said on the floor of the convention—wise words, witty words, foolish words. This work will be consulted as long as the 1970 constitution remains in effect, for the light it will shed on passages in the new constitution. What did we mean by this section or that? Lawyers and judges and legislative bodies will be governed in their thinking and action by what we said, deliberately or carelessly. For me the work will have a very special value. As I peruse it, I will have to ask myself again if the many months and great energies we devoted to running for election as delegates to the convention, attending its sessions, campaigning for the adoption of the constitution were worthwhile. As I have said, this was the great experience of my mature life. But did it mean as much for the people of the State whom we purported to serve? Again, I think the answer is in the affirmative; but to be sure, what we produced will have to be tested by time and experience, in a generation other than mine.

fifteen

Nathan Leopold—After Stateville

The first half of my book, *A Handful of Clients*, deals with Nathan Leopold. Certainly, the Leopold case in all of its ramifications was the most interesting and significant in my professional career. In a sense, it gave additional meaning to my life. As I said in my book, I encountered many people up to the time of publication—strangers even—who would stop me in the street and ask, "How is your client getting along?" They seemed to assume that, in what was then thirty-four years of legal practice, I had had one client, Nathan Leopold. Additional years have gone by since then, and I have been involved in many matters of moment, but the *Leopold* case is still the one with which I am most closely associated in the popular mind and among my colleagues. I do not resent or regret this. After all, Clarence Darrow, who lived for a long while and had many celebrated courtroom battles, is still primarily associated with the *Leopold-Loeb* case. It is something to be a postscript, or even a footnote, to the life of the legendary Darrow.

I have told of the letter that was given to me by Leopold on the very day of the parole hearing in 1958. It captures the heart of his case and personality perfectly. With his letter, Nathan gave me the letters, long treasured by him, that he had received from Darrow. I still feel deep emotion as I reread Nathan's words, now that he is gone:

> I have long had in mind to ask you to accept these Darrow letters [the only ones that he had ever received from the great lawyer]. . . . It seems particularly fitting to give them to you now. For, while I am writing this on the 2nd, you will be handed the envelope containing them on the afternoon of February 5, just after you have finished pleading my case before the Parole Board.
> There are so many reasons why you are the one person in the world who should have these letters . . .
> These are externals. But there are so many fundamentals in which you and Mr. Darrow are kin. In your basic kindliness, in your deep understanding and charity, in your genuine sympathy for and love of your fellow man. Perhaps most strikingly in the enthusiasm you and Mr. Darrow share in espousing the cause of the underdog . . .
> There is, of course, a far more personal reason why I am anxious that you should have these letters. For if this hearing turns out as we hope it will, you will have succeeded in the seemingly impossible task of bringing Mr. Darrow's efforts of 30 years ago to the only conclusions which can give them significance. Just after Judge Caverly handed down his decision that September day in 1924, I turned to Mr. Darrow and told him that I didn't know whether to thank him or to forgive him for saving my life. I still don't know, Elmer.
> For up to now it hasn't been a life he saved, in contradistinction to an existence. It is you who, if we are successful, will have given me back my life. It is you who will have given meaning to what Mr. Darrow did so many years ago.
> For if you succeed, I may still have the opportunity of justifying my existence—of making of it a life.
> Succeed or not, the effort you have put forth has been superb. How very fortunate I am in one lifetime to have known and been defended by Mr. Darrow and by you.

There is a sort of legend that, as a young man, I was associated with Clarence Darrow in the original trial of Richard Loeb and

Nathan Leopold in 1924, and that, thereafter, I strove repeatedly to get Leopold out of prison, and finally succeeded in 1958. While I knew Darrow in 1924, I had not yet entered law school, and I did not become involved in any way in Leopold's life until 1952. Before that, there had been a slight reduction of Leopold's sentence because of his being a part of the wartime malaria experimentation at Stateville, making him eligible for parole consideration, for the first time, in 1952.

Initially, I represented him in connection with his book, corresponding and meeting with the editor and attorneys for Doubleday. At that time, another lawyer had filed a petition for executive clemency in Leopold's behalf. Leopold expected this proceeding to fail. When it appeared that it might succeed, he asked me to step into the matter. As gracefully as possible, I succeeded Varian B. Adams in the summer of 1957. Although we were led to believe that Governor Stratton might commute the sentence, and at least one newspaper proclaimed it, he concluded that another application for parole was the proper method of terminal rehabilitation, despite the fact that, in turning down parole in 1953, the Governor's Board had given Leopold a "set" of twelve years, making him ineligible even to apply for parole until 1965. Leopold had no hope that a new application, or rather, a petition for rehearing, would be entertained. I was far more optimistic about the matter than he. We filed a veritable book of thousands of words—and a rehearing was granted, but the actual hearing was set for months later, in February, 1958.

We put in an enormous amount of preparation, as if the destiny of the race, and not merely one man's freedom, depended upon our efforts. We had an extraordinary group of witnesses: Carl Sandburg, then at the height of his fame; Ralph Newman, a close friend of Leopold's oldest brother; Father Eligius Weir, who had known Loeb and Leopold from the beginnings of their imprisonment; Dr. Marvin Sukov, a psychiatrist who had known Leopold at the prison; Helen Williams, who had first counseled him in connection with the prison correspondence school; John Bartlow Martin, the popular writer on penology; Dr. John Pick, who effected rehabilitations through plastic surgery; and others. Despite the high quality of the other witnesses and the mountainous mass of documentary material we introduced—six or seven volumes of it—Leopold was his own best witness. At the hearing years previously, Leopold had been a very bad witness. He could not account for the commission of the crime to anyone's satisfaction. We, therefore, concentrated on developing his ability to persuade the Board; for we knew that another failure on his part could be fatal. He might die before he had another chance. Those who read the chapter entitled "A Target for Five Men" in my book *A Handful of Clients* will get a vivid picture of the grilling to which Leopold was subjected and how well he handled himself. He showed that his criminal conduct was probably induced by the disparity between his intellectual and emotional ages. As we phrased it, he was an intelligent savage.

We were able to convince the Board to permit the five-year period of supervision to be served in Puerto Rico, instead of Illinois or elsewhere in continental United States, where the publicity would have been unendurable. The Church of the Brethren, under the inspired leadership of Dr. W. Harold Row, one of the few authentic saints I have ever known, sponsored Leopold's parole by giving him a job as a medical technician at its hospital at Castañer in the heart of Puerto Rico. He was to receive room and board and $10.00 each month. His success on parole was as great as his success in prison. Just as his offense was "the crime of the century," his efforts in Joliet and Stateville and later in Puerto Rico resulted in the rehabilitation of the century.

Three times I went to Puerto Rico during Leopold's stay there, and each time I got a different sort of view of him. The first time was in 1958, within weeks of his release from prison. My wife, Ceretta, had died only a month and a day after the release and, of course, I was in a doleful state. My children insisted that I had to go there to recover from the blow. I could not help dwelling on the fact that this was the trip that Ceretta was supposed to have taken with me, and had dreaded. While I was with people, and particularly Leopold, I was deeply interested; alone, I brooded. Fortunately, I was with Leopold most of the time. I saw him in his surroundings at the Brethren General Hospital in Castaner and I talked with everyone who knew him. They were delighted with his skill and devotion. The chairman of the Puerto Rican Parole Board, Judge Umpierre, assured me that he really did not belong on parole; that he was completely fit for freedom. Leopold was less secure, privately, than he publicly professed. He was in dread of what might happen if he stumbled in his work. He said to me: "I am in deadly fear that I might hurt some child by my ineptitude. I could not live through that." He was worried, too, because he was in charge of the drugs and narcotics: "What if somebody steals some narcotics and I am blamed?"

A year later, I visited him again, this time with my new bride, Mamie. I was a totally different person and so was he. He lacked the sense of personal insecurity that he had felt the previous year. He was confident of what he could do, and somewhat critical of others. He was annoyed by the parole restrictions still placed on him. What is freedom if one cannot travel without permission to the neighboring Virgin Islands, cannot marry without permission, cannot be out late, or drink, or own an automobile? I promised that I would continue my efforts to relieve him of all these burdens.

He was the best host imaginable. He extended himself to make our visit a happy one. He and Jeanne Hall, one of his American visitors, arranged a great feast for us, a gourmet's delight in every way. He wandered with Mamie and me through the *jibaro* country and elsewhere, pointing out people he knew, birds, vegetation, bits of lore. It was a delightful experience for all of us.

Some months later I went to Puerto Rico with Harold Gordon in connection with Leopold's deposition, taken by our opponents in the *Compulsion* case. We stayed at Leopold's apartment and saw him in his role as host and housekeeper. He had a domestic, named Amerika, do the heavier work, but he did the cooking and the lighter work fairly competently. Most of our meals we had at restaurants or at the apartment of Trudi Garcia de Quevedo, his future wife. There was one jarring note almost immediately—on the wall of Leopold's bedroom, there were two pictures almost side by side, mine and Richard Loeb's. (I was comforted somewhat later when Leonard Lyons, the columnist, reported in an article in the *Saturday Evening Post,* after Leopold's marriage, that in the foyer of their apartment my picture was alongside of Clarence Darrow's. The Loeb picture was not mentioned.) Even more jarring was Leopold's impatience and temper. Gracious most of the time, when angered for however little reason, he could be sharp indeed in response, even toward me. He seemed to have an almost feverish desire to taste everything in life, whether good or bad; excess seemed to be his norm at times.

Upon my return to Chicago, I renewed my efforts to get him off parole, as the restraints galled him so very much. He was given permission to marry Trudi. He had said that he would not marry her until he was truly a free man, but his mind was changed. The two, so different in many ways, remained married to the end of his life.

After five years, he was finally released from parole and restored to his full civil rights. Governor Kerner wrote to me: "By his conduct to date, Nathan Leopold has set an example of rehabilitation and service. I hope that Mr. Leopold's future life as a free citizen will continue to justify the parole system and be an encouragement to others who are presently serving in our prisons." Later, when Kerner was interviewed after he resigned as governor, he said that the results of two criminal cases gave him the greatest joy—the restoration of Leopold and the commutation of Paul Crump's death sentence. I reminded the governor that Leopold's success proved the folly of capital punishment.

The principal result, in a way, of Leopold's being released from legal restraints was that he became a much-traveled individual, going to all of the places of the world that he dreamed about during his more than thirty-four years in prison and five more on parole. He went to Europe two or three times, to Latin America, to the South Pacific, and around the world, as well as on many trips to the States. He had an almost uncontrollable urge to be up and around, even when his diabetes made walking painful to him. At first Trudi would accompany him on these trips, but she could not stand the pace, and he would go alone. Wherever he went, I heard from him, in glowing terms. He constantly urged me to emulate him in this ceaseless journeying back and forth. He dared to do all sorts of venturesome things. When he was in Singapore, a journalist mentioned that he was going to Saigon in the midst of the carnage of Vietnam. Without a moment's hesitation, he accompanied the journalist and saw our involvement at first hand.

He went to the various Church of the Brethren conferences in different parts of the nation and to meetings abroad. He was sometimes tempted to become a Brethren in fact as well as in spirit, so grateful was he to that wonderful brotherhood of believers in peace, social service, and justice. Dr. W. Harold Row, who had induced the Brethren to sponsor his parole, continued to be his inspiration to the end of both lives. They died just weeks apart. In an issue of *Brethren Life and Thought*, published in 1965, there was a magnificent article by Leopold, entitled "The Ministry of the Brethren in the Years to Come." The editor introduced the article in these words: "Nathan Leopold, though of the Jewish faith, writes as from the inside of the church. The hundreds who heard him speak at the 1964 Annual Conference will recall his eloquent and moving tribute to the Church of the Brethren, and his reasons for not joining the church. In this article, we have asked him to write in love and concern for the church, telling us of the directions the Brethren should go."

Much of the article should be quoted. I confine myself to two passages:

> One of the most charming traits of the Church of the Brethren since its beginning has been its dignity, its quietness, its reserve. Brethrenism never has been, and I think it never

can become, a religion of drum-beating, of noisy, insistent evangelism. This is just not the nature of the church. Should it ever attempt to adopt methods of this kind, it would cease to be Brethrenism. And yet reserve, too, can be carried to extremes. There is also a scriptural text about hiding one's light under a bushel. The fact is that, though the church has existed in the United States for a quarter of a millennium, the vast majority of Americans have never heard of it! Is this the efficient preaching of the gospel to every creature? . . .

Indeed, the pastor who preceded the present incumbent was a Puerto Rican, who spoke no word of English. And yet the young volunteers serving at the Brethren Service project attended every service: Sunday morning, Sunday evening, Wednesday evening. Many of them, upon their arrival in Puerto Rico, knew not a word of Spanish. They attended every service, although they could not understand a word of what was said. Once I asked a young volunteer just why he sat through so many hours of a service he could not understand. Somewhat surprised by my question, the young man replied that he was bearing his witness. A wonderful concept, and one I have meditated upon a great deal in the years that have passed since I asked the question.

In the same way he strove to drive home valuable lessons about the tasks of penology. He contributed to a symposium on prisons and correctional law published by the *Nebraska Law Review*. Joining such diverse persons as Senator Roman L. Hruska and Dr. Karl Menninger, he wrote under the title: "What Is Wrong with the Prison System?" It is an article written long before Attica, and should be read by all who wonder why our prison system does not reduce the incidence of crime.

He wanted to write a book about the years which followed his release from Stateville. He felt that he could not write it unless the work was commissioned by an outstanding publisher and he was paid a substantial advance. Now and then interest was aroused in the project, but never were his terms met, and he wrote only a few pages, none too promising, of the projected work. Perhaps he did not have another book in him. He should have written of his experiences out of prison, if only for himself, confident that there would be many readers in time if he wrote something worthy of his years of freedom.

He was truer to himself when he wrote a little book about the birds of the area, published by the University of Puerto Rico, despite there being no financial reward in it for him. He was wiser, too, when he devoted countless financially uncompensated hours to help the Brethren Hospital at Castañer, even when he was no longer employed by it; and when he visited with lepers throughout the Caribbean; and when he tried to help young people to get jobs, education, opportunities of all kinds. There was a time when he thought of adopting a child. This might have been a redemptive experience for him, and I have often regretted that his mind was changed. He sought for thirteen and a half years to make up for all that he had lost during more than thirty-four years in prison. The responsibilities of parenthood might have been more rewarding than marriage. They might have removed some of the abrasiveness that remained with him to the end.

Leopold never ceased to be on trial. At times the world expected too much of him, and some were too critical. He expected too much of himself, but was not always self-critical enough. His life will be studied for what it can teach us about the good and bad possibilities of human beings. He was a puzzle even to those like me who knew him best.

From about April, 1971, until the end of his life, Leopold's health was bad. He went from one cardiac difficulty to another; he was in and out of hospitals. He always had to carry around medication for emergencies and had to have a source of oxygen close at hand. A person of his intelligence must have realized that the end was approaching, but he gave few objective signs of it. He did things on an excessive scale or planned to do them in a prodigal manner. He was going to go to Europe; he was going to visit the dying Harold Row in Washington, and me, still relatively robust, and members of his family, as well as friends here and there—indeed, in every part of the country. He was going to see the venerable Helen Williams, still bright and concerned as she neared her ninetieth birthday. He was going to go to Los Angeles to learn if he could straighten out the son of his one-time comrade in prison, David Fulford. He ate excessively, he drank too much, he smoked without pausing, he agitated himself and everyone around him. At the same time, by way of semi-humorous contrast, he constantly lectured me about taking better care of myself. He would write letters telling me how very much I was over-doing and that I ought to take more vacations and that I was precious to many people, including himself. He would telephone and tell me the same thing. At the same time, he violated every word of caution that he offered.

Finally, he got to the Chicago area. Almost immediately, he telephoned me. He was in very great distress. He wanted me to arrange for a thorough examination by a heart specialist. I consulted with the deeply concerned Abel Brown and we agreed upon a renowned cardiologist who insisted that Nathan had to come to the Heart Pavillion at the Michael Reese Hospital to stay for a period of time. In spite of his distress, Nathan agreed to this rather reluctantly. Almost before he was in the hospital, he wanted to get out of it so that he might attend the memorial services for Harold Row, who had just died; he wanted to complete arrangements with the Brethren for his work abroad, and he wanted to travel. He stayed for several days in Michael Reese Hospital. Abel Brown and I visited him frequently. My wife, Mamie, saw him more often. The great surprise was his brother Sam's concern. Sam, who at first was not going to see him at all, saw him almost daily.

The time arrived for Nathan's release from the hospital, a time set apparently by him rather than the physician. He was going to spend some hours with Mamie and me before we left for our annual visit to the Theater Festival at Stratford, Ontario.

Instead of resting, he continued to converse with me almost compulsively, as if he felt the need to unburden himself on every subject. He told me of his plans for seeing young David Fulford, the Brethren people, Helen Williams, and others. The only remark he made which indicated even a subconscious knowledge of his inevitable destiny was his reference to the fact that I was trustee and executor under his will, which I had not seen, and that he had made arrangements for giving his body to the Medical School in San Juan upon his demise.

With Mamie the conversation only intensified. Mamie drew him out in other areas, in which I was somewhat more reticent. They looked through the window at the birds that frequented our back yard, because of the water and seeds and shelter and baths that Mamie had provided. When an unusual bird appeared, Nathan would say something with respect to it. All the while he smoked, smoked, smoked. Every now and then he would show signs of physical distress, but he brushed them aside.

About 10:00 P.M. or so, Nathan announced that he was going to bed. This was an early hour for him. About 1:00 A.M., it was clear that Nathan was in trouble once again, and I quickly roused myself. The doctor, whom we called, arranged immediately for Nathan to be re-admitted to the Michael Reese Hospital. We drove him there, carrying the oxygen tank, the medication, the mass of luggage. During most of the ride, I had the feeling of impending disaster. I thought that the chances were great that we would arrive at the hospital with a corpse. Because of the lateness of the hour and security problems in that part of Chicago, we had to go to the one emergency entrance that was available. Nathan was placed on a portable bed and was driven by a nurse through the vast underground facilities of the hospital, as I walked beside him. I had never seen those great ominous stretches at the hospital. I was jarred as policemen on motorcycles or on foot came by us periodically. At last, we arrived at the Heart Pavillion and he was taken upstairs. I was told that there was no point in remaining, that he was in reasonably good condition and would receive prompt attention.

At frequent intervals, we called during the few days we were out of town and were reassured about Nathan's progress. He was still in the hospital when we returned. By then, he was persuaded that he ought to cancel his plans to go to California and other parts of the country and to return immediately to Puerto Rico. He did go to New York and then went on home. When I did not hear from him for a few days, I got apprehensive. My fears were confirmed. He was back in the hospital, having suffered another attack. I never talked with him again and never received another letter from him, but I did hear from Trudi. She was by no means reassuring. One Sunday night, I received a long-distance call from Trudi's sister, Anita. Nathan had just passed away, and Trudi was too ill to talk with anyone. She wanted me to notify the family and closest friends, like Ralph Newman and Abel Brown.

Though I was one of the two or three men closest to him in the last years of his life, I did not feel that I understood everything there was to know about him. I knew all of the facts about externals, and yet the inner truth escaped me. I knew that he had participated in one of the most notorious crimes of the twentieth century, yet I could not think of him as any sort of criminal, let alone a murderer. There was so much that was both appealing and unappealing in him—the gratitude that never dimmed, his utter impatience with those he regarded as inferiors, the continuing prejudice against blacks, the obsession with time and movement and activities, the refusal to accommodate himself to the necessities of his condition, the glaring contradictions in his character and temperament, the great intelligence mixed with naivete. I thought of incidents in our friendship, of the problems we had surmounted, of those that remained unresolved. I could not sleep because of the thoughts that crowded upon me. The simple truth is that I could not have slept in any event, because within minutes of my learning of Nathan's death my telephone began ringing. The calls came in throughout the night from newspapers, radio stations, television stations. Everyone was apologetic for disturbing my rest, but all were persistent. Nathan would have been pleased that, in his death, he was still news.

sixteen

Fighting the Death Penalty

Just as the struggle against slavery in the United States was the touchstone of humaneness in the nineteenth century, participation in the battle against the death penalty was the test of sensitiveness and civilization in the twentieth century. I would sometimes fantasize about addressing the Illinois legislature and persuading it to vote for abolition, or arguing before the Supreme Court and having them declare the death penalty cruel and unusual punishment, as indeed it is. I did far more than fantasize.

For fifteen years, there was hardly a day when I did not do something to advance this cause in which I believed so devoutly. I made speeches before live audiences and over radio and television, and in my daily conversation with all sorts of persons I reasoned over the matter. I sought to persuade every one who would listen and some who would not. I wrote articles and reviews for newspapers and magazines and every possible forum, little or big, influential or not. I attempted to get organizations to take enlightened stands on the issue. I formed or joined with many groups involved in the cause. I participated in cases to prevent or set aside death sentences, whether directly as attorney of record or as attorney for a so-called friend of the court (*amicus curiae*). I was part of proceedings for executive clemency. I corresponded with and on behalf of doomed men. If any one died by act of the State in my day, I died with him. If any one survived, I rejoiced with him. It was my privilege to play a not-inconsiderable role in the fight against capital punishment. It is not often that one lives to see such cause triumphant. I have had that joy, and not because of longevity.

One of the often-repeated charges that troubled me most was that my Jewish people, at least in ancient days, had believed steadfastly in death for certain offenders—"an eye for an eye, a tooth for a tooth," as it was styled. Whenever I could do so, I told public audiences and private gatherings of the real attitude of ancient Israel toward the death penalty. I told of the many prescribed safeguards—the banning of circumstantial evidence, the requirement of eye witnesses who had warned the offender of the consequences of his deed, the prayer and fasting before deliberation in a capital case. I liked to point out that the old rabbis had said that a court imposing a death penalty once in seventy years was a tyrannical one, so that the extreme penalty really did not exist in Israel at the time of Jesus.

When asked at the Illinois Constitutional Convention if I would have imposed the death penalty upon the Nazi war criminals at Nuremberg or Eichmann in Jerusalem, I answered that I would not have done so.

Had I never met or been involved with anyone who had been convicted of murder, I am sure that my role in the battle against capital punishment would have been different. Society, rather than the individual murderer, is the chief concern, but we learn about social needs, lapses and lacks through observing at first hand those upon whom society looks askance. Had I never been involved in the Leopold and Ruby cases, the Crump and Witherspoon cases, and others less known but equally important in their effect upon me, I could not have shown the understanding and resourcefulness that have been required in this crusade against a social evil—murder and all violence, capital punishment and all mindless reaction to crime. And the personalities of those who have been my closest companions in the fight—persons like Willard J. Lassers, Lois Weisberg, Gene Lovitz, Hans Mattick—have determined, in some way, what I have done and its measure of success.

"What does he want?" Meyer Levin complained when Nathan Leopold sued him in connection with the novel and moving picture named *Compulsion*. "To be paid a royalty for the creativity of murder?" That was a peculiar sort of remark for Levin to make in view of his often-proclaimed view that Leopold was so rehabilitated that he ought to be released from prison. If Leopold's "was the crime of the century," Levin had said, his release "would be an example of the correction of the century. This man who became the symbol of crime can be the symbol of correction."

I have represented seven murderers in recent years (in addition to those for whom I filed *amicus* briefs), partly by choice and partly by happenstance, and I am startled by their similarities as well as by their differences. Five of the seven have truly been creative men, not in their crimes, to be sure, but in their temperaments. Leopold wrote an account of his prison experiences which some have called the best book of its kind in our day. The *Saturday Review* devoted three critiques to it in one issue. Paul Crump has written poems, stories, letters, that show a writer in the throes of birth, however some may minimize his only published novel, *Burn, Killer, Burn!* Bill Witherspoon has a facility of expression that has enabled him to publish more stories and articles than any other prisoner of whom I know since the days of O. Henry—with the possible exception of Chessman. And one who shall here be nameless (because his case is unreported and I must respect his privacy) edited the *Joliet-Stateville Times* (the penitentiary publication) and contributed to it many pieces of excellent prose.

I have said much about Jack Ruby in my book, *Moment of Madness,* and elsewhere. One aspect of Ruby's situation I would like to underscore, because it is a principal ingredient of the homicides with which I am familiar and an argument, I believe, against capital punishment. If the assassin of the President had been moved at around 10:00 A.M., as widely announced, Ruby, who came upon the scene after 11:17 A.M., could not have killed him. And if there had been any measure of good sense in the Dallas police-department methods of guarding and moving Oswald, nobody, including Ruby, could have gotten close enough to Oswald to shoot him. Had Ruby not taken certain pills that morning, he would not have been so overcharged as to be capable of violence. Finally, had a destitute employee, a stripper in his nightclub, not awakened him by her telephone plea for money, he would not have arisen early enough to be on hand at the Western Union office near the police station, the one such office open that day in Dallas.

Chance, chance, chance—this characteristic of the Ruby case was an ingredient of the other killings, save, possibly, for the one by Loeb and Leopold. The latter's cellmate, whom I was instrumental in having released from prison, had never associated with criminals until he lost a finger in an industrial accident and, with it, his job. He went, unarmed, to burglarize a supposedly unguarded apartment. By chance, the elderly occupant was home. Paul struck him with his fist, and left. The victim, by chance, had a bad heart, which gave out, and he died. Paul was persuaded—foolishly—to plead guilty of murder and was sent away, his life ruined.

Witherspoon was carrying a foreign revolver, with which he was unfamiliar (it was not his own), when chance overtook him. He was not in the process of committing any crime; he had done no wrong in Chicago after his arrival from Michigan. With little or no reason for it, a woman drinking companion sent the police after him. Either in panic or, as he claims, accidentally, as he was giving up his gun, he shot Officer Stone, and the death penalty followed, because it is murder compounded when the victim is a police officer.

So I might spell out the details of the other cases. When chance is not involved in the commission of the crime, it figures in the apprehension of the criminal, as in the Loeb–Leopold case (except for the little-used glasses which fell, unobserved, from his pocket, Leopold might never have been apprehended). Above all, chance dominates the trial, the penalty imposed by the court, and, especially, whether or not it will actually be carried out. I have often said that the chief thing wrong with capital punishment is that it is like a reckless game of chance, a legal lottery with the results more random than in gambling houses.

Thousands kill in this lawless land. It is a dreadful thing, this propensity for violence, made more calamitous by the damage done to our system of justice. Of the thousands who kill, only a proportion of them are caught and go on trial for their lives. (I am thinking of the days prior to June, 1972.) The worst killers, the hired professionals, are almost never caught. Conviction and the degree of punishment bear little or no relationship to the merits of the case. If you have the wrong color of skin, come from the wrong family, and live in the wrong part of town; if you have the wrong lawyers or judge or jury; if you have killed the "wrong" person (police lives are more sacred than those of infants or women); if you don't make the right deal with the State's Attorney; if he is trying to climb to higher office on your corpse; if any of a dozen fortuitous circumstances are there, or lacking, the result will be different. Only a small proportion of the total used to get the judgment of death; many of these sentences were overturned because there was an error in the record (a wrongful search, a faulty confession, prejudicial conduct by the State); others, like Paul Crump, survived by reason of executive clemency. In the end—I am referring to the preabolition period—some few were executed. In Illinois, typical of the country as a whole, only three men in fifteen years died in the electric chair. Some states had no executions for many years; a growing number were abolition states. The answer was not to set the clock back by demanding more executions.

It is morally wrong to maintain the roulette-wheel type of injustice, and it is constitutionally wrong, too. When I first suggested that capital punishment is always a civil-liberties issue, because its fortuitousness negates due process, many of my colleagues disagreed with me. But then the American Civil Liberties Union, at the behest of the Illinois Division, went on record in making abolition of the death penalty an article of constitutional faith and the United States Department of Justice, under Ramsey Clark, issued, for the first time, what may well be an historical pronouncement against capital punishment.

When the last death instrument has been demolished, and jaundiced judges may no longer destroy men, gifted writers who capture the spirit of an age in their works, men like Koestler and Camus, will perhaps be tempted to compose parables about the small people who tried to make themselves into giants by being arbitrary bestowers of life or death. They will be shown to be moral pygmies in all their deeds.

The fortuitous nature of life and death was illustrated for me by some happenings in Austin, Texas, at the time that I was attempting to get Jack Ruby's death sentence set aside. That brilliant young law professor Paul Rothstein, who had been my son Ted's classmate at Northwestern University Law School, invited me to address his criminal-law class on aspects of the Ruby case. In walking to and from the classroom, I had to pass the very tower which, not long afterward, became the vantage point from which a deranged young man shot at passersby, killing or wounding many of them before he himself was killed. I might have been one of his numerous victims had I addressed Paul's class on a later occasion, not at all unlikely because of my relationship with him and the continuing nature of the case.

William Witherspoon was represented in what appeared to be the last stages of his court proceedings by Julius Lucius Echeles, one of the most unusual of criminal lawyers in my day, a singularly articulate and able advocate, who had an almost perverse capacity for getting himself into difficulty. The Illinois Supreme Court had affirmed the Witherspoon conviction and death sentence. He had attempted the *habeas corpus* route in the United States District Court and had failed there. Now all that remained was an effort at executive clemency.

On earlier occasions, Witherspoon had urged me to represent him, but I had been reluctant to get into his case for what I thought were good reasons. I did not think of myself as a criminal lawyer, despite several successful criminal matters, but others seemed to regard me as a skilled practitioner. Echeles himself asked me to become associated with him. If I would take the lead, he would be of every assistance to me. I yielded, and filed what some regarded as a very strong petition for clemency.

At this point I was taken completely by surprise. I had cautioned Witherspoon to do nothing without my prior approval. Suddenly I learned that he had filed another petition for a writ of *habeas corpus* in the Federal court—one can file successive petitions. It came before Judge Parsons, who presumably did not know that I was involved in the case. He appointed Albert Jenner, Jr., and two or three of his young associates, including Thomas Sullivan and Jerold Solovy, to represent Witherspoon. They did their usual highly competent job. Jenner and his associates are notable for their devotion to nonpaying, as well as paying, litigants. They take more unpopular cases, involving public issues, than any other Establishment firm, and often enough they win. By now there is a long list of their efforts and triumphs.

This case did not at first appear as if it would be one of their successes. Judge Parsons told them to go back to the State courts to exhaust their remedies. This they attempted to do through one of the most intricate and far-reaching petitions I have ever seen. I often refer to it as a model when one is not sure as to how to achieve the result one is after. The Witherspoon attorneys lost in the Circuit Court and lost in the Illinois Supreme Court as well. Their last recourse before going back to Judge Parsons was an application to the United States Supreme Court for a writ of *certiorari,* where the chance of success was slim. The likelihood was that Witherspoon's fate would be back in my hands, and I would have to persuade the Board and the governor to spare his life. The sour aftertaste of our success with Crump might adversely influence the result, but we had to try and try, not only for Witherspoon's sake, but as part of our continuing effort against capital punishment.

Largely at my urging, the Illinois Division of the American Civil Liberties Union decided to file an *amicus curiae* brief in connection with Witherspoon's application to the United States Supreme Court for the reversal of his death sentence. The A.C.L.U. asked me to prepare this brief in its behalf and, as a matter of course, I agreed. Thus, once more I was speaking for Witherspoon, while he had the added advantage of representation by Albert Jenner, Jr., and his associates.

I felt that my argument was clear and decisive. All studies, I said, show that the people of this country are steadily becoming more and more opposed to the death penalty. Competent studies show that the death penalty is not a deterrent to the commission of murder, and a large majority of the leading authorities in the penal and social sciences favor the abolition of capital punishment.

Illinois and every other state where the death penalty is not mandatory leave it to the unfettered discretion of the jury to determine when the death penalty is appropriate, I said. The courts flatly refuse to give the jury any guidelines to follow in capital cases, due to the fact that the courts themselves are given no guidelines in making this determination. The absolute discretion of the jury or trial-court judge will not be reviewed upon appeal unless it clearly shows a great departure from the spirit of the law or unless the penalty is manifestly out of proportion to the nature of the offense.

In Illinois, as elsewhere, I said, the governor is given the exclusive power, by the State Constitution, to commute sentences. As in the case with jurors and judges in imposing penalties, no standards are given to the governor to guide him in making this fatal determination. Thus, executive clemency is a matter of grace, which may turn upon any one of a number of fortuitous circumstances. From it, there can be no appeal.

It has been established that those persons who have no scruples against the death penalty are biased in favor of the prosecution, thus stacking the deck against the accused in one situation where he has the most to lose. This exclusion of a substantial part of the population precludes the defendant from having his case heard by a cross-section of the community, depriving him of due process of law and an impartial jury.

Capital punishment must be examined, I said, not as if it were one among many punishments society chooses to impose upon its offenders, but one awful in contemplation and irrevocable in result. In Illinois in this twentieth century, there have been at least four verified cases of innocent persons being convicted of murder. One of them, Lloyd Eldon Miller, was within several hours of execution, a reprieve having been refused by the governor and the State Supreme Court. Ultimately, the United States Supreme Court reversed the state courts in a scathing opinion, highly critical of the prosecution. Miller is now a free man.

On June 3, 1968, the United States Supreme Court handed down a ruling in the *Witherspoon* case that was of inestimable importance. At first I thought that it marked the speedy demise of the death penalty. I still think that, if one has to pick out that ruling of the highest court that best foreshadowed what occurred only four years later, it would be the *Witherspoon* ruling, delivered, for six members of the Court, by Justice Stewart. The whole opinion begs for quotation.

Very early, Justice Stewart, once mistakenly regarded as one of the less-enlightened members of the Court, got to the point of the case:

> The issue before us is a narrow one. It does not involve the right of the prosecution to challenge for cause those prospective jurors who state that their reservations about capital

punishment would prevent them from making an impartial decision as to the defendant's guilt. Nor does it involve the state's assertion of a right to exclude from the jury in a capital case those who say that they could never vote to impose the death penalty or that they would refuse even to consider its imposition in the case before them. For the State of Illinois did not stop there, but authorized the prosecution to exclude as well all who said that they were opposed to capital punishment and all who indicated that they had conscientious scruples against inflicting it.

He then went on:

The petitioner contends that a State cannot confer upon a jury selected in this manner the power to determine guilt. He maintains that such a jury, unlike one chosen at random from a cross-section of the community, must necessarily be biased in favor of conviction, for the kind of juror who would be unperturbed by the prospect of sending a man to his death, he contends, is the kind of juror who would too readily ignore the presumption of the defendant's innocence, accept the prosecution's version of the facts, and return a verdict of guilt. To support this view, the petitioner refers to what he describes as competent scientific evidence that death-qualified jurors are partial to the prosecution on the issue of guilt or innocence.

The data adduced by the petitioner, however, are too tentative and fragmentary to establish that jurors not opposed to the death penalty tend to favor the prosecution in the determination of guilt. We simply cannot conclude, either on the basis of the record now before us or as a matter of judicial notice, that the exclusion of jurors opposed to capital punishment results in an unrepresentative jury on the issue of guilt or substantially increases the risk of conviction. In light of the presently available information, we are not prepared to announce a *per se* constitutional rule requiring the reversal of every conviction returned by a jury selected as this one was.

He explained further:

If the State had excluded only those prospective jurors who stated in advance of trial that they would not even consider returning a verdict of death, it could argue that the resulting jury was simply "neutral" with respect to penalty. But when it swept from the jury all who expressed conscientious or religious scruples against capital punishment and all who opposed it in principle, the State crossed the line of neutrality. In its quest for a jury capable of imposing the death penalty, the State produced a jury uncommonly willing to condemn a man to die.

And finally:

> Whatever else might be said of capital punishment, it is at least clear that its imposition by a hanging jury cannot be squared with the Constitution. The State of Illinois has stacked the deck against the petitioner. To execute this death sentence would deprive him of his life without due process of law.

Much too soon Witherspoon came up before the Illinois Parole Board, which turned down his application for release.

About a year later another parole hearing was set and again Jerold Solovy was in charge. This time he asked me to appear as a witness. I thought that I would present my views in narrative form in about a half hour and then be on my way. Instead, Solovy conducted a very interesting direct examination in order to enable me to tell of my connection with the case and my reasons for believing that Witherspoon ought to be released on parole without further delay. When Solovy completed his examination, Theodore Fields, the chairman of the Board, whom I knew quite well, proceeded to question me at great length, as did two other members of the Board. They brought out my entire philosophy of penology and had me defend each point that I made. In the course of their interrogation, their views on Witherspoon became apparent, enabling Solovy to gear his further presentation to satisfy the Board's doubts. But, again, the Board turned down Witherspoon—the impending election of 1972 may have been an unexpressed reason. Chairman Fields said to Witherspoon at one point: "It is not a question *if* you will be paroled, but *when*." I suspect that by the time these words appear, Witherspoon will be in the free world. He will probably do a good deal of writing and it would surprise me greatly if he failed to give a good account of himself.

Many people take a quite rational view of crime and punishment in normal circumstances. But let there be a public clamor for heavy punishment by reason of newspaper hysteria or for other reasons, good or bad, then the ordinary sensible person caves in and becomes so blind with rage as to be unable to view a particular situation with his usual good sense. Opposition to capital punishment must not be based upon the merits of any individual; for there are no good murders and no virtuous murderers; the taking of human life is reprehensible, whether it is done by an individual or the State. One must not decline to take a stand on principle because the case is a bad one, over which people are greatly agitated.

Willard Lassers and I confronted that difficulty boldly after the Illinois Supreme Court affirmed the conviction and death sentence of Richard Speck, charged with the brutal slaying of eight nurses. We did not like the violation of the *Witherspoon* rule as to jurors having scruples against the death penalty in his case any more than in less distasteful cases. We felt that the courts had violated Speck's constitutional rights in that respect, regardless of his guilt or innocence. There was no problem in persuading the Illinois Division of the American Civil Liberties Union and the Illinois Committee for the Abolition of Capital Punishment to file an *amicus* brief in his behalf when Speck petitioned the United States Supreme Court for relief from the death sentence.

We expressed ourselves forcibly:

> Of course, *amici* do not know if petitioner *Speck* is actually guilty of the heinous crime of which he was convicted; but this *amici* do definitely know—that few individuals, fewer juries, very few courts are capable of the constitutional objectivity and faith required in a case of this dire nature. Perhaps only the Supreme Court of the United States is capable of rising above the blind and blistering emotions engendered in the present situation in order to pass the necessary constitutional judgment upon what appears to be a deliberate, if understandable, evasion of a basic and righteous principle this court has solemnly proclaimed in the *Witherspoon* case. This is why this court should grant *certiorari;* otherwise, the *Witherspoon* case,

stillborn, will no longer be of any force or effect, and overeager, if not unfair, prosecutors, courts and juries will feel free to let primeval prejudices alone govern in shocking cases where even the worst person is entitled to society's most enlightened judgment. There is no point in proclaiming a constitutional principle if it is to become rhetoric rather than reality when one's emotions are sufficiently aroused. It is not simply for *Speck* alone, but for all persons, guilty or innocent, who face the verdict of their peers, that we contend. We must make certain that there is no vitiating of a constitutional right where, as here, the very horror of the facts suggests irrationality upon the part of the perpetrator.

The gist of our brief was that the Illinois Courts, like courts in several other states, had virtually nullified the *Witherspoon* rule as to jurors on really insubstantial grounds. We declared that three Illinois capital defendants—Speck, Moore, and Mallett—were being deprived of their constitutional rights to its benefits, and about seventeen others faced similar deprivation, the list growing with each new case. We also asked the Court to consider whether the unitary trial—where guilt and punishment are decided in one trial—and the absence of judicial or statutory standards for imposition of the death penalty comport with constitutional standards. The latter issues were those involved in *Maxwell vs. Bishop,* then before the highest court.

In that case, Willard Lassers and I did a very unusual thing. We filed not one, but two, *amici* briefs, the one, as usual, for the Illinois Division of the A.C.L.U. and the Illinois Committee for the Abolition of Capital Punishment, and the other for several religious groups—American Friends, Lutheran Church in America, Church of the Brethren, United Church of Christ, Disciples of Christ, Episcopal Church, United Methodist Church, Greek Orthodox Archdiocese of North and South America, the American Ethical Union, and the United Presbyterian Church. In both briefs we argued that the imposition of the death penalty in a unitary trial is a deprivation of life and liberty without due process. In the A.C.L.U. brief we went beyond this argument and declared, also, that the imposition of the death penalty in the absolute discretion of the jury, uncontrolled by standards or direction of any kind, violates due process. We urged, in the words of the *Witherspoon* ruling, that the practices of which we complained "stacked the deck" against the defendant in a capital case, where special care ought to be exercised because of the finality of the result. I liked especially the profoundly moral undertones of our closing words in the brief we wrote for the religious groups:

> The unitary trial in capital cases unfairly prejudices a man on trial for his life and thus constitutes a deprivation of due process of law. It confronts the defendant with a needless moral question—shall he ask for mercy before being judged guilty and while asserting his innocence? It requires the jury to decide the awful question of life or death when frequently deprived of full knowledge of the human being before it.
>
> The unitary trial is a bar to an effective plea by a human being for understanding and for mercy. We plead for the right to make such a plea. As we show compassion, so may we receive compassion. In the words of Amos (5:15) let us "establish judgment in the gate; it may be that the Lord God of hosts will be gracious unto" us. In the words of Micah (6:8), let us strive "to do justly and to love mercy." These words of Scripture encompass our plea.

The Supreme Court sent the *Maxwell* case back to the State courts for determination on the basis of *Witherspoon,* rather than the issues on which the Court had accepted the case for consideration. This is often done by the Court when a matter is not ripe for determination or the justices cannot agree upon a result.

At the same time the Court accepted the *Crampton* case from Ohio and the *McGautha* case from California for consideration on the same issues—the unitary trial and the absence of standards. Meanwhile, the sentences of death in the various cases were held in suspension like hundreds of swords of Damocles.

In the *Crampton* case, Willard Lassers and I again filed two *amicus* briefs, the one for the Illinois Division of the A.C.L.U.

and the Illinois Committee for the Abolition of Capital Punishment and the other for various religious groups. Our briefs raised substantially the same points as in the *Maxwell* case, and the language was similar. We felt that we had to emphasize and re-emphasize certain basics to the Court. If they were not influenced in the one case, they might be in the other case. The Court was known to accept what once it had rejected.

On May 3, 1971, the Supreme Court handed down its opinions in the *McGautha* and *Crampton* cases, bitter disappointments to those of us who had so long contended against capital punishment. Justice Harlan delivered the opinion of the Court and it had the surface indicia of scholarship so characteristic of Harlan. "We conclude," he said, "that the policies of the privilege against compelled self-incrimination are not offended when a defendant in a capital case yields to the pressure to testify on the issue of punishment at the risk of damaging his case on guilt." "The constitution," he concluded for the majority, "requires no more than that trials be fairly conducted and that guaranteed rights of defendants be scrupulously respected. From a constitutional standpoint, we cannot conclude that it is impermissible for a State to consider that the compassionate purposes of jury sentencing in capital cases are better served by having the issues of guilt and punishment determined in a single trial than by focusing the jury's attention solely on punishment after the issue of guilt has been determined." In the end, Justice Harlan suggested that the juries in the two cases before the Court, "unassisted by standards," reached the right results, sparing one defendant and dooming the other. Justice Black, in a brief, almost curt, opinion concurred with Harlan. "The constitution," he said, "grants this court no power to reverse convictions because of our personal beliefs that state criminal procedures are 'unfair,' 'arbitrary,' 'capricious,' 'unreasonable,' or 'shocking to our conscience.'" Was this, indeed, Black speaking? The Court had no right to end capital punishment, he said; that was in the province of the legislative power. Justices Douglas, Brennan, and Marshall dissented, but the situation was discouraging, notwithstanding the Court's agreeing to decide cases at last on the basic issue—whether or not the death penalty is cruel and unusual punishment under the eighth amendment to the Federal constitution.

Before the Court had handed down its ruling in the *McGautha* and *Crampton* cases, I wrote another article on the death penalty for *The Nation,* published in its issue of January 11, 1971. In a sense it anticipated the ruling and what was to follow. I wrote:

> The Court seems to be reluctant to consider the direct issue as to whether capital punishment in any and all circumstances and for any crime is constitutional. That argument stems from the ban on cruel and unusual punishment. It seems to fear the far-reaching consequences of what some Justices, past and present, believe is inevitable. In the end, facing the issue directly may well prove the easiest way out.

On June 28, 1971, the United States Supreme Court granted the petitions for writs of *certiorari* filed on behalf of Richard Speck and other condemned men from Illinois, New Jersey, Texas, Louisiana, Washington, Ohio, Florida, and Massachusetts. At the same time, without further briefing or argumentation, the Court reversed the judgments, insofar as they imposed the death sentence, and remanded the cases for further proceedings, on the basis of *Witherspoon, Maxwell,* and one case in which we were not involved, *Boulden.* Justice Black, to our continuing dismay, dissented, as he had in *Witherspoon* and similar cases. It was hard to think of this staunch libertarian as refusing to meddle with capital punishment because of his devotion to what he believed the Founding Fathers had decreed.

Lassers and I filed a brief in behalf of Lyman Moore. He wrote a letter, wholly typical of him, a letter which made me happy all over again that I was in his corner in the fight for his life:

> Dear Elmer Gertz: A copy of your brief and argument arrived Tuesday. It has been read and re-read by the "Death Row Supreme Court" which, as you know, is probably the most critical, pessimistic and suspicious court extant. The unani-

mous decision was "IT'S GREAT." Words like eloquent, persuasive, forceful and emphatic were (rightly) used. . . .

While we were awaiting the judgment of the United States Supreme Court in the assorted death cases before it, a ray of hope arose in California, which, in recent years, has had one of the most enlightened supreme courts in the nation. With only one justice dissenting, he rather shrilly, the California Supreme Court declared the death penalty cruel and unusual punishment under the California constitution and thus unconstitutional. Just a short time previously, the Court had rejected such argument by a vote of four to three. We felt that this ruling from the state having the largest number of persons under the sentence of death was bound to stiffen the will of at least some justices on the highest court of the land in favor of abolition. We did not think that the ruling by the highest Texas court in favor of the constitutionality of the death penalty would overcome the California ruling. What ultimately leads up to a landmark ruling in any area of the law is at once quite visible and invisible, certain and subtle. When the result is known, one can see all sorts of reasons for its inevitability.

The atmosphere was far from cheerful among those of us in the vanguard of the fight. Willard Lassers and I filed our usual *amicus* brief in these latest cases, but Willard, in particular, despaired of any favorable ruling by the Nixon Court.

Our brief, I thought, went substantially beyond our earlier arguments. It was a combination of practical and legal reasoning and the highest moral appeal. We closed with a passage from Deuteronomy. We reminded the Court that Moses, shortly before his death, in his final charge to his people declared:

"Today I offer you the choice of life and good, or death and evil . . . I offer you the choice of life or death, blessing or curse. Choose life . . ."

We asked the Court, too, to choose life and good, and we gave them good reasons for their choice.

The decision was handed down on June 29, 1972. In the cases of *Furman, Jackson,* and *Branch,* from Georgia and Texas, the

Court declared *per curiam* that the imposition and carrying out of the death penalty in those cases constitutes cruel and unusual punishment in violation of the eighth and fourteenth amendments.

Justices Douglas, Brennan, Stewart, White, and Marshall filed separate opinions in support of the judgments. The Chief Justice and Justices Blackmun, Powell, and Rehnquist filed separate dissenting opinions. The disparity of viewpoint filled the pages of a sizable book. Seldom was the Court more divided.

Is the death penalty really at an end? Only time will tell. Meanwhile, 600 human beings are now alive who otherwise would have rotted in unhonored graves. And society, at least for the time being, is no longer a killer of killers. It has risen to a stature that makes possible more rational solutions.

Perhaps now we will learn that prisons should be intended for rehabilitation, rather than punishment alone; for teaching offenders the ways of useful life, rather than the barren ways of crime. In the process, society may learn that it, too, has much to reform and remake, so that it may become a hearth and haven and hope for all human beings and for itself.

seventeen

The Many Lives of Libel

Almost from the beginning of my career as a lawyer, in the early 1930's, to this very moment, I have handled one libel case after another. The subject is a recurring theme. It has been instructive to me. It tells me much of myself as a lawyer and as a person, and I think it has meaning for the profession and the larger public. I cannot tell all of the story, but enough to give it flavor.

I learned many things from being a libel lawyer and chiefly that one does not grow rich in the State of Illinois by representing plaintiffs. The big money is made in the defense of libel, representing the newspapers, particularly the *Chicago Tribune.* Some of the great legal and practical obstacles in Illinois have been created by reason of the prodigious influence of the *Tribune.*

There is a rule of law unique to Illinois; no other state has it. It is called the innocent-construction rule. In essence this rule declares that if the words published about the plaintiff, the words which he regards as defamatory, may reasonably be given an innocent—that is, a nondefamatory—meaning, then they must be given such meaning by the court as a matter of law, and the case dismissed. This is so even if the words might also reasonably be given a defamatory meaning. The choice is not left to the jury as to which reasonable meaning should be adopted. One can see at once the advantage this gives to powerful newspapers guided by highly competent counsel.

I was the attorney for the unsuccessful plaintiff in a case that helped establish the rule that was largely a death knell for libel cases in Illinois, even before *The New York Times vs. Sullivan* case and its progeny ended many actions for defamation on a national basis. My case did not involve the *Tribune,* but a local Hearst newspaper. I represented a scholar and author of considerable distinction, named Maurice Parmelee. He was connected with a Federal agency as an economist. This was surprising in view of the controversial nature of much that he wrote. His book on nudism was the subject of a celebrated obscenity suit, and he wrote about Communism and other controversial subjects. This aroused the interest of Westbrook Pegler and other Hearst writers who were prone to see Communists in and under every bed in all governmental agencies. Of course, it was precarious for Dr. Parmelee, a government economist, to be thought of as a Communist; this was libelous per se, as lawyers say. Of course, too, it was precarious for a government employee to sue a powerful newspaper, but Dr. Parmelee was nothing if not courageous.

The Hearst attorney, Floyd E. Thompson, and I conferred in Judge Harry M. Fisher's chambers about the case. The conference lingers in my memory these many years for a variety of reasons, not all connected with the case. Floyd Thompson, as a relatively young man, had been a justice of the Illinois Supreme Court, a candidate for governor on the Democratic ticket and the President of the Chicago Bar Association. Now he was a senior member of a leading law firm, which represented the Hearst newspapers and other large corporations. Yet there was something arid, unexciting, and unconvincing about him. I remember him saying, almost querulously, that, despite his reputation and the size of his firm, he could not afford to buy a new fur coat for his wife.

Judge Fisher was the most remarkable jurist who had ever sat in the courts of Chicago. He had been born in Eastern Europe and had come here as a very young man. He had been known to the Douglas Park–Lawndale community for years; first as a struggling immigrant employed as a cap maker, and then as a leader in the Jewish community and a rising political force. In time his Eastern European accent had been transformed, as if by a miracle, into an Oxford accent. He spoke so perfectly, so deliberately, that his phrases could be parsed on the spot.

Judge Fisher's great virtue was his willingness to break new ground. He was the author of landmark decisions, both in criminal and civil law, and often enough he was upheld by the reviewing courts. He believed that the law was a living, growing thing.

Judge Fisher was a special favorite of the press. He had written opinions in protection of the right of newspapers to be critical of public officials long before *New York Times vs. Sullivan* so drastically reduced the possibility of recovery in libel cases. He believed strongly in the marketplace of ideas, and was very sensitive to any effort to cut down or limit the newspapers' right to speak out.

We discussed my complaint in the *Parmelee* case in the light of the Judge's well-known views. To my surprise, the Judge found the first count of the complaint, which I regarded as rather weak, as strong, and the other count, which I regarded as strong, he thought so weak as not to state a cause of action. He overruled the motion to dismiss the first count and sustained the motion as to the other count.

In the course of discussion, we reached a settlement as to the first count. I thought it was a very modest figure, but I was assured by the house counsel of the Hearst newspapers, Kurt J. Salomon, that it was the largest amount the Hearst papers in

Chicago had ever paid in settlement of a libel suit. Strangely, they would not settle as to the other count and I was compelled to appeal it.

Everything in life seems to be interconnected with something else, either of the past or the future. At the time of this litigation, I did not know that my daughter, then a youngster, would be the next-door neighbor in Highland Park of the Kurt Salomons. In later years, we sometimes reminisced about his time as counsel for the Hearst papers and my battling with them in this and other cases.

In my brief in the Appellate Court of Illinois, filed at the April, 1950, term, I stated the situation as succinctly as the legal necessities permitted. (I think it is helpful to the lay reader to tell of litigation, now and then, with the prolixity and technical phraseology of the pertinent legal documents.) The offending libel, I said, consisted of an article written by Westbrook Pegler, a famous columnist, which, as the amended Count II alleged:

(1) characterized plaintiff, Dr. Maurice Parmelee, as a Communist or as closely in sympathy with and promoting the theories and objectives of Communism;

(2) impugned his patriotism;

(3) accused him of a crime involving moral turpitude (the writing and circulation of depraved, or obscene, books);

(4) reflected upon and impaired his occupational and professional standing; and

(5) otherwise tended to expose him to public hatred, contempt, aversion, or disgrace.

The article, I continued, was published by defendant, Hearst Publishing Company, Inc., in the *Chicago Herald-American* and various other newspapers of general circulation throughout the United States on or about June 2, 1948.

All of the facts are admitted as a matter of law, I said, by the defendant's motion to dismiss the complaint, as are the allegations with respect to the laws, regulations and public practices against Communists.

I then briefly summarized our theory of the case, as required by the court rules.

Then I gave defendant's theory of the case.

Defendant contended, I said, as fairly as I could, that the article complained of does not state that plaintiff was or is a Communist, fellow-traveler, Red, or adherent to or sympathizer with Communists or Communism, or that he was or is guilty or convicted of a crime; that plaintiff seeks to enlarge the meaning of the article by innuendo; that there was no actual malice, spite, or ill-will on the part of the defendant and no special damages; that the words were not written of the plaintiff in his business or profession; and that the article was fair comment.

It was now up to the Appellate Court to resolve the conflicting contentions.

The argument before the Appellate Court was proof that one can never tell in advance what such a tribunal thinks or does. It is only in retrospect, after one has seen the actual opinion of the court, that one can really size up the oral argument or what it portended; then it is too late—except for future guidance.

In my characteristic reviewing court manner, I was discussing with the court what I regarded as the outrageous nature of the abuse of Dr. Parmelee by the Hearst newspapers. One of the justices, either Kiley or Lewe, remarked at this point: "You are rather hard-hitting yourself, Elmer, in what you write." I smiled, foolishly pleased that the justices had read my articles and reviews. I then went on to explain the differences between what I had written and the defamatory publication against Dr. Parmelee. There was no inkling as to how the justices reacted. Later I knew that, consciously or subconsciously, they had given me a preview of their thinking.

Floyd Thompson did not argue the case before the reviewing court, nor did Kurt Salomon. Instead, that task was handled by Roger W. Barrett, highly competent son of the great Lincoln scholar and collector, the lawyer, Oliver Barrett, a friend of Carl Sandburg's. Roger and I were quite friendly, without being intimates. We treated each other with becoming deference and could be much more frank with each other than most lawyers. Roger congratulated me on my argument and seemed quite discouraged by his own. "It seems to me, Elmer, that you are sure to win," he said as we parted. How wrong he was was indicated on June 30, 1950, when the Appellate Court handed down its opinion, written for the court by Justice Kiley. The opinion, quiet and confident in tone, summarized the pleadings. It then gave the gist of the Hearst maneuver:

> The motion to dismiss asserted that there was a failure to state a cause of action for words actionable *per se* [in themselves] or actional *per quod* [by reason of the circumstances]; no allegation showing special damages, financial injury, or malice, nor that the words were written of plaintiff in his business or profession, nor that any statement was made with intent to injure plaintiff's name or reputation or to induce public hatred of him; and that the article dealt with a matter of public interest and was fair comment and criticism.

When fancy legal language like *"per se"* and *"per quod"* is used, one looks for trouble. It came soon. Justice Kiley indulged in all sorts of verbal gymnastics, then went on:

> The question is whether count two, based on the article, states a cause of action in libel. This involves the question not whether the meaning ascribed to the words by plaintiff was libelous but whether the words used were capable of conveying the meaning which plaintiff ascribes to them. The article does not directly refer to plaintiff as a Communist, etc. Plaintiff argues that the article read as a whole is capable of conveying to an ordinarily reasonable reader the meaning that he is a Communist or a Communist sympathizer. We believe that no ordinarily reasonable reader could understand the language used to mean that plaintiff was a Communist, etc. Any implication of sympathy with Communists arises out of the charges against the Department of Commerce. The language clearly places plaintiff in either the Department of Agriculture or the Bureau of Economic Warfare. Plaintiff relies principally upon the language in the first paragraph of the second part of the article. It is plain that the term "malignant Communists" forms one species of the genus "wild people." We think that what was said about plaintiff in the first part of the article rather excluded him from the "malignant Communists" species and left him under the genus "wild people" in a species "strange company."

> We conclude, on this claim, that the words in the article are not capable of conveying to an ordinarily reasonable reader the meaning that plaintiff is a Communist or Communist sympathizer, etc. . . .

Justice Kiley then went on in the same somewhat involved but logical manner:

> We think that there are no words in this article which in themselves are capable of conveying to the ordinarily reasonable reader that plaintiff was engaged in or advocated depraved private or public practices. We believe that the statements that the plaintiff wrote disgusting and depraved books is a statement of Pegler's opinion of the books. These books were matters of public concern . . . and in the absence of a bad motive (solely to harm plaintiff) . . . the expression of the opinion was not actionable libel. . . . There is nothing alleged from which we can infer that Pegler's opinion was expressed solely to harm plaintiff. . . .

Finally, the opinion disposed of the claim of special damages (in libel *per quod*):

> . . . The rule is that in such a case special damages must be alleged. . . . Plaintiff's allegations of special damages are wholly insufficient because they are too general and the motion to dismiss did not aid the allegations. . . . Special damages must be alleged with particularity. . . . It is not enough for plaintiff to allege generally that as the result of the article his professional standing or employment has been jeopardized or rendered insecure or that he has suffered financially through declining circulation of books and cessation of requests for new manuscripts or that he has incurred liability for legal fees and expenses. . . . We have in mind the rule of pleading against alleging evidentiary facts. The requirements for actionable libel are strict in the interests of protecting freedom of expression.

There, in the last sentence, is the real basis of how the opinion was reached. It is this thinking which has led virtually to the demise of defamation as a cause of action. If the law is still alive, however faint the breathing, it is due, at least in part, to my professional activities, as we shall presently see.

If the Parmelee complaint had been upheld, I was prepared to prove at the trial all sorts of bizarre and damaging facts about Pegler which had been dug up by Max Swiren and Ben Heineman, two friends of mine in the legal profession, who had been successful in other litigation involving Pegler, filed in the Federal Court. Heineman then was much involved in civil rights and was collecting a huge volume of material on racial restrictive housing covenants, not yet banned as unconstitutional. One could not know that he would soon become a successful operator of railroads, making it difficult for him to carry on his earlier public interests.

Pegler's malignant articles about Dr. Parmelee appeared in newspapers throughout the country. Pegler was then at the height of his infamy as a columnist. Dr. Parmelee was by no means his chief target. That great woman of my generation, Eleanor Roosevelt, was a constant object of Pegler's malice and misinformation, and there were others, including the President of the United States.

I tried to induce leading lawyers in various cities to file suits on behalf of Dr. Parmelee, with very little success. One of President Roosevelt's sons, Franklin, approached by me, turned down the representation, with at least some reluctance. That doughty old warrior for civil liberties, Osmond K. Fraenkel, took the case; Marvin Holz, a labor lawyer in Milwaukee, later a judge, took another case. I worked with both of them, without favorable result. The difficulties in contending against the press were not confined to Chicago. Some notable victories were won by others, chiefly in the South and New York, where the old English repugnance to assaults on reputation prevailed. The victories were fewer in number even there as the years went on.

While I was involved in the Pegler litigation, I could not help recalling that, unknown to him, I had helped establish Pegler's reputation as a hardhitting columnist some years earlier. I was with the Arvey firm at the time. A couple of lawyers of my acquaintance had asked me to work with them on a matter involving my old friend, Carey McWilliams, then representing a faction in a Hollywood union that was trying to get rid of the strong-arm characters who were tyrannizing the rank and file and running the union for their personal enrichment, rather than truly helping the membership. One of the unsavory characters was named Willie Bioff, and he had come from Chicago. Could I find out if he had had a bad record here?

Using the magic words of reference to Arvey (he himself did not know of my involvement in the matter), I went to the State's Attorney's office and the police and dug up evidence that Bioff had been a panderer, a burglar, a bad man generally. One of the famous Chicago police detectives, Captain Shoemaker, old "Shoes," as he was called, reminisced, knowingly, about the man. I got the records and set down all that I learned and sent it on to Los Angeles. There the attorneys, who were trying to rescue the union, decided that the most effective means of using the material was to turn it over to a columnist with a wide audience—Westbrook Pegler. He used the material effectively, indeed. The result was that it was found that Bioff was a fugitive from justice in Illinois; he had not served a prison term to which he had been sentenced. When an effort to extradite him was made, Bioff was represented by one of Arvey's pals. It was then learned, for the first time, that I had been involved in the gathering of data about Bioff. Fortunately, I had asked one of Arvey's top political associates if there were any reason for my not working on the matter. He knew no reason. And I had billed for the matter through the firm. Thus the embarrassment was not mine.

Bioff went to prison, later bore witness against some of those with whom he had worked, and went into hiding. His enemies pursued him relentlessly, and, ultimately, he was blown to bits when a bomb was placed in his automobile.

Pegler's reputation grew and, characteristically, he called some of the very persons who had assisted him, Carey McWilliams, for one, Communists! My name was, apparently, unknown to him and I escaped his malice, even when I was the attorney in suits involving him.

Most Chicago lawyers and, I suppose, lawyers in other cities are in almost mortal fear of opposing newspapers in litigation, especially in libel actions. Either through principle or foolhardiness, I have always been known as a person with little hesitation about suing the press or writing about it. I have discussed my writings about the press elsewhere in this book. This is the place to tell about my suits, some of considerable interest and a few of great significance. I have not confined my activities to the *Chicago Tribune* and the Hearst press. I have had cases involving the Field newspapers—both the morning *Sun-Times* and the evening *Daily News,* despite my being a sometime contributor to both and a friend of the editors. I hope that this is not mere perversity. It does not seem to have harmed my relations with them, a tribute to them as much as to myself.

One day a debonair young attorney named Basil Lambros, once of Chicago, now of Los Angeles, called upon me with a lovely lady, named Cora Galenti. She was far older than her looks, I was told. Appropriately, her profession was the rejuvenation of faded females. It seems that the *Chicago Sun-Times* had just published articles which the lady and her handsome counsel claimed had defamed her by declaring that acids and other dangerous ingredients were employed in her rejuvenation process. Would I file suit against the *Sun-Times*?

It happened that at this time the *Tribune,* long the self-proclaimed foe of frauds and quacks, had just published an article or two in praise of another rejuvenist, written by that long-time exposer of the shoddy, Norma Lee Browning. Had this led the *Sun-Times,* by journalistic illogic, to expose Cora Galenti? We would soon see. For I filed suit, with Basil Lambros as co-counsel. The complaint was notable for its spelling out of special damages.

The *Sun-Times* was represented by one of the most distinguished of Chicago law firms, Isham, Lincoln & Beale, of which the martyred President's eldest son had been a member. Other firms had changed their names with each generation of new partners; not this one; its best lawyers were content to bask in the Lincoln luminosity. The one actively in charge of the defense of the Galenti case was Robert Hanley, a young, personable and highly competent trial lawyer, who had been my son Ted's instructor in trial practice at Northwestern. He was assisted by A. Daniel Feldman, a recent law-school graduate. This in itself was remarkable. When I began the practice of law, few established firms would employ Jews.

Both sides immediately got down to the essence of the case through the arranging of depositions, particularly of Cora Galenti, the plaintiff. I knew that we would stand or fall by how well or ill our client did when subjected to the close scrutiny of a good cross-examiner like Hanley. The heart of the case was whether or not Miss Galenti employed acids in her rejuvenation treatments. She assured me that she did not use carbolic acid (phenol) or any similar dangerous ingredient, and I believed her; otherwise I would have not filed the suit. There were other issues as well, relating to licenses and legal difficulties.

I never learned definitively where the whole truth lay; for we soon settled the suit, not for a fantastically large sum, but far more than I had obtained from the Hearst paper for Dr. Parmelee.

In my forty years as a lawyer, I have met some remarkable practitioners of my craft, but not as many as one might expect in a profession that numbers many thousands. By any test, Morris Ernst is near the top of the list in anyone's group of fascinating characters. Morris is first and foremost a personality, and then a professional. He would attract attention in any calling. The great range of his interests is almost unmatched in our profession. It is difficult to believe that this great civil libertarian was born in the deep South in a period when one did not expect constitutional enlightenment. His early training was not in the law, but in industry. Somehow, he fought his way to the top in law. His first national reputation came through his efforts with the American Civil Liberties Union. Almost from the beginning, with Roger Baldwin, he was a leader in that advance guard of the fighters for the Bill of Rights. When he triumphed in the "Ulysses" case, in the 1930's, it looked for the moment as if literary censorship was at an end. The case is still a beacon of hope for those who would free all forms of expression from the shackles of the censor.

Morris loves human beings and is sometimes unfastidious in his choice of those he will champion. This has caused the raising of eyebrows, and more, at times. He could be at one and the same time a confidant of President Roosevelt, exchanging letters on an almost daily basis, and an associate of the great bankers, men like the Morgans. He is as proud of his service on the banking board of New York as his work with the American Civil Liberties Union.

If Morris has one strong antipathy it is to the extremists of the left. He is as sensitive to Communists as some people are to Fascists. He has departed from organizations he once cherished because he feared that they were in danger of being taken over by the extreme leftists.

We have been on the same side of some legal matters and have been on opposing sides in others. He is a resourceful fighter, but always fair and generous. His duels with the members of his law firm are fascinating to observe. He seems to have trained them to speak up to him. I have heard that lovely and talented lawyer, Harriet Pilpel, dispatch some of his ideas rather well. He is intrigued by such differences. Morris and Harriet have forwarded cases to me involving first-amendment rights. The most interesting of all matters that I have handled through them was the *Insull* case, in which the son and namesake of the one-time utilities king sued the Scripps-Howard newspapers and other publishers and authors for libel. Morris' firm represented the ancient and honorable firm of Harper and Bros. and they asked me to defend that company and one of its authors against a libel charge bound up in one suit with the charges against various newspaper and book publishers and authors. I felt elated, indeed, when I got a telegram from Harriet congratulating me on a brief I had filed in that case, which, as it happened, produced a quick victory.

During the second year of the Century of Progress exposition at the lake front in Chicago, the Ford Motor Company arranged for nightly performances by a symphony orchestra. There were at least two persons who attended virtually every night—Samuel Insull, the fallen utility tycoon, and I. We did not attend as companions; indeed, I did not know him. My only connection with his empire, somewhat remote, was to persuade Ceretta to buy a fur coat instead of investing in Insull Utility stock, as her sister Fae and others were urging her. Instinctively, I was suspicious of Insull's piling of entity on top of entity; it seemed to me to be highly artificial and dangerous. There followed, not long after, the financial collapse of his empire, his flight to Greece, his extradition to this country, his trial, and disgrace. It was high drama, tragedy, too; and, not having lost anything myself, I could feel a degree of sympathy for him, sensing that he, like many others, was the victim of the perilous financial structure that had been created. I was especially sympathetic as I observed him at the Ford symphony concerts. It was clear that he, who had once dominated the opera establishment in Chicago, dearly loved music. He seemed to hang on to each note almost wistfully, as if it were all that he had left to him. He retreated modestly into the background, approaching nobody and approached by none. Despite my great curiosity, I said nothing to him, although I have a faint recollection of having nodded to him, in a friendly manner, once or twice, perhaps more. Insull was very much part of the history of my generation, and I became part of his history, as well, through defending the libel action brought by his son many years later. It was a case of great consequences in the history of the law and it grew naturally out of the Insull story.

From the moment I began the practice of law, I was very much aware of Chicago's largest and most powerful law firm, then known as Kirkland, Fleming, Green, Martin & Ellis. It has gone through many changes of name and personnel, but it remains unique, not only in Chicago, but nationally. No firm has its peculiar influence and pervasiveness. It was founded by Robert R. McCormick. He was not then a Colonel, only an alderman and Czar of the Sanitary District and about to assume his family position, with Joseph Medill Patterson, in the leadership of the

Tribune, Chicago's inimitable newspaper, ruthless in its determination to be the first in journalism and to permit no diminution of its power. Naturally, McCormick's firm represented the *Tribune,* a potent and lush plum for any group of lawyers.

When assistant to two masters in chancery in the Arvey firm, I got to know many of the Kirkland lawyers, young and old. With some of them I became quite friendly. I think that Andrew Hamilton was my favorite. We were close to each other in age and temperament, and I liked his careless crop of red hair and humorous and relaxed speech. Later I got amusement from observing that Andy, a Protestant, was the attorney, on behalf of his firm, for the Catholic Bishop of Chicago. That stood me well when an eminent liberal bishop decided that he did not have to pay for the lavish decorating of his church by a Jewish painting contractor. Andy interceded in my behalf and my client was paid, not in full, but enough to rescue him from a financial crisis. Andy and I and the men in the Chancery office ruminated over the situation. It struck us as ironic that a prince of the Church, noted for his advanced views and broad tolerance, would be so cynical in his approach to money.

Long before I had ever opposed the *Tribune* law firm in any litigation, I had friendly relations with Howard Ellis, a senior partner of the firm, who was in charge of media matters. When I wrote and researched about George Sylvester Viereck, I thought it would be helpful if I had access to the depositions of Mayor William Hale Thompson that Ellis had taken in the course of the continuing litigation and battling between the *Tribune* and Big Bill. Ellis was graciousness itself in permitting the use of that material and much besides. Thereafter, we were nominally opponents in several cases, but it was always other members of the firm who did the actual work.

One would normally not think of the specialty of libel law as a dangerous one. I had reservations on that score when I received a telephone call from a disbarred lawyer, informally representing a notorious man, reputed to be a leading member of the crime syndicate in Chicago. His client was about to be released from the county jail, where he was serving a sentence, if memory serves me, on a highly technical charge. I did not know if other accusations against him were true, but I was sure that he should not have been convicted on such slender grounds in this instance.

Just before the call, I had read in at least one newspaper that the man had once committed a very brutal murder in which he had hung his victim on a meat hook, after viciously assaulting him. Of course, I did not know if the charge was true, and I was not going to convict anyone without trial. I was assured by my caller that the charge was untrue and grossly defamatory. Suit would be brought on the matter.

"You are the only lawyer in Chicago with guts enough to represent such an unpopular person and to bring suit for him against a newspaper," I was told. I cannot say that this compliment filled me with enthusiasm. I was not too communicative; indeed, scarcely audible. My caller went on: "Will you see my man when he gets out of county?" I decided quickly that, at the very least, I ought to see the man.

A few days later he called upon me. He did not look the monster he was reported to be. He gave me an account of his health. Apparently, he was dying of a multiplicity of causes. He talked of various matters, including the lies and libels of the press and the sins of their craven allies in the State's Attorney's office. Then he got to the point. One newspaper in particular had invented an utterly untruthful story that he had murdered someone. He had done no such thing and could easily prove it. He wanted to sue the paper for libel and collect as much as possible. I was the only lawyer who would dare handle such a case, he repeated in the words of his friend who had called me earlier.

What do you say when such appeal is made to you? I explained the law relative to libel, especially the defenses newspapers have in such cases. I told of the practical difficulties. I recalled what Don Reuben, the *Tribune* lawyer, had done to a person in similar circumstances when that person had brought a suit. Reuben cross-examined him so mercilessly in a pretrial deposition that he was forced to drop his suit. I then explained that injury to a good reputation is the gist of a libel action—when one's reputation is not good, regardless of the truth, one is unlikely to recover. Defense counsel like Don Reuben could trample upon one's life until nothing were left of it. My would-be client saw the point, and that was the end of the matter.

There was a bloody aftermath. My would-be client was indicted, several years later, charged with the murder of an associate a decade earlier. (Murder has no statute of limitations. Charges may be brought at any time.) A short time before the trial was to begin, he was "executed," in gang-land fashion, in the garage adjacent to his home. He was now definitely beyond the reaches of the laws as to defamation and murder.

Several years later, by way of contrast, a different sort of person called upon me to represent him in a proposed action for defamation against another Chicago newspaper. He was the head of a crime-fighting agency and, therefore, a public official. He had been maligned in his private as well as his public life, and he was indignant. I could share his indignation, but persuaded him of the foolishness of suit in his situation. The legal and practical obstacles were much too great for him. He went on to attain higher status, despite his journalistic detractors.

I would like now to tell of several relatively recent libel cases in which I have been opposed by Don Reuben—the ill-fated case of Dr. Myrtle Farnsworth against the *Chicago Tribune,* a landmark in the law of libel which had extraordinary and wholly irrational consequences at the Illinois Constitutional Convention; two cases against the prestigious credit reporting agency, Dun & Bradstreet; and a case involving a gentleman named Seymour Zeinfeld, which illustrated for me, in unforgettable fashion, that one must never lose hope in any law suit, no matter how poorly one may seem to be faring.

There was a basic constitutional issue in the *Farnsworth* case—whether a trial court could refuse to instruct a jury in the very words of the freedom of speech section of the Bill of Rights of the Illinois Constitution of 1870. I wanted Judge Dieringer, who presided at the unfortunate trial, to submit the following instruction to the jury:

"Truth is a defense in a libel action only when published with good motives and for justifiable ends."

The judge refused to follow the Illinois constitutional provision because he was persuaded by Don Reuben that it was federally unconstitutional by reason of *New York Times vs. Sullivan* and later cases.

The *Tribune* had published a series of articles about medical quacks, and they had singled out my client, an osteopath, for special, not to say venomous, attention. They had said all sorts of mischievous and defamatory things about Dr. Farnsworth, which we regarded as utterly untrue and patently malicious. They had, in effect, hounded her out of her profession.

The pretrial maneuvers in the case went on for a long while. They included the taking of the depositions of Dr. Farnsworth and of a mysterious personage named Madame Lopez, who had an extraordinary and not wholly helpful influence upon my client. The depositions were painful to me as illustrative of Don Reuben at his sharpest. At one point, he taunted Dr. Farnsworth by saying to her: "You are a quack! You are a quack!" I was old-fashioned enough to believe that no person, least of all a woman, ought to be subjected to such treatment by any lawyer, let alone a skillful and eminent one like Don Reuben.

The trial was stormy, indeed. At one point, Judge Dieringer threatened to commit me for contempt, my one such experience, particularly shocking because I was not conscious of having uttered one disrespectful word. I had simply persisted in maintaining a viewpoint different from Don's.

I think the case was lost at the trial level largely because of some amazingly damaging testimony by a famous neurosurgeon, Dr. Joshua Speigel. Under the careful guidance of Reuben, Dr. Speigel demonstrated why he believed that Dr. Farnsworth's treatment of certain diseases was highly improper and why he discredited the so-called Drown machine, a diagnostic machine much criticized by the medical profession—alleged to have been employed by her. I knew and had great respect for Dr. Speigel, a specialist highly recommended by my own physician brother. Yet, I cross-examined him as vigorously as I could. I brought out that he confined his practice to neurosurgery and knew little about some of the ailments that Dr. Farnsworth treated, and that he had never studied osteopathy, Dr. Farnsworth's field, and knew little about it. He also conceded that he had never seen the Drown machine and had never studied it. Yet, I must admit, that his testimony was very effective in the light of his medical qualifications, experience, appearance, and assured method of testifying.

Still, in my opinion, many errors were committed at the trial and I felt, particularly in view of the constitutional provision already quoted, that we ought to prevail on appeal. For example, I had clearly proved that the author of the articles had done insufficient research, had deliberately misstated many basic facts, and was determined to harm Dr. Farnsworth.

At this late date, there is no point in dwelling upon all of the facts, as the Illinois Supreme Court decided the appeal adversely to us essentially on the constitutional issue. The justices urged that health is a matter of the greatest public importance and that newspapers, therefore, had the right to deal bluntly with medical quackery and would be protected against judgments in libel suits, as long as they were not malicious in the actual sense, even if they were not accurate in what they published. The court ruled that the provision in the Illinois Constitution of 1870, protecting truthful statements only when they were "published with good motives and for justifiable ends," was federally unconstitutional. This was the first case, Federal or state, that had gone that far. Constitutional protection for the public discussion of public issues has since become accepted law and the case is frequently cited. Now public officials, public figures, and public issues can be discussed, even inaccurately, with little fear of a backlash of libel litigation.

Somewhat after the *Farnsworth* decision, I became chairman, as I have narrated, of the Bill of Rights Committee at the Sixth

Illinois Constitutional Convention. When our committee discussed the freedom-of-speech section of the Bill of Rights, I pointed out the constitutional consequences of my defeat in the *Farnsworth* case. Much to my amazement, the committee persisted in retaining the federally unconstitutional language. I could not believe that a committee, largely dominated by able lawyers, would thumb its collective nose at the Supreme Court of our state. The committee counsel, Dallin Oaks, who generally did not intrude, urged the committee to follow the law. I drew up a minority report, joined in by several other members. I felt confident that, in plenary session, the full convention would go along with me and reject or revise the objectionable provision. It refused to do so. And so it has come to pass that the Illinois Constitution of 1970 has a section known in advance to be federally unconstitutional.

I had better fortune in the two Dun & Bradstreet cases in which Reuben opposed me. One of them, involving a builder, Reuben was glad enough to settle when we boxed in his client irretrievably. The other one, involving the publisher of a trade journal, Reuben would not settle. He obtained a summary judgment for the defendant, Dun & Bradstreet, in the Federal Court before Judge Parsons and we appealed. The United States Court of Appeals reversed the summary judgment and sent the case back for trial on the merits and we won, only to face another appeal. The case is unresolved as yet.

In some respects another case in which I take tremendous satisfaction is not a great one, like the *Leopold* or *Ruby* or *Tropic of Cancer* cases. The man I represented, Seymour Zeinfeld, is a fine but not famous person. The amount involved is not staggering, the issues fairly common. True, the case has become an important one because of the rules laid down by the Illinois Supreme Court, and it is frequently mentioned in the legal treatises. The suit was filed in 1959. The final order was not entered until May, 1972. The thirteen years of litigation had amazing ups and downs in the Circuit Court of Cook County, the Appellate Court of Illinois, the Supreme Court of Illinois, and then again in the Circuit Court. It was deader than Marley in each court on more than one occasion and it came to life again, through my maneuvering, and died again and again. Victory was repeatedly snatched from defeat, and then lost. There was surprise and perfidy at every turn and, in the end, victory, final and complete.

Seymour Zeinfeld was a life-long friend and business associate of David H. Ratner. At first their relationship was almost idyllic, but gradually they seemed to have lost confidence in each other as business associates, without any decline in their friendship, so far as Zeinfeld could see. Ratner had risen in the trucking world and, at the time involved in our suit, he was the president of the Hayes Freight Lines and associated companies. He was a millionaire. Zeinfeld was the controller and treasurer of the companies. In May, 1957, Zeinfeld told Ratner he was leaving the companies. Ratner urged him to take a long vacation and then to return to the business. This he declined to do. He left on June 28, 1957. So sure was he of Ratner's friendship that he constantly discussed with Ratner the various business opportunities that he was considering.

His negotiations followed a peculiar pattern. Each prospective associate would be deeply interested at first, and then, after discussing the matter with Ratner, his interest would terminate. Finally, Zeinfeld decided to leave the trucking industry and go into the construction business in the Park Forest area. He applied for a mortgage on a home in Park Forest and, as a matter of course, listed Hayes Freight Lines as his former employer. The mortgage company sent in a form for verification of employment only, and Ratner himself, instead of simply verifying the former employment, sent in a letter, stating: ". . . Mr. Zeinfeld was the controller of Hayes Freight Lines for seven years and as such was in complete charge of the books and records. After leaving the company we discovered there was a substantial amount of money owed the company. Upon tracing him he offered to compromise. Under the above circumstances it is difficult for me give him any reference."

This shocking letter, utterly false in its basic statements, caused Zeinfeld to lose the opportunity to get a mortgage and adversely affected him generally. He was sickened to think that his old friend and business associate would sink so low. He consulted his brother-in-law, a tax lawyer, and that devoted man took him to Don Reuben, who explained that his firm could handle only the defense of libel actions, not the prosecution of them. Don recommended me as an able and tough plaintiff's lawyer—neither the first nor the last time that he had done so.

I filed a two-count complaint on February 5, 1959, the first count for libel and the second for malicious interference with contracts, employment, and business. We realized that we had insufficient hard evidence to support the second count, but we believed that we could obtain it with diligent efforts. Of the first count—libel—we felt confident. There could be no real defense to it.

The two defendants were represented by the David Axelrod firm, their counsel in the highly specialized trucking utility field. They filed motions to dismiss our complaint, and these were overruled. There followed extensive depositions and much additional gathering of information, and the case finally came up for trial before Judge Joseph Butler. Meanwhile, Ratner had called in the Isham, Lincoln & Beale firm to represent him, in nominal association with the Axelrod firm. Bob Hanley, assisted by Dan Feldman, was in charge. We felt thoroughly prepared for trial, as we had lined up several good witnesses, and the legal situation was satisfactory from our viewpoint. Suddenly, Hanley renewed the motion to dismiss the libel count and for summary judgment on the second count, the one grounded in malicious interference. Judge Butler at first indicated that he was going to overrule the motion to dismiss the libel count and then suddenly allowed it, and we would normally have been out of court. I induced him to permit us to make various offers of proof as to what our evidence would be in the event there was a trial. These offers made out what I regarded as an airtight case on the libel count. I recognized that, while Ratner had probably done all that we charged, it would be difficult to establish the case for malicious interference. But we decided to appeal on both counts. We felt that the Appellate Court of Illinois would find for us on the libel count at the very least and send the case back for trial on that count.

We briefed and argued the appeal as carefully as we could, with the aid of my friend Sidney Z. Karasik, who used to work with me, now and then, on appellate matters. I had employed him in the *Tropic of Cancer* appeal. I felt doubly confident because, while the appeal was pending, the defendants offered us a substantial sum in settlement. We turned it down because we regarded it as insufficient. Imagine our shock when, on April 25, 1967, the Appellate Court, in an opinion written by Justice Burke, sustained Judge Butler's rulings against us. We felt that Justice Burke's opinion was singularly weak as to the libel count. Based as it was on the so-called innocent-construction rule, it cavalierly read into the defamatory language a nondefamatory meaning which, we felt, was a complete misreading of the language of Ratner's letter as well as the law. Still, we knew that there was no point in asking the Appellate Court for a rehearing. It would simply repeat what it had already said. The Appellate Court seldom changes its collective mind.

But we were not going to abandon the matter. We decided to ask the Supreme Court of Illinois for leave to appeal. Such leave is very seldom granted—perhaps once in twenty or so cases. In all such applications, reasons must be set forth rather persuasively in order to induce the Court to reconsider what the first reviewing tribunal had done. We said, in our petition: "In the humble opinion of counsel, this is the most important libel case that has been presented to this Court since *John vs. Tribune Company* . . ." The *John* case, which had been lost by Karasik, was one in which the court stretched the innocent-construction rule far beyond my *Parmelee* case and all other cases. We had to make the Supreme Court see that, despite the innocent-construction rule, we had a situation, in the Zeinfeld case, that cried for correction. We summed up our reasons with persuasive preciseness and then argued them at considerable length. The Court agreed with us that we should have leave to appeal, an extraordinary result, as we have indicated. But it was only tentative. We still had to brief the matter. The other side had the right to respond. Then the case would be argued orally before the court, and they would ultimately decide our fate. If it were adverse to us, there would be little, if anything, that we could do. It was not the sort of case that normally could be carried to the Supreme Court of the United States.

At last the Supreme Court handed down its opinion, a shocker from our viewpoint. In effect, it reversed the Appellate Court on the merits of the libel count by holding that the language of defendant's letter was actionable as a libel *per se,* that the complaint was legally sufficient and that the letter was only conditionally privileged as a matter of law. This meant that if the defendants were in bad faith, as defined by the authorities, they had no privilege and we could recover a substantial sum. But, alas, the Court affirmed the Appellate Court, after saying all these fine things, on a purely technical pleading matter—that we had not formally denied the affirmative allegations made by the defendants in their answer! Apparently, some law clerk of the justices had overlooked that we had, in fact, denied all of the so-called affirmative allegations. As explicitly as possible, we called the denials to the Court's attention in a petition for rehearing, and, to our joy and its credit, it corrected the situation. Its final opinion reversed the Appellate Court opinion and remanded the case for trial. The likelihood of getting such result was about 500 to 1, at the very least, and we felt triumphant, indeed.

Around this time, Hanley left the Isham, Lincoln & Beale firm, and Feldman was in full charge of the matter. We immediately began negotiations for a settlement, both of us feeling that such was the only sensible course. If we could not settle, we would go to trial. The matter was further complicated by my being away from the office frequently because of my duties as chairman of the Bill of Rights Committee at the Illinois Constitutional Convention. When I returned to the office on a full-time basis, I prodded settlement negotiations by a motion for summary judgment on the issue of liability, for I had become persuaded that we were truly entitled to such judgment as a matter of law. We seemed very close to a settlement when, suddenly, the erratic Ratner discharged the Isham, Lincoln & Beale firm and retained the Kirkland firm, the same firm that had recommended me to Zeinfeld in the first instance.

There followed some of the most hectic and disheartening maneuvering that I have ever experienced. When I could not reach a settlement with Don Reuben and Larry Gunnels, I strengthened my motion for summary judgment and filed a strong brief and supporting documents. Thereupon the Kirkland firm filed a motion for the summary dismissal of the suit. I felt that this was purely strategic and I believed their brief was weak. I was especially confident because the motions were assigned to Judge Nicholas Bua, one of the very best men on the Circuit Court by reasons of his legal knowledge, integrity, and judicious bearing. We argued the matter thoroughly before Judge Bua and, to my displeasure, he opined that it was a very close case. He took it under advisement and then numbed us by a ruling that, despite the closeness of the case, he was dismissing it. Was all to go down the drain after all? We were prepared to appeal once again to the higher courts. Would it never end?

I cannot begin to narrate all that happened thereafter—the additional briefs, supporting documents and motions, the additional arguments, the additional settlement negotiations, Judge Bua's intervention toward achieving a settlement, despite his adverse ruling. At one point the judge insisted upon having both Zeinfeld and Ratner appear separately before him in his chambers. As a result of what Ratner said to the judge, the latest settlement offer was kicked over. The judge then wanted the parties to appear in court for the taking of their depositions. They appeared rather reluctantly. Ratner testified in such fashion as to outrage us and, apparently, the judge, with the result that, after so many years, the case was finally settled for many thousands of dollars. We regarded it as a great moral victory, as well as possibly a financial one. Considering the time and effort I put into the matter, the fee was a modest one, but it was sweet. I have seldom rejoiced more in a result. I still rejoice in it. I regard it as a high point of my legal career.

During much of the same period of time, I was deeply involved in another libel action that had promising beginnings but a dismal end. Gordon Novel's case against Jim Garrison, the notorious District Attorney of New Orleans, and *Playboy* magazine had much significance, but Novel was as difficult to deal with as Zeinfeld was easy. In some respects, it is distasteful to write of the Novel case, but I feel that I must do so, because of the issues involved.

A young man, Novel came into my office at a time when I was deeply interested in the New Orleans District Attorney's prosecution of Clay Shaw for alleged participation in a conspiracy to assassinate President Kennedy. I regarded Jim Garrison's actions against Shaw as bad-faith persecution, rather than legitimate exercise of any proper function of the prosecutor's office. I had met Shaw and liked him very much. He impressed me as a literate, liberal, rather gentle person, who could not possibly be involved in conspiring to kill anyone, least of all a President whom he admired. So when Novel told me of the defamatory falsehoods that Garrison had uttered against him in the course of an interview published in *Playboy* magazine dealing with the Kennedy assassination, I readily agreed to represent him without the immediate payment of any fee. Garrison had charged, in effect, that Novel was a part of the conspiracy. I did not know then that I would become deeply involved in a situation with innumerable legal, factual, financial, and psychological difficulties. Above all, I did not know that my client was himself a character so complicated, despite his apparent openness, that one could not really know him. I scarcely think he knows himself.

First of all, there was the matter of obtaining jurisdiction over Garrison in the United States District Court in Chicago. After all, Garrison was a public official hundreds of miles from Chicago;

and there was the legal obstacle created by the *Insull* case in which I had been one of the attorneys. Judge Miner had held, in the *Insull* case, that the Federal court in Chicago had no jurisdiction over nonresident publisher defendants where distribution to a minimal extent was involved. We maneuvered long and effectively on the jurisdictional issue, through affidavits, briefs, interrogatories, admissions, documentation, everything in the realm of judicial discovery. After a long delay, Judge William J. Campbell ruled, on January 2, 1969, that the court had jurisdiction, not only over the publisher of *Playboy,* but Jim Garrison as well. Judge Campbell's long memorandum, subsequently published in the official reports, is of great importance in its differentiation of our case from the *Insull* case, and for its discussion of Federal jurisdiction. It left us quite optimistic as to the future of the litigation.

I have before me as I write these words the thirteen-page docket of the District Court, relating to this case. It lists innumerable requests for admissions, exhibits, answers to interrogatories, stipulations, orders, answers to our complaint, motions to dismiss and other motions galore, efforts to take an interlocutory appeal after Judge Campbell's ruling that he had jurisdiction, transcripts of proceedings, notices to take depositions, deposition after deposition—I cannot begin to recite what each party did, or attempted, in this wildly contested case. We took the depositions of Hugh M. Hefner, head of the *Playboy* empire, A. C. Spectorsky, his chief lieutenant, Murray Fisher, a topflight editor, and Arlene Bouras, chief copy editor. I overcame my embarrassment at this interrogation of friends of mine like Hefner, Spectorsky, and Arlene Bouras; and they understood, too. Hefner and Spectorsky both remarked that they would like to see more of me when the case was at an end. I had known Spectorsky since his days as literary editor of the *Chicago Sun.* I thought both men were amazingly candid in what they said in response to my questioning. They admitted that they had serious misgivings as to the wisdom of publishing the Garrison interview.

The defendants went after Novel with the vigor and thoroughness that their anger and bankroll permitted. He was questioned for endless days. His deposition runs into hundreds, if not thousands, of pages. It is so long and embarrassing in language that I dare not look at it. Gordon Novel has a natural flow of obscenity and indiscretion, apparent in almost every page. What he said might make a very remarkable article, whether of fact or fiction or something defying precise definition. In turn, he amused, angered, embarrassed, and puzzled me, no less than our opponents.

Initially, the defendants' motions for a summary judgment of dismissal of our case were denied by Judge Campbell—the court reserving the right to reconsider its ruling. Then, after innumerable delays, for few if any of which I was responsible, the case was set for trial at a time when I was scheduled to go to Miami Beach to attend the celebration of the fiftieth wedding anniversary of my brother, Sol, and his wife, Augusta. I was refused a continuation of only a few days, and planned to have my associate, Wayne B. Giampietro, handle the case in its early stages. Then Jim Garrison moved for a continuance and it was allowed. But the case never came to trial. The defendants moved for a reconsideration of their motions to dismiss the case and this was granted, largely on the basis of Novel's being a public figure and having thrust himself into the vortex of public discussion. Judge Campbell wrote a long memorandum in support of his viewpoint.

I should tell of other libel actions in which I have been involved. Invariably, when I have represented *defendants* I have won, more easily in recent years than before *New York Times vs. Sullivan*. When I appear in court to represent defendants, the judge appears to be shocked that Elmer Gertz, the celebrated plaintiff's counsel in libel actions, actually defends such cases as well. It is as if a southpaw should turn out to be ambidextrous.

I had an easy time with a group of educators. They were the larger part of the faculty at a high school in Chicago who were disturbed by a small but highly militant dissident element on the faculty. They wrote a letter to the Assistant Superintendent of Schools, urging some sort of remedial action. The letter was read at a closed meeting by one of the teachers. Thereupon he was sued for libel. The rest of the faculty agreed to back him up, financially and morally. This case I was able to win on a mere motion to dismiss, because the suing parties could not correct the constitutional defects that I pointed out in their complaint. Essentially, what I said was that the parties were public employees and that grave public issues were involved, so that all that was said was privileged, unless it could be shown that there was actual malice. I contended that the elements of malice had to be spelled out in the complaint, and not merely at the trial.

I have saved for the very end a case involving myself personally. In ruling on this case, the lower courts went to the utmost limit in immunizing the most despicable defamer of character from the evil consequences of his utterances.

One day in April, 1969, Mary Giampietro, wife of my young associate, told us that a pamphlet had been thrust upon her while she was shopping in her neighborhood. It turned out to be a reprint of an article from the extremist John Birch Society publication, *American Opinion,* in which I was described as a "Communist-fronter," "Leninist," and participant in various "Marxist" and "Red" activities. The article was induced by my participation in several civil suits against Richard Nuccio, a Chicago policeman who had shot and killed a nineteen-year-old lad named Richard Nelson. The John Birch Society publication falsely charged me with being part of a Communist conspiracy to harass the police generally and Nuccio in particular.

Enraged, I broke my rule against personal participation in litigation and sued the John Birch Society magazine in the local Federal Court. In denying the defendant's motion to dismiss the suit, Judge Decker held that the publication was libelous *per se* as a matter of law. He was troubled whether or not I was a public figure. "Don't tell me," he said, "that Elmer Gertz is just another lawyer." When no one on the jury panel recognized my name, he was persuaded that I was not a public figure within the meaning of *The New York Times* case. The libel was published and the suit filed before I contemplated running for election as a delegate to the Illinois Constitutional Convention.

Wayne acted as my attorney and did extremely well, winning a $50,000 verdict in my favor. We claimed only punitive damages. My witnesses included Frank Greenberg, the President of the Chicago Bar Association, my old friends Eli Fink and John Ligtenberg, and one of the attorneys for Nuccio, who affirmed that I was an attorney of very good reputation and had not participated in any conspiracy against Nuccio or the police generally.

In due course, the defendant filed what is known as a motion for judgment notwithstanding the verdict—that is, to set aside the jury verdict and dismiss the suit. To our shock, Judge Decker changed his mind, declared that I was a public figure at the time the libel appeared and that public issues were involved. He, therefore, granted the defendant's motion. Outraged, I appealed. The United States Court of Appeals kept the case under advisement for many months—from January 31, 1971, to August 1, 1972—and finally sustained Judge Decker. My petition for a rehearing and for reconsideration by the entire court instead of a three-judge panel was denied. I decided to carry the matter to the United States Supreme Court.

Judge Kiley wrote: "It is with considerable reluctance, however, that I concur. The reluctance is due to my fear that we may have in this opinion pushed through what I consider the outer limits of the first-amendment protection against liability of non-'public figures' in their personal privacy."

The court was good enough to call me "a reputable lawyer." It assumed, too, that "the article was libelous *per se* as a matter of Illinois law and that its author was either deliberately or recklessly mendacious."

What deeply troubled me is that the court failed to recognize that, assuming the validity of all that was said by it, I was still entitled to the opportunity to attempt to prove the actual malice or gross recklessness of the Birch Society publication. It had continued to distribute the libelous article for a year after suit had been filed. At worst, the case should have been reversed, so that I might establish these things in the trial court; otherwise, in my judgment, there is a denial of due process. Hence my appeal to the United States Supreme Court, which, to the surprise of some people, granted *certiorari.* On November 14, 1973, my associate Wayne argued the case, with some brilliance, before the Supreme Court in Washington, while I talked on censorship at Southern Illinois University in Carbondale, as part of the activities in connection with a Henry Miller Exhibit, derived largely from my Miller material. It is premature to declare the effect of either appearance.

The basic question remains—where do the rights of the individuals begin and end in view of the first-amendment protection of speech? If the right of freedom of utterance is absolute, as Justices Black and Douglas have contended, then there is no right to prosecute for obscenity.

This, too, is an area in which I have been prominent. It may properly be asked if I can express belief in utter permissiveness in the one area without conceding it in the other as well. I have represented authors, publishers, producers, distributors, and others in a vast variety of obscenity cases in all parts of the country, almost invariably with success, either at the trial level or appeal. I believe strongly in complete freedom of expression, as I have said in my pamphlet, *Books and Their Right to Live.* Some find it hard to reconcile this attitude with a belief in libel laws, however limited in scope. It is a subject that I shall be glad to debate.

eighteen

A Sabbatical Leave-taking

As I write these final words of my memoirs, I am approaching my sixty-seventh birthday. There was a time, long ago, when I would have regarded this as the beginning of senility. When one devotes full time to the practice of law, full time to the teaching of law and full time to writing, one does not have time to ask about the meaning of the passage of years.

That is the advantage of being asked to write an autobiography. Perforce, one must give thought to the meaning of what has happened. At first, I was shocked when urged to do this book; then I was pleased; then I took it as a challenge, not unlike other challenges that I have faced in an eventful life. How does one avoid mock humility without appearing to be vain? How does one prevent an autobiography from becoming little more than a chronicle of names, dates, and places? Remembering that one must tell, at least in general outline, what has happened, how is basic meaning given to the chronicle?

Henry L. Mencken used to say that there is no such thing as a dull autobiography; that even a clergyman can write one interesting book—about himself. I prefer to think in the manner so meaningfully utilized by Henry James in one of his better stories. A man constantly thinks of himself as on the verge of some great adventure. He articulates his feelings to a friend from time to time. Years go by, but the great adventure never comes to pass. For the man does not know that it is not by whim or fancy that one scales great heights, but by arduous climbing, which gives one little time for contemplation of the greatness that is to be. A man may go through life quietly, calmly, with humility and grace and never realize what he has accomplished. He may give no thought to anything except the living of each day so that it is a fulfillment of his personality and needs.

Day by day I observe my six grandchildren and their parents. I watch hesitant steps growing into confident strides. I observe lisping inarticulateness becoming fluent speech. I see how each person, young and old, is utterly dissimilar to every other person, despite our utilizing the same senses in similar surroundings. I cannot help thinking of the days before World War I, when I was a child. Those days are as near as yesterday, as close, almost, as today. As I was then, I am today. I am still filled with wonder and eagerness and joy and with an unwillingness to bear any burden of anger or vengefulness.

What we have dreamed about eventuates, but it is all part of the process of growth, not of volition. As the Bible declares, by taking thought we do not add to our height. It is by daring to live that we become men.

Certainly, the years bring changes, both superficial and real. The golden curls of my childhood have turned into sparse hairs, more nearly white than gray. The make-believe of babyhood has become the sometimes-sad reality of maturity. But, in the end, triumph and tragedy are both part of one process, inevitable, irreversible, individual. Hopefully, it will remain a memory when one is gone.

There are differences that are superficial. Where once one had to fret about money, the means to do things, one is freed from such worries. Where one had taskmasters, now one is one's own master and one learns that there is no master more severe than self. Now and then one may be easy, self-indulgent, but demands are still made, out of the necessity of becoming what one wants to be. Ambition does not have the roar and sweep of one's youth, but it is still there, disguised in forms not always recognizable.

I sit in my law office each day, taking only the cases that I want to take, trying to be a lawyer for more than cash considerations. Now and then I have to ask myself if I am swerving from this goal. But the kind judgments of friends and of strangers persuade me sometimes that I am using the law as an instrumentality for something beyond personal satisfaction. I can argue cases before reviewing tribunals and feel that I am among my peers, reasoning with them, and teaching the truth, now and then, to judges.

I sit in my classrooms at the John Marshall Law School and try to give some meaning to the strivings of young persons. My school has the largest enrollment in the State of Illinois. Dean Noble W. Lee sought for fifteen years to get me to teach there. He assured me that I would derive more satisfaction from imparting knowledge to the young than from exhausting myself in the courtrooms. He is right, but I do not regret those many years of turmoil when I was able to persuade judges and juries of the rightness of causes in which I believed. I am conscious that my students look upon me as more than just another instructor. To them, at the thresholds of their careers, I am somewhat of a legend. This does not stop them from questioning me sharply when I say something that disturbs them. I refuse to lecture to the students. I insist upon Socratic discourse between teacher and taught, even when my classes are much too large. And there is the constant quest to learn new things in order to impart them to the students. How does one make them understand, truly, that one must always be a student, no matter how long one has practiced in the profession?

I sit at home, with a yellow legal pad on my lap, writing, or more often printing, the words of reviews, articles, books. I find it difficult to write when I am too comfortable. A desk would make my thinking too formal. I print because my writing has become illegible, where once it had sharpness and fluency. I print because, once upon a time, I was a student in a technical high school. That school constantly comes to my mind, although I never intended to become an engineer. An architect perhaps, but never an engineer.

I vary this routine of the practicing and teaching of law and of writing by public appearances, over radio, television, and sometimes in person. I do not speak as often as in the past, but I still enjoy it—never from manuscript, seldom with notes, always with a kind of free flow of ideas. I sometimes surprise myself by what I say. Despite the spontaneity of my talks, they appear well organized, the sentences parse.

I am not as active in community or professional organizations as once I was. But I still find it difficult to resist public challenges. One day I am on a citizens committee to find an alderman for my ward. Another day I am working, as for years in the past, on adult education as the most necessary of community responsibilities. With Bernard Shaw, I believe that when one ceases to grow one ceases to live, even if the burial rites have not been performed.

It is relatively easier for me to brush aside all responsibilities and rush off to some near or distant point—Russia, Scandinavia, Israel, Greece, perhaps China, any country, anywhere; or near at home, Stratford in Canada and Minneapolis in the United States, in order to attend theatrical performances that are better than anything commercial Broadway produces. The theater is still one of my great passions. One of my secret hopes is to write a play, perhaps about Brook Farm. I dream, too, of writing several juveniles, the desire strengthened when I read to my grandchildren. They have their parents' great joy in my playacting as I read to them. Dana's insatiable appetite for the words uttered by me is very much like the glee her mother showed, more than thirty years earlier, when I read about good and evil animals and nice and naughty people.

Unlike my ancient grandfather, with whom this book began, I think of the past as well as the future. Like my wordly wise father, I know that today is the best that we have. I cherish it. At the same time, there are definite plans that I have, as well as timeless dreams.

I am doing articles for a couple of encyclopedias, and those who liked my book on the new Illinois Bill of Rights have asked me to do an over-all account of the Illinois Constitutional Convention of 1970; and I have been asked to pen a portrait of Peter Tomei as the introduction to a monograph on the work of his committee at the convention. Peter died suddenly, at age thirty-six, shortly after the approval of the new constitution, an inheritor, surely, of unfulfilled renown. No limits could reasonably have been set to his possible achievements. He seemed to have everything—brains, drive, friends, family, and potentials —and then he was nothing; he was dust that would soon be scattered and forgotten. Is that the whole story of everyone, no matter how ancient and wise and honor-laden he becomes?

As one soberly contemplates one's own life, as one shudders at the thought of Peter's fate, one cannot help asking what, if anything, one has done and its meaning. I sometimes think that fortuitousness, chance, is the residuum of it all. Had I not been absorbed in the American Civil War, and had not Nathan Leopold's oldest brother shared this interest with me, I would not have handled Leopold's efforts to get out of prison; I would not have achieved my greatest professional success, my greatest personal acclaim. Had I not become known for my successful efforts for Leopold, had I not been a Jew, had I not been associated at one time with Jack Arvey in the practice of law, I would not have been asked to work on the Jack Ruby case. Were I not a friend of a friend of the president, briefly, of Grove Press, I would not have become the attorney defending *Tropic of Cancer* in a multiplicity of obscenity cases, and thereafter cases involving other books, magazines, and movies. My chance appearance with Russ Meyer on a radio program led to my being asked by him to represent him in efforts for *Vixen* and other robust films.

Chance paid a similar role in more important areas of my life. Were not my first wife, Ceretta, so committed to assisting parents and children to adjust to life, she would not have been involved in the automobile accident that led to her death. Had I not gone on the only blind date of my life, I would not have married Mamie and would have missed much joy and creativeness.

I could give instance after instance of the fortuitousness that has been the main ingredient, perhaps, of my life. I might say, with some astrological fanatics, that all is written in the stars; that the interplay of the planets determines what we are, what we do, what we become. This would be an easy answer and, undoubtedly, as false as most glib responses.

I think I see a more meaningful pattern to the fabric of my being. I am what I am because there are threads and patches, self-sewn, that add up to it. Expressed otherwise, I have been tending since my first conscious breath toward the sort of life that I have led. When I was little more than a baby, I said that I wanted to be a great man. That does not mean that I am one. But it does mean that I have always had the instinct toward achievement, toward making something of myself. One can have this drive and do little. Perhaps, when it is all added up, I have done little. Perhaps, there is only what St. Paul has described as the blare of brass, sound without substance. I may be forgotten before I am gone, as billions before me. It is enough that I have felt the same sort of quickening that a mother feels in her womb. I have cried out that I am alive. I have moved my limbs meaningfully. I have felt emotions, thoughts, joys, sorrows. Every moment I have tested life. I have said with my Jewish compatriots—"L'chayim"—"To life!" I still lift a glass and a full heart to life. I always shall.

About the Author

Best known as a lawyer, Elmer Gertz has made waves in literary circles with books, pamphlets, book reviews, magazine articles, radio plays, as publisher of a weekly newspaper. His range of interests is best indicated by some of the organizations he has founded or joined and headed: the Civil War Round Table, the Shaw Society (Bernard, that is) of Chicago, the Decalogue Society of Lawyers, the American Jewish Congress, and the Public Housing Association. An avid theater-goer all his life, he has an almost equal interest in gourmet dining (though his wife says he talks more food than he actually eats).

His chief joys are his wife, his three children, and his six grandchildren. As for accomplishments, he is proudest of the State of Israel Prime Minister's Medal, awarded to him in 1972.